REQUIEM FOR THE RESISTANCE

REQUIEM FOR THE RESISTANCE

THE CIVILIAN STRUGGLE AGAINST NAZISM IN HOLLAND AND GERMANY

HERMAN FRIEDHOFF

BLOOMSBURY

First published in 1988
Copyright © 1988 by Herman Friedhoff
Bloomsbury Publishing Ltd, 2 Soho Square,
London W1V 5DE

Reprinted December 1988

British Library Cataloguing in Publication Data

Friedhoff, Herman
Requiem for the resistance: the
civilian struggle against Nazism in
Holland and Germany
1. World War, 1939–1945—Underground
movements—Netherlands 2. World War,
1939–1945—Personal narratives Dutch
I. Title
940.54′492′0924   D802.N4
ISBN 0–7475–0173–4

Phototypeset by Cambrian Typesetters, Frimley, Surrey
Printed in Great Britain by
Biddles Limited, Guildford and Kings Lynn

PICTURE CREDITS

All pictures are from the author's collection apart from p. vi top left courtesy of
Mosaik Verlag, Berlin; p. vi top right courtesy of Ullstein Bilderdienst, Berlin; p. v top
and bottom, p. vi bottom, p. vii top, middle and bottom courtesy of the Rijksinstituut
voor Oorlogsdocumentatie, Amsterdam.

DEDICATION

To the memory of Dr Herman Bernard (Stuuf) Wiardi Beckman, Dr Carel Abraham, Theo Cramer, and all those whose creative lives were cut short by nazis.

To the future of my sons Falco, Dennis, Sander, Gijsbert, Andrew and Jolyon, and all those who will have to help prevent a recurrence.

ACKNOWLEDGEMENTS

The following people have been helpful in one way or another. They will forgive me for lumping them together in alphabetical order without indicating the nature of their contribution. My gratitude makes no distinction.

Rupert Allason MP (the author Nigel West, London), Iradj Bagherzade (London), Dr Floris B. Bakels (Bussum), Drs David Barnauw (Amsterdam), Jan H. van Borssum Buisman (Haarlem), Hugo Brunner (Oxford), Jane Carr (London), Dr Pierre H. Dubois (The Hague), Drs Falco Friedhoff (Ossenzijl), Sir John Hackett (Coberley, Gloucestershire), Dr Günther Hadding (Gütersloh), Marijke Halbertsma née Wiardi Beckman (Aerdenhout), Drs A. A. M. (Ton) van der Heyden (Naarden), Bob Horan (Adderbury, Oxon), Annelies & James Kels (Haarlem), Christa Laird née Falck (Oxford), Dr Brian Martin (Oxford), Ambassador Oliver Miles (Oxford), D. W. Moisson (London), J. K. (Keith) Oldale (London), Roger Schlesinger (London), Baron & Baroness de Smeth (Schilde, Antwerp), John Swanzy (Oxford), Carla & Frank Thooft (Rotterdam).

When I was a publisher tributes from authors were never printed. After all, it is the publisher's job to support his authors. Times have changed and so have customs. But I hope that tycoons will never obscure the vital special relationship between publisher and author. As a gamekeeper turned poacher I am therefore happy to record in print my thanks to Bloomsbury Publishing Ltd, a young and vigorous team which does not need naming of individuals.

I must, however, name John Man of Oxford, freelance author and editor as well as friend. His convivial yet exacting guidance helped me create this final text.

CONTENTS

CONTENTS

PREFACE

In the following pages I have tried to convey the colour of life during the resistance to nazism. The subject threatens to be drowned by an avalanche of books on World War II, almost exclusively on military matters. Even books on the Resistance concentrate on its military aspects – the spying, the sabotage, the links with British secret services. But in Holland – and Germany – these links were tenuous for most of the time and virtually non-existent for some.

Our resistance was almost entirely civilian. We had lost the military battle. We lacked the ammunition for counter-revolutionary activities. Sabotage only brought instant and ruthless reprisals on innocent bystanders. Spying for military purposes was useless as no Allied armies came anywhere near to benefit from it, until the autumn of 1944. And in the meantime – for five long years – we faced the all-pervasive presence of nazis, representatives of a once civilized nation who had supped with the devil.

Evoking the feel of life in those days nearly half a century later involves immersion in ephemeral detail, much of it prone to the distortions which the passage of time inflicts. Fortunately, the past decade has seen the publication of documents which put our experiences in a perspective we then lacked. This explains the recent preponderance of publications. It has also made this book possible. But to rely on documents can be misleading. Experts differ in their interpretation – even description – of the same events. Moreover, whereas some documents have become available, others have not and many

ix

will never surface for they have been destroyed. That was the fate of most of the documents which could have helped me to refresh my memory; we could not let them fall into the hands of the Gestapo. For much of the book the only evidence stems from my memory and that of the few survivors. Little information remains concerning most of the principal characters. The only objective proof to show me that my own experience was not a dream is a newspaper announcement, a call on behalf of the *Sicherheitsdienst* (SD) for my arrest. Most of my friends – the principal characters in the story that follows – are dead.

This leads to another problem I faced when writing. Relatives and friends of those who died are still alive and while their memory will be as flawed as mine, their recollections of people and episodes may well differ from mine. To avoid causing distress I have therefore disguised a few of the characters by giving them false names and different looks, occasionally by attributing to them actions that were not theirs.

In addition, in order to evoke as powerfully as possible the texture of life under nazism, I have adopted a narrative style that owes more to the techniques of the novelist than to those of the academic historian. I wanted to entertain as well as to inform. After all, the times were replete with drama and I was there whereas today's historians were not.

For all these reasons I call the result a dramatized memoir, not a formal history. But I hope it will be a contribution towards history and redress an imbalance in the formal accounts that threatens to present future generations with a warped picture.

As a participant, the only way I could credibly achieve this was to chronicle my own experiences and those of my close associates. Yet to leave out the context and narrate just another adventure story would be deceitful as well as frivolous, like presenting the walnut as a shell without the kernel. For the context determined the adventurous experiences to a large extent. I hope that the reader wil be happy with the mixture of personal narrative and historical analysis. Those who still feel uncomfortable should bear both the reality and my aim in mind.

PREFACE

I have made sure that the following pages are authentic. Mine is a true picture even where not exact. As a record of our wartime experiences it is as truthfully and as passionately recalled as memory and consideration will allow.

Prologue
THE PHANTOM FROM THE PAST

'Is that Herman?'

At times the telephone throws up peculiar questions. This one was superfluous too, for I always announce my full name at once: to leave whoever calls in no doubt about my identity. The use of only my first name – rare in my hometown of Oxford – made the caller someone familiar. Yet the gentle male voice with a slight American accent was unfamiliar. I racked my brain in silence, then chose a reply that would not reveal my failure to recognize his identity.

'It is indeed,' I said guardedly.

The caller next reverted to Dutch, with a distinct upper-class accent.

'This is Alexander.'

It did little to enlighten me. During the war 'Alexander' had served as cover for *my* real name, to confuse the Gestapo. I also knew several Alexanders, in my native Holland as in my adopted Britain. Slowly it dawned on me that most Alexanders used abbreviations like Alec or Alex, Sandy or Sander, even Lex as I had also been called. This Alexander waited patiently, clearly aware that my brain needed time to work its way to the unexpected truth. If he were the one I now suspected him to be, why should he phone after four decades of silence? So instead of showing my growing excitement I replied cautiously:

'Alexander Paul?'

'That's it. You've got there.'

'From New York?'

'Correct. All the way.'

We had been friends before and during the war. Soon after he had made his home in New York while I made mine in England, and we lost contact. Even Christmas cards had long ago been discarded as meaningless. Now, in a flash, the past came back, images toppling over each other, of the lanky, blue-eyed teenager I had liked and of the authoritative man-of-action who had inspired me through the war, even though I did not always know what was going on. It was typical of Alexander Paul to keep me guessing.

'Where are you calling from?'

'London. Brown's Hotel.'

'How did you get my number?'

An irrelevant question perhaps, but one which gained me a breathing space while I searched frantically for a train timetable. For I had a sudden urge to recapture those distant days of World War II.

Alexander mentioned a publishing colleague, then he added: 'I've got a problem and it relates to the war. I'd like to talk to you about it. But, of course, you may not want to dig all that up.'

I would not have wanted to, but for a curious coincidence. Six months earlier, in the autumn of 1983, I had been one of sixteen presented with the Resistance Cross by Prince Bernhard of the Netherlands in Rotterdam. In Holland there is nothing strange about a delay of nearly forty years in an award for wartime services. We never wanted one and those sixteen were among the last bestowed. One of my partners from those days was among the recipients, Amanda, a beautiful lady then as now. But Alexander, the only other one alive, did not attend. We discussed him though and assumed he had received his Cross from the Dutch ambassador in the USA. Three thousand miles is a long way to travel for a recognition he did not really need.

Meanwhile I had found the train timetable. So I told Alexander I wanted to see him, of course, which train to take from Paddington, and added I would collect him at Oxford station. Then, as an afterthought, I said:

'But how will I recognize you? D'you still have that handlebar moustache?'

'Alas, the years have reduced it to a conventional size.'

'My moustache has gone completely.'

Moustaches were once significant. Mine was, because when I wanted to hide my face as well as my name from the Gestapo it refused to grow beyond a weak imitation of the strong male image to which I felt entitled. (Some years later, in less martial circumstances, it blossomed when I did not feel strong at all.) Alexander's was, because it succeeded beyond expectation and created a martial image to which he did not aspire. (It also nearly cost him his life.)

Alexander continued: 'But I'm still six foot three. Don't worry. I'll know you when I see you.'

'Will you be alone? Stay the night?'

'I'll be alone but won't stay the night. Just reminisce and hopefully set up another meeting.'

I collected Alexander from the station. Neither of us had any difficulty in recognizing the other. His height never seemed exceptional – though once it too helped the Gestapo – as he is well proportioned. He now stooped slightly, though not from age but from many years of politeness to smaller breeds of diplomats at the UN, where he had worked long and successfully. His hair had thinned considerably and greyed, though it still retained some of the crinkles that women found so attractive. Presumably that was why, surprisingly, he wore a hat which he had eschewed when he had abundant wavy hair. The moustache was grey too but quite firm, the nose as before long and aquiline, the eyes with the same humorous twinkle. He still showed that aristocratic appearance, reminiscent of an El Greco portrait. There was no doubt about his identity, nor, he kindly said, about mine. I am only reasonably tall, missing six feet by a hair. At the time I had less luscious hair than Alexander, and blond, but more of it is now left.

We talked. As of old, jocular remarks abounded, only interrupted briefly by a reference to the cause of his visit: a phantom from the past. The phantom appeared in the form of a letter from an old lady to the editor of the *New York Times*. There had been a laudatory editorial on the occasion of Alexander's retirement from the UN, which had prompted the lady to write that all was not entirely unblemished in his wartime past.

'Mr Paul would no doubt want to forget at least one episode where his role has been less than honourable, as he will perhaps in retrospect acknowledge. I have no wish to elaborate, as that might seem to detract from his undoubted achievements, only to point out that none of us is perfect.'

Such random accusations would not have been published but for the sender's status in American society. The outspoken widow of an equally outspoken Supreme Court Judge, she was much admired by Alexander's acquaintances as well as by many in the country at large. Alexander was puzzled, for he realized that he had never even spoken to her although they had often been at the same functions. She must have avoided him. But why? What was she referring to? What did she know? What had she been told? And by whom?

How seriously did Alexander take the letter? A silly question considering that he flew across the Atlantic to seek solace. Yet, having read the letter to me, he adroitly moved away from the war and concentrated on raking up our boyhood past and our pursuits afterwards, thus preventing me from enquiring about the years in between. He had dropped a stone in a quiet pond but seemed content merely to watch the ripples create their intricate patterns. As I drove him back to the station I ventured to ask what he thought the letter referred to.

'No idea, my friend. That's why I want to talk to you at some length. Strange things happened in those days, things we took in our stride then. But perhaps now we would see them differently. Perhaps they would look absurd, or sordid, or irresponsible.' He paused, frowning.

'Is it because you want to silence the lady of the letter?'

'Not really. She won't be shut up easily anyway. No, I always believed we actually achieved something. Now I'm beginning to wonder.'

So much had gone wrong in the resistance that pinpointing achievements would be like the search for the proverbial needle in the haystack. Still, there was more: the human dimension.

We met again a month later in a Cotswold country hotel, when spring had softened the dreary winter and walks had become a gentle pleasure rather than a hearty duty. In the course of a happy fortnight Alexander told me his story and I recounted mine. Together we raked over details of our pasts which had long ago been relegated to obscurity. Two separate stories emerged, but which linked in more ways than we had suspected. We discovered they were complementary, each life-history supplementing the other to form a fairly full picture of the resistance in its varied aspects.

During those years Alexander nearly died twice and escaped with his life several more times in jeopardy. Since the war he had had a glittering career and now lives in the full public glare. I too had had my lucky escapes, less spectacular than his but some of them equally traumatic. There are surely phantoms in my past but no one will bother to query them; none of my actions since the war had caught the limelight, nor had my wartime exploits. My postwar career as a publisher had been exciting only to myself. But someone had queried Alexander's past. When it caught up with him he wanted the comfort of a comrade in arms from those distant days. It would be useless for him to explain his predicament to his current friends. They were not involved in the issues, would not appreciate them and could not therefore provide a satisfactory answer. They might be sympathetic but their sympathy would be for the present person not its past incarnation.

When we started our rambling recollections I soon found out that Alexander felt as though he were locked up in a cage of which the gilt had tarnished. As a resister and intelligence agent he had earned many decorations, among them an honorary British DSO and OBE as well as the Dutch equivalent of the British VC. Had he been taken in, by his own success?

More surfaced. We were surprised to discover that both of us felt haunted by our resistance past. A curious phenomenon for there seemed little rational reason for it. After all, forty years of fairly normal existence should have wiped out the memory of the five abnormal years. We had survived these in good health and reasonably good spirits. Also, millions were involved in World War II, thousands of survivors could tell stories as harrowing as ours, or more, and many did. Why then this haunted feeling? After the war soldiers returned to civilian life and could reminisce with a clear conscience and clean hands, mostly. They had done their job. So had we. We too should have felt satisfied.

'Ah,' said Alexander, 'there's the rub. We were civilians, not soldiers.'

'So what? In a war, where's the difference? We did our duty like soldiers.'

'True. But soldiers are told what to do in all circumstances. We weren't.'

I nodded. It was a good point. We had no guidelines, no clear instructions. We had to fumble and grope for them.

'And we couldn't act, we could only react,' he went on. 'We couldn't do much to defeat the nazis, only help prevent them from defeating us.'

This triggered something in my own mind. 'Yes, we always remained part of our own society. We were always aware of its weaknesses and always planning improvements.'

'That's it.' Alexander became excited too. 'We faced arrogance and evil. And witnessed ordinary, decent people sup with the devil . . .'

'. . . and determined to renew society so it could never happen again.' I felt again the bitterness of lost chances, the youthful commitment and the lingering disappointment.

'Yes,' Alexander concluded, 'we worked hard at it. And most of those committed to renewal died.'

That haunted us: the lack of understanding, the lack of a sense of achievement, in addition to the death of our comrades.

I had forgotten having played such an important part in his life. I remembered that there was friendship and that this had been tested during the war and had deepened as a result. Although Alexander was nearly three years older than me, other connections had closed the gap. His brother Peter and I shared a class at school and much homework. As a result I often visited their sprawling early-eighteenth-century house, full of mysterious corridors and stairs. It was attached to an even more mysterious museum of which their father was keeper. Besides some exquisite art and ancient scientific and technical instruments – some of them huge – it boasted an observatory through the slender dome of which light spilled down onto the gloomy apparatuses below. We raced up and down winding stairs and along endless corridors and landings and played hide-and-seek among the dinosaurs of the industrial revolution. Alexander joined in these voyages of discovery and played bogey, scaring us by jumping out from some shadowy recess.

He was considered extremely clever because he attended university and read law as well as history, an unusual combination in those days. Peter and I grappled with mathematics for our secondary school finals, but Alexander lacked a head for what he called 'sterile abstract calculations'. However, he did have an astonishing memory for events past and present, which he effortlessly arranged in logical patterns that far outstripped our comprehension. We were not impressed by his seemingly artless power of analysis, for it did nothing to help solve our more scientific problems. Still, we realized he was someone special.

His very name underlined this: Alexander Paul. The first was intended to honour Alexander of Macedonia who spread Hellenistic culture across the world, built bridges to Asian cultures and transcended tribal, national and other bigotries. His surname was a coincidence. In the seventeenth century it was intended as a *middle* name to honour the apostle Paul who set christianity on its world-conquering course. Unfortunately the scribe forgot to enter his forebear's surname. Alexander tells everyone who asks that he is descended from Adam, has inherited some of his peculiarities – diplomatically avoiding specifics – and that he could not care less what his ancestors had been or were supposed to have been. The mixture of genes and their mutations were bound to result in unforeseen specimens of Pauls at some stage. He felt content to be associated with such illustrious members of the human race as

Alexander the Great and St Paul. It did not involve any genes but provided mental stimulus.

We held our talks in an old manor house, converted into a comfortable hotel, with exposed beams and blazing fires. We went walking in the undulating countryside and the weather remained generally kind. What had started as a private round of recollections turned into a wish to let others participate. Not because our experiences are more exceptional than those of others but because Resistance as an aspect of World War II is little appreciated today. The plethora of books concentrates on the military and political aspects and has crowded out the purely human aspects we were engaged in. Yet it was Resistance that laid the foundation for the rebuilding of Europe.

Resistance had a validity of its own. It was the people's revolt that made the astonishing postwar recovery possible. Victory on the battlefield could so easily have led to another Versailles. In some ways it did. The military efforts were, of course, of vital importance, but Resistance grew independently and remained primarily a rebellion of ordinary citizens against what they came to perceive as evil. We were involved emotionally, as the German resisters were. We stood face to face with the nazis every day for five long years. To us evil was more tangible than the word used so easily from a distance by the belligerents.

Contrary to popular belief, Resistance originated with the people of Europe's occupied territories, including Germany. It was not initiated by the Allied secret services and only fed by them spasmodically. Armies, navies and airforces could not help us. We had to face nazism alone, make up our minds about what could be tolerated alone, assess alone the practical possibilities of action and face the consequences alone. This was the context of our defence of human dignity and of human values.

For that reason I have included much of Alexander's experiences in this memoir. We both realized that memory can play tricks and that hindsight intrudes. This did not unduly worry us, for the basic truth survives errors of detail, just as basic strengths survive incidental weaknesses. Much as our

basic identity survives the havoc that ageing perpetrates on our
physical appearance, witness the instant recognition when
Alexander and I met at Oxford station in our late sixties after
last seeing each other in our early twenties.

Chapter One
THE END OF INNOCENCE

When war broke out on 1 September 1939 the shock produced no more than a ripple in our peaceful lives. We rushed home from a family holiday in the Belgian Ardennes. The Dutch government called up trained army conscripts, just in case. That was all. The German army marched eastward into faraway Poland, and France and Britain simply and honourably declared war on Germany two days later. Shortly after we were informed that Poland was conquered and split up between two unlikely allies. Nothing more. The French and the British did not move eastward and the Germans did not move westward. No clash of arms occurred anywhere near us. So we relaxed.

We could not anyhow believe our *dolce-far-niente* was really threatened. Nor was it. After a fortnight of frantic drilling of creaky civilians in ill-fitting uniforms Alexander went back to his university. I was too young by a few months to be called up and, having recently passed my secondary school finals with some odd but pleasing results, took what I felt to be a well-deserved rest at the beach.

Holland's west coast boasts an almost endless sandy beach with only some flimsy dunes to protect the green pastures beyond – and below sea level – with a few ancient dikes to fill the gaps. The weathergods showed clemency and offered an Indian summer which allowed us, who lived nearby, to enjoy the beach without tourists.

During those eight months of quiet before disaster struck – the phony war – several events occurred which proved significant for Alexander and me. On 28 August Queen Wilhelmina had joined hands with Belgium's King Leopold in a worldwide appeal for sanity and peace. It did not deter Hitler. Queen and king tried again on 7 November, this time reminding the belligerents to respect neutrality. This second unusual venture into international politics was preceded by some frantic activities inside the Dutch royal palace in which only a handful of people were involved, among them Dr Herman Bernard Wiardi Beckman, a friend of my parents.

The queen harboured few illusions about these royal interventions, but she felt they had to be undertaken. Wilhelmina seemed determined on the more active role that her ancestor William of Orange had played in the sixteenth century but convention now frowned upon. She witnessed 'the stealthy drift of civilization into politics. Politics, however important and unavoidable, is always a secondary function of human life.' Wiardi Beckman had quoted these words of Huizinga to the queen when trying to articulate her feelings during the talks about the second royal appeal. He completed the quotation: 'Politics can never be either the essence or the ultimate pursuit of civilization. Its aims are limited, its views restricted, its results provisional, its means clumsy and inefficient, and its preponderance merely a "cursed spite".' These words came to be repeated often during the next few years to remind politicians amongst resisters of the relativity of party ideologies.

The next event was clearly related to the royal efforts. I noticed that Alexander had disappeared. This did not immediately become apparent, for during the week he was at his digs in Leyden. The explanation came in a most peculiar way.

Late in September my girlfriend Amanda and I were on the beach with friends. Amanda in her swimsuit could not avoid showing her gorgeous figure, nor did she want to. Part of the fun for boys was ogling girls and for girls to ogle boys, though girls also ogled other girls. One girl we had not met before attracted a lot of attention. She could not hide her boyish figure nor her height of over six feet and she stressed this unusual combination by keeping her body straight and almost stretching it, unlike most tall people who tend to slouch. She also walked majestically on the balls of her feet as if she were wearing high-heeled shoes. Later we discovered she also did this off the beach. In addition she wore make-up, her full lips accentuated by lipstick, her eyes shadowed, her long nails painted, though all carefully applied. Hardly any girls used make-up on the beach, few sparingly at parties. It seemed a challenge to convention, which was no doubt the intention. Yet, somehow, this unorthodoxy made her beautiful.

One of our friends was in animated discussion with her. While we looked rather obviously at her, she kept casting glances at Amanda's protruding bosom. I winked at our friend, who took the cue and introduced her: 'Laura van Alblas.'

Laura, in a deep voice, added: 'I'm Alexander's cousin.' And continued staring unabashedly at Amanda's breasts. It made Amanda blush through her suntan and fidget. I now recalled that Alexander had once mentioned Laura, although vaguely and in a way that made us wonder whether she was a relative or his girlfriend.

Amanda recovered quickly. 'But we haven't met before, have we?'

Laura now took her eyes off the breasts, either satisfied or out of politeness. 'I'm mostly in Leyden, at the university,' she explained.

We then sat down and talked lightheartedly until everyone went for a swim, everyone except Laura. While Amanda threw herself about exuberantly in the waves, I got out early and went to Laura. She smiled, looking me up and down.

What she then said came as a surprise. 'I've got to talk to you about Alexander. But not here.' Whereupon she invited me to her place and gave instructions on how to find it. 'Bring your luscious girl,' she added in a hushed voice, for the others were returning.

Amanda shook her endless curls, a motion I never stopped admiring. As she began to dry herself, I whispered Laura's invitation to her. She nodded, and I told Laura we would come.

Laura left by car, we followed on our bicycles, more slowly, pedalling into a rising wind. The meeting was to have monumental repercussions and would change the course of our lives. We lost our innocence, in more ways than one, as adolescents as well as politically. The cataclysm of the war accelerated the gentle process of growing up.

Our schooldays in the mid-1930's were sunny. We grew into adults untrammelled by the clouds that beset teenagers today. If there were any clouds they remained in the minds of our elders and out of our sight. And even our elders did not view them with apprehension. The thunder of the financial upheaval of the 1920's had finally died away. My father, whose career at the Ministry of Works had been crudely cut short, was re-established as a respected architect. Any future crisis would surely be minor by comparison.

Born in August 1920, I had been too young to be aware of these traumas, even though they affected my parents. Nothing shook my happy innocence. Our school curriculum did not include contemporary affairs: we stuck firmly to Napoleon. And left politics to the politicians. I had plenty to keep mind and body busy. Outside school there were sports, music and, eventually, girls. And to link all these activities there was the bicycle.

It was the age of the bicycle. Everyone from the age of three had one. I cycled to school twice a day and used it to go to all my other activities. Sometimes I even rode with my cello strapped to my back. Travel had never been a problem in our small flat country, where distances are usually measured in single miles. Trains, medium-distance tram-trains and short-distance trams took care of longer journeys. We liked to believe the bicycle was a Dutch invention, an understandable fallacy, for Holland was – still is – the most cycle-dense country in the world. The bicycle was certainly to prove of vital significance during the war.

Few people owned cars, neither my parents nor the Pauls nor any of our neighbours. The large houses around us lacked garages. Incongruously, our smaller house did have one. My father – then the city architect of Haarlem – had designed the house. He said the garage was to store bicycles, for the present at least, though of course as an architect he had an eye to the future. I suspect he had also had his eye on my maternal

4

grandfather's long black Hispano-Suiza, a majestic, rather funereal vehicle, accommodating a chauffeur behind a solid glass partition. Sadly, between the design of the house and its construction my grandfather died, the car was sold, and the garage remained a bicycle shed.

Another vital tool for the resistance also reputedly derived from a Dutch invention: printing from movable type. The romantic story relates how a merchant and printer of book-blocks – L. J. Coster – cut letters from the bark of a beech to amuse his children. This had happened in 1440 in a wood close to my home. His statue still graces the main square of Haarlem. As with the invention of the bicycle we seem to have been duped, though I still find it hard to concede the honour to Gutenberg. However this may be, the newspaper became an indelible part of the resistance along with the bicycle.

For a professed non-intellectual in a world of men with degrees my mother coped well. She did this by making virtue out of necessity and letting the males have their way, ensuring her sway over the family by insisting on excellence and enjoying the results. She gave up playing the violin when my father's proficiency at the piano soared. She staunchly supported my determination to take up the cello at a very tender age. She later chose as my teacher an expatriate Spaniard, Thomas Canivez, a friend of Pablo Casals. I therefore had the privilege of watching the two practise duets in front of a huge mirror and of receiving double expert advice. We had musical evenings and weekends, and went to concerts, often at the Concert-gebouw in Amsterdam.

Music continued to play a major part in our life and fulfilled a special role during the war. The only jarring note occurred when my second cousin introduced jazz into our classical climate. The juvenile Swing Papas began their brief existence in our home, with me at the piano. Parental discord gradually subsided when they noticed my attempts to restrict practice and performance to their absences. Fifty years on, the same cousin – Peter Schilperoort – still leads its postwar successor, the Dutch Swing College Band.

My mother also encouraged me in finding my religious feet. We were not really practising Christians. My father belonged to one protestant denomination, my mother to another. When they went to services they did so together with us children, alternating between churches. But the endless sermonizing and the humourless pomposity bored me and I lacked any religious feeling. This saddened my mother. So when my English teacher, despairing of my ever mastering that alien language, jokingly suggested an alternative way to achieve some proficiency, my mother took it seriously and sent me to the Church of England.

The small chapel was – still is – an ugly Victorian building squeezed between elegant seventeenth-century houses on one of Amsterdam's narrow canals. The sermon lasted less than ten minutes and the singing was faster and more enjoyable, due in part to the presence of a choir. Afterwards the vicar, having detected a bass voice, asked me to join the choir. Flattered, I accepted.

During one service I had a revelation that must have been similar to that of Saul on the road to Damascus. I saw a vision, a lingering image of a smiling Jesus sitting on a rock in the desert, praying and beckoning. The image and the feelings it aroused – as strong now as then – influenced my attitude in the resistance. Religion also motivated many others, the Paul brothers, Wiardi Beckman. Not that any of us indulged in endless theological discussions, but in our endless discussion about resistance tactics and goals we started from the same christian premises.

In one area my mother did not hold sway, although she took a keen interest in it, as did my father, though for different reasons. Girls came early into my life, at the age of six when I went to primary school and was seated next to a girl called Tineke on a twin bench. Tineke quickly became a steady companion outside school as well, in effect my first girlfriend. The kisses were exchanged were mere pecks on cheeks, but surely as meaningful as more elaborate physical contacts later on. I never completely lost track of her, though we moved to different schools as we grew up. I found her again in the dark days of 1943, by which time she had blossomed into a beautiful and very desirable young woman. She and her husband then gave me much needed sanctuary from the Gestapo.

As a girlfriend Tineke was succeeded by many others. Gradually kisses veered towards lips and eventually hands were used as well. I remember my bitter disappointment at seventeen when the splendid breasts of a much coveted girl turned out to be mostly made up of cottonwool.

The Paul brothers introduced me to amateur dramatics and this signalled a dramatic turn in my love life. Mostly I acted in supporting roles as I was considered essential as a 'good filler'. Which is how I came to meet the girl who shared much of my wartime life and effectively saved it.

It had taken me some time to recover from the cottonwool breasts. But girls had again come to mean bosoms and bottoms. I am afraid I have to admit that I went for mere size then. Alexander, however, behaved in a more discerning way, not only because he was older but because he valued other attributes besides physical ones. Not that he was prim or superior. He just had a wider choice. His girlfriends were invariably beauties, mine just jolly nice, except one.

That one exception was kindly passed on to me by Alexander, not because she was not well-endowed – which she was – but because he wanted a change and so did she. Her parents had chosen well when naming her Amanda for she was indeed 'lovable'. She particularly liked virgins – an implausible term for a male – whom she took pride in initiating in the delightful enjoyment of life's marvellous gifts. I shall always be grateful to her for my own initiation, the pleasant surprise one Sunday afternoon in my empty home of my erect manhood being guided by nimble fingers to her soft yet strong womanhood and there galloping off without help or hindrance.

Amanda was not only superb as a lover. She was sharp and witty and a beauty: of medium height with large black curls down her back, dark brown eyes that sparkled like fireworks, an almost Grecian nose, most unusual in our predominantly blond and widenosed population. She was uncomplicated, with a great sense of fun and of humour. She acted with us in our plays, she giggled on the sidelines when I exhausted myself on the hockey pitch and she came to our musical sessions, not as a performer, nor even as a listener, but as a spectator. For she was fascinated by people and their often erratic behaviour, and displayed an insight into human character which I still lack. In all this sex helped, as it always will, even though its role is mostly wrapped up in obscurities that are meant to reduce its importance but tend surreptitiously to increase it instead. Its moments had to be stolen anyway and it did not provide the only bond between us.

A little before this introduction to love in its all-embracing sensation I had my first encounter with politics. It had been precipitated rather unconsciously in Amsterdam, where we lived for a few years in a fairly desirable district. The area came to attract displaced people from Germany, most of them Jews. Initially this early experience with what came to be known as 'the Jewish question' merely concerned their status as fugitives. We commiserated with them and made friends with several. Generally they behaved impeccably and sought to integrate themselves with the indigenous population. Most of them were well-off and sophisticated.

When more of them arrived — many thousands — the situation subtly but distinctly changed. They began to stick together more and more, gradually forming enclaves, and their Jewishness became the subject of endless discussions. This irritated us gentiles, though for its cliquishness and not primarily for its Jewishness. Any group of people which consolidates itself — whether religious, racial or social — tends to irritate by its exclusiveness. Such exclusivity habitually brings in its wake requests, then demands, for special privileges outside the confines of church or hall. It offends those left out and leads to hostility. In our tolerant society then hostility remained confined to a very few gentiles whom the majority did not take seriously. Anti-semitism never really found root in Holland, nor did the nazism which fed on it. Only a handful of expatriate Jews contemplated moving on to America, even when the threat of a German invasion of Holland became acute. My family had by then returned to Haarlem, where the first real political clash occurred.

One day four classmates turned up in the uniform of the nazi youth organization. They were sent home to change. This created a stir, for one of the fathers took his son, still in uniform, back to the school and into the classroom. The teacher did not know how to handle this breach of protocol. My friend Peter Paul – a few seats away – then stood up and said to me in a clear voice: 'Come on, Herman.'

Baffled, I loyally got up and followed Peter to the door. Here he whispered some instructions in my ear. In unison we then said loudly:

'We protest and are going to report to the headmaster.'

We were unclear about the precise reason for the protest, but it resulted in a mass exodus which left the unfortunate teacher dumbfounded and alone with the nazis, the son and the father, who were just as surprised by this unexpected development and as much at a loss.

The headmaster took us back into the classroom, closed the door, called for silence and addressed the father.

'Sir, I'd like to remind you that parents are only allowed in classes at my invitation.'

We giggled, the father was about to comment when the headmaster continued: 'There's also a rule that prohibits pupils from wearing boyscout uniform.'

This silenced the father but unleashed exuberant laughter from the class. The father took his son by the arm and strode out, mumbling something about politics being more serious than scouting. No more disturbances followed. Three of the nazi boys returned to normality, the fourth did not turn up any more. Peter and I were gently reprimanded in the privacy of the headmaster's study, but also thanked for having saved the teacher from worse embarrassment.

This incident occurred at a time when the Dutch nazi party had already started on a downward slope. It had been founded in January 1933 as a grouping of predominantly right wing people rallying behind a cry for stronger government and with fairly innocuous means to achieve it. Some 600 joined. The next year it grew to 21,000 and early in 1936 to 52,000, when it fell back to half that number at the outbreak of war. In 1935 it received 8% of the popular vote, a sensation in our fractionalized country. In 1939 this too was halved. The reason for the upsurge was the call for strong government without attaching racist strings. Even Jews joined. The reason for the slide was the introduction late in 1936 of the very racial theories left out at the start. Also, smartly uniformed men began to be seen marching through the streets in a fashion clearly copied from nazi Germany. A few family friends had initially joined them but left, disappointed.

All this did little to make me politically conscious but it upset my sense of history. Hitler came to be compared with Napoleon. This puzzled me for I admired Napoleon. I do not recall having any particular feeling about Hitler, nor about friends professing a preference for strong government. After all, my image of Napoleon made him a strong leader, even a great one. The comparison upset me because Napoleon figured in my estimation as a civilized man whereas what little I had heard about Hitler made him out to be uncultured and rather a bully. Also, Hitler was not married and had no mistresses, whereas Napoleon had two wives and many mistresses.

We Dutch claimed recognition for a third 'invention' which conditioned our attitude before and during the war, in addition to the bicycle and printing, albeit of a different nature and this time rightfully so. Hugo Grotius is generally conceded to be the father of international law with the publication in 1625 of his *Law of War and Peace*. Ever since, Holland has been preoccupied with the legal aspects of international relations. And this preoccupation deflected attention from the real threat. For we preferred to ignore the sabre-rattling that was going on in Germany and continued to rely firmly on the settlement of disputes between states by the power of argument rather than by military might. Like their British opposite numbers – Baldwin and Chamberlain – the two Dutch prime ministers who dominated the interwar period – Colijn and de Geer – were applauded for their statesmanship, for it procured stability and peace. After all, that is what we all want at all times. We too had our prophets of doom like Churchill in Britain, but in Holland they were not to be found in politics.

It was the Professor of History at our most ancient and prestigious university – Leyden – who sounded warnings of impending disaster, and as early as spring 1935. Johan Huizinga turned his considerable analytical talents from the

Middle Ages to the contemporary scene when he published a 'diagnosis of the spiritual suffering of our time' in his *In the Shadow of Tomorrow*. Its opening sentences echoed throughout the country – and beyond – for the next decade.

'We live in a crazy world. And we know it. No one could be surprised if the madness suddenly erupted in a frenzy which left the people of Europe dulled and infatuated, the engines running and the flags flying but the spirit departed.'

Reprint followed reprint and by the time the war engulfed us few households were without a copy. Most of my teenage friends read the book, as I did. My parents counted Huizinga among their friends. When the nazi avalanche reached us I sometimes sat at his feet. As the text so clearly reflects our mood at the time, a few more extracts follow.

'The cohesiveness of our social order is everywhere in doubt. A vague fear for the future has crept in, a feeling that civilization is in decline and may even collapse. What seemed certain and holy has become unsettled: truth and humanity, reason and justice. We witness forms of government that do not function any more, systems of production that break down.'

And elsewhere: 'Two great cultural gains on which we pride ourselves – education for all and instant publicity for all events – contain the seeds of degeneration. Undigested knowledge impedes judgement and stands in the way of wisdom.'

My undigested encounter with the Jewish question described earlier made me relish his account of race: 'The neglect of the critical faculty is best illustrated by the current racial theories, which coordinate biological and cultural elements. If spiritual qualities form part of race, then, logically, similar talents point to similarity of race. The Jews and the Germans are both extremely gifted in philosophy and music, therefore the semitic and germanic races are similar. And so on, as you like. The example is ridiculous but not more absurd than many views now widely held.'

Huizinga particularly voiced his concern 'that the state is not subject to moral criteria, is outside morality, in fact amoral. The worship of success in economical affairs makes it possible to eliminate indignation in political judgements. A political

11

system that was initially despised, then feared, gradually becomes acceptable, even admirable. Injustice, cruelty, moral constraint, oppression, disloyalty, deceit, perversion of justice? But the streets are clean and the trains run on time. This illustrates the deceptive tendency to reverse a valid judgement. A healthy state organization is characterized by order and discipline. Reversal: therefore order and discipline imply a healthy state system. As if sound sleep alone proves righteousness.'

It is easy to see how our attitude came to be dominated by spiritual arguments, not by power politics. What happened across our eastern border came to be discussed in terms of cultural values, not brute power.

One politician who appreciated the reality was Wiardi Beckman. I called him 'Uncle Stuuf', 'uncle' in accordance with the prevailing custom which separated close friends from friendly acquaintances by granting the former honorary family status. 'Stuuf' was a nickname which referred to his peculiar upper lip, 'stiff' if you wish. I liked him, but only just. He formed part of my parents' world and remained on the fringes of my life until June 1940. I suppose I sensed the special qualities that made me worship him later, but school, sports and Amanda prevented them from penetrating any deeper.

Uncle Stuuf came from an ancient patrician family. Like several such scions in the early decades of our century he felt a deep concern for the plight of the 'new slaves' of the industrial upheaval. For him this had its roots in the christian religion, indeed followed logically and emotionally from Christ's perception, though not necessarily from the precepts and dogmas which the passage of centuries had imposed upon His clear vision. Uncle Stuuf translated it into political activity.

Born in 1904, he opted for the social democratic party while still at secondary school when he defended the party's leader, who in 1918 had appeared to call for a revolution and a republic. A strange start to a prestigious career, for Uncle Stuuf was neither a revolutionary nor a republican, just very much aware of the class system, the sharp division between the privileged and the non-privileged, not only resulting in appalling misery but also in an awful waste of talent. He never pretended that the underprivileged would by definition inherit the earth and be the better rulers. Nor did he ever promise that misery could be eliminated everywhere forever. It was to him much simpler: the then prevailing system prevented the unfettered development of whatever talent resided in the underprivileged masses. As a christian and a historian he knew that such talent had never been confined to any ruling class. A firm believer in excellence – in today's jargon an élitist – he felt that any barrier to personal achievement other than personal limitations was wicked, stupid and stultifying. He was a radical and fervent evolutionist, but a democrat not an autocrat or a communist. Indeed, he abhorred communism as much as nazism, as much as the prevailing system which made democracy a fraud. His defence of the inexcusable remarks of his leader nevertheless impressed by its subtlety: he scathingly pointed to the despicable situation of the underdogs and the dire need to alleviate conditions which 'would otherwise lead to revolution and the despatch of the queen'. An interesting opinion in view of the future affinity between the conventional queen and her radical subject. At Leyden University he was much in demand as a debater of great intellect. History was his subject, Huizinga his professor. A strong bond came to be forged between them, even though the older man was rather conservative and almost agnostic. Their bond, despite such schisms, provided a pointer to Uncle Stuuf's future value for the resistance. A doctorate followed. When he became my 'uncle' at 33 – I was seventeen and completely un-interested in politics – he was the editor of the largest daily newspaper in Holland and a member of the Upper House of Parliament.

Wiardi Beckman had difficulty in mixing with the very people whose cause he championed, out of shyness not arrogance. Few people realized he was shy, for his fiery speeches at large meetings inspired his 'slaves'. He linked the defence of human dignity with the undignified, almost inhuman treatment of his listeners and he did so with sound historical analyses. He impressed both his educationally under-nourished party audience and his sophisticated political opponents. This curious – and rare – combination made him a choice for the triumvirate which introduced Prince Bernhard into Dutch society after his marriage in 1937 to Crown Princess Juliana. It was also to lead Queen Wilhelmina to pick him as one of her secret advisers in the autumn of 1939.

'Fiery' describes him adequately, warts and all. Once I eavesdropped on a discussion at our home. I saw Uncle Stuuf gesticulating wildly and my father looking suitably impressed, but also worried. Clearly the subject was the danger of national socialism in general and Hitler's territorial claims in particular. Unwittingly my father echoed Huizinga:

'But Stuuf, the trains run beautifully on time and massive motorways are built. There's no unemployment and people work diligently. Germany seems to have left the traumas of defeat behind.'

'Indeed,' retorted Uncle Stuuf, 'but to what purpose? You won't like it when that purpose is revealed.'

I had no idea what he meant.

'What can one do?' asked my father ready to accept expert wisdom.

'Prepare,' shot back Uncle Stuuf.

'How?'

'By doing what they do: building roads and bridges, and arms.'

'But I can only build houses and schools and churches.'

'Fair enough. But don't be impressed by their silly slogans. Read Huizinga again. Some of us will have to resist. Prepare mentally.'

The words conveyed little to me. But I remembered them when the years of innocence were gone.

During the ride from the beach to Laura's home Amanda shouted: 'Alexander's just an excuse. She wants my tits.'

Panting, I shouted back: 'I'll be their protector.'

'You don't stand a chance with her around.' Amanda had not taken long to size Laura up.

After cycling for some half an hour we had found our way to the big iron gates at the entrance to Laura's home. A long drive through trees that protected us from the wind brought us to a huge rambling house. Clearly successive owners had built on and on. We caught our breath. Laura stood in the monumental entrance porch, looking very distinguished, in high heels, waiting impassively while we swung off our bikes. Towering nearly a head above Amanda and inches above me, she took us into a vast room with vast sofas, vast easy chairs and lots of little tables, lots of comfort but little character.

While we took in the room, Laura said: 'My parents are away for the weekend. The maids have the evening off, but they've prepared some food. Let's have a drink first.' Not a bad deal, for Amanda and I had merely reckoned on sandwiches on the beach. Had Laura planned our visit? Later she called it a lucky coincidence.

'Cigarette?'

'No thank you,' I replied quickly, looking round.

But Amanda took a cigarette and sat in one of the sofas, pulling me down beside her. Laura poured out the drinks and put the glasses on little tables. She then sat down opposite us, opened a box, took out a large cigar, lit it and looked us over. I was astonished and must have shown it, for she smiled at me and blew smoke up towards the ceiling.

'People never know what to make of me,' she said suddenly. 'Neither did I, until a couple of years ago. Like everyone else I've got my sexual feelings, perhaps more than most.' We seemed to be in for a confession. 'I realised I could only compete with shapely girls like Amanda by accepting my peculiar features and accentuating some of them. I didn't like stares of pity and awkward silences. That is why I do what I do. After all, Amanda shows off her special features. Though she's a natural beauty. My legs are quite shapely, so I wear high heels and people actually notice them. My hands are nice too, so I grow my nails. And I smoke cigars because minute cigarettes look ridiculous in my hands. They're nicer too, die easily and can be relit any time. Very useful when you want something for your hands to play with, as most people do.' It did look elegant on Laura. 'People still look, of course, but not out of pity. They wonder, as you did.'

Amanda stopped her. 'It certainly works. You do catch the eye.' Then, as if to assert herself: 'But you stared at my chest.'

'We're quits then,' Laura laughed.

I felt slightly uneasy at this weird rivalry. 'OK, you're both lovely. Now what's this about Alexander?'

'I went to the beach because Alexander told me that's where I'd find you.' Noticing my blink of surprise, she asked: 'Does that shock you?'

I regained my composure. 'Not shocked. Intrigued.'

'He's in Berlin. Apologies for the secrecy, but it's all a bit hush-hush. Please don't tell anyone else.'

'Of course we won't if you don't want us to,' Amanda slipped in. 'But what's special about Berlin?'

Laura did not reply directly, but looked at me. 'Promise you won't tell.'

Still not taking her seriously I held up my right hand. 'I do most solemnly swear to keep a secret a secret.'

Laura paused. Then she said: 'Alexander's preparing for the war.'

'You must be joking,' I exploded. 'He's anti-war.'

'Of course he is, but he's even more anti-nazi.'

'There won't be any more war,' Amanda chipped in lightly. 'The Germans have already got what they want and don't need to go through Holland to get at France.'

Laura now became very serious and said emphatically: 'On the contrary, we know they'll go through Holland and Belgium.'

'Know?' I asked, astonished. 'And who are "we"?'

'Well, I'm part of it. We've had endless discussions. Surely you know the general idea. My mother and Alexander's are sisters. My father's in the navy. I've just got my degree, history. Huizinga was my professor. Wonderful man. So you see, I have to be part of it.'

I did not see. What exactly did she mean? She smoked her cigar, pensively, stalling on an explanation. We sipped our drinks and waited. Amanda moved slightly away from me, clearly concentrating, probably sensing the turn events would take. I had no idea. Laura stared at us through the cigar smoke, while I wondered what to make of this extraordinary woman.

'You've got lovely breasts, Amanda,' she said suddenly.

Unabashed, Amanda replied: 'I know, Laura. They keep telling me.'

'You probably think I'm flat-chested. But that's not quite true. Mine are like pancakes, though several layers of them.'

Although fascinated by this strange new turn the conversation was taking, I was also slightly embarrassed. 'What's all this about?' I interrupted. 'What about all the hush-hush stuff?'

'Give me time, will you? I'll tell you in due course,' she replied and opened her eyes wide. 'It's nice to find you so attractive. You've got sexy legs, Herman.'

Before I could compose myself Laura came over and sat between us. As I shuffled sideways she began stroking my thigh. She then turned and touched Amanda's breasts, gently. 'We're in for it,' I thought and looked at Amanda, questioningly. She nodded, then to my utter surprise took her sweater off, displaying her splendid form. Laura was captivated: she cupped a hand around one of Amanda's breasts, lightly explored its circumference and held the nipple for a moment. Then she pulled back and took off her own sweater to reveal the pancakes. And gave terse instructions.

'Grab them, Herman. And take your shorts off.' I did as I was told. Laura's breasts were large in diameter, with little depth but quite firm, in fact rather pleasing. Though I must say I preferred Amanda's.

'That's lovely. Don't be gentle. Press harder.' Not everyone tells you what to do. I obliged and at once found myself part of a tangle of legs, arms, hands and fingers, in addition to breasts. The next thing I remember is Laura standing above me.

'What do we do with Herman?' she asked Amanda and then answered her own question by taking her pants off and simply straddling me.

I was the first to recover. 'Thank you, Laura,' I said rather formally. 'Can we now get on with the hush-hush?'

She did not reply at once, then said playfully: 'You've got to learn a lot yet, you idiot. Why can't you relax and enjoy it? There's no need to be quite so single-minded.'

Amanda too had recovered. 'Well,' she said, backing me up, 'you do mix business with pleasure rather.'

Laura reacted instantly. 'One can't always do what you call

business without pleasure. Sex is a very sound test of people's character.'

This dictum was a pointer to the future, though I did not realize it then.

Laura went back to her chair and relit her cigar, ready for further disclosures. 'You know,' she said rather ponderously, 'there's no stopping Hitler.'

I shrugged. 'He certainly acts like a lunatic. Where do we go from here?'

Laura blew smoke to the ceiling before replying. 'There's not much to tell yet. We must be prepared and I want to prepare you. First, absolute silence. Secondly, you'll be part of a small group. There'll be a few more. It's called a cell. If the Gestapo infiltrate or arrest one of us, they won't know anything about the wider organization. If we're careful it'll keep the Gestapo from knowing, hopefully forever. They're very professional. So should we be.'

'Will Alexander be in our cell?'

'No. He'll be doing other things and you shouldn't talk to him about it.'

I had only a vague idea what she meant and was still confused by the erotica.

'What's wrong with the Germans anyway?'

'Nothing except that they supported Hitler. Many Dutchmen admire what Hitler has done too. They've closed their eyes to the unpleasant bits. No omelettes without breaking eggs, that sort of argument. But we think it's the other way round. What good he appears to have done is calculated to achieve evil goals. He's developed concentration camps for evil purposes. First he incarcerated opponents, then what he calls ungermanic people, and soon it'll be Jews. And when the camps fill up he'll have to get rid of the overflow. That'll start the wanton killing. He'll do the same wherever he goes. Alexander told me that the SS went in behind the army into Poland. The army was told to shut its eyes. The massacres are going on there now.'

I was much impressed by this, my first introduction to the reality of war-time politics. The atmosphere had changed completely. No more erotics. We did not question Laura for we had nothing to question her with. I did not see what action could follow, but it did not seem to matter. Laura would tell us what to do.

As I now know, Alexander had been asked by Uncle Stuuf to contact a professor at Berlin University under the cloak of enquiring about the possibilities for a postgraduate course. Uncle Stuuf remembered the academic as a strong anti-nazi and also a friend of Hans Oster, then a lieutenant-colonel under Admiral Canaris, head of the Abwehr, German military intelligence. He knew Oster to be anti-nazi as well, for Oster had supplied the Dutch military attaché in Berlin with details of Germany's plans for invading Holland and Belgium. As a bonafide student Alexander would make a less conspicuous emissary of the queen than a well-known politician. The reason for this delicate mission was not to test Oster but to support his warnings. The Dutch government had chosen to ignore them and Uncle Stuuf felt it useful to sound out these military men about the chances of preserving Dutch neutrality, with the support of the queen.

Alexander travelled by train. He recalled with glee that on his first journey at the end of September he encountered hostile questioning at the border. It gave him his first lesson in how to stand up to bullies. The train had been halted at a tiny station inside Germany. There were two guards, both tall and muscular. They wore the high-peaked cap prevalent in nazi Germany. Alexander confessed that he could never forget these nazi caps, symbols of mindless arrogance.

Flipping through his passport, one of the guards asked: 'What are you doing in this train? Don't you know you're in Germany now?'

'Of course I know,' Alexander replied casually. 'I'm on my way to Berlin.'

'What for?'

Alexander remained polite. 'A course at the university.'

'Why? There's a war on.'

'My passport is in order and surely entitles me to enter Germany.'

'Ah,' came the chilling retort, 'but we're entitled to refuse entry to enemy aliens.'

'I didn't know Holland was involved in your war,' said Alexander icily, though still civilly.

The guard squared his shoulders and raised his voice. 'We decide who our enemies are.'

Alexander somehow found the courage to cover his anxiety and shout back. 'I'm a student! You have no right to refuse me entry! Show me your papers and I'll lodge a protest!'

At which to his relief they moved on. In Berlin Alexander was received most politely, though coolly. Why was a mere student of law being used for such a delicate mission? As he pointed out the delicacy of the queen's position, Alexander realized that he was ill prepared. There had not been enough time, nor did he know enough about the people he met or their circumstances. Luckily he was invited to return.

When he arrived home again, Uncle Stuuf agreed that by their reticence Oster and the professor had intimated that they too were in a delicate position. They were probably risking their lives, not just their reputation. Possibly they also had other problems on their hands. Uncle Stuuf therefore arranged a letter of introduction from the German ambassador in Holland, an old-fashioned diplomat not keen on the nazis.

Within a few days Alexander was on his way again. His rapid return with the letter impressed the German anti-nazis. They were also visibly relieved, for Alexander's mission turned out to be only diplomatic. Oster consequently introduced him to his political assistant, Dr Hans von Dohnanyi, a deeply religious and sharp-witted 37-year-old lawyer with whom Alexander quickly made friends. Dohnanyi appreciated his young Dutch colleague's seriousness, intelligence and dedication. The two also shared a sense of humour, so singularly lacking in nazis. Although caution still prevailed, Alexander obtained a fairly full situation report, valuable in itself though not very helpful for his mission.

Dohnanyi explained that while many Germans were in no way nazis, most of them felt they had to accept small doses of the new *Weltanschauung* or political philosophy. It would prevent worse from happening if they stayed the course. Dohnanyi said it proved difficult to convince these potential allies of the danger in this attitude. 'It ignores the old Roman warning *principiis obsta*, that things must be nipped in the bud as they would otherwise get out of hand and all would be swept away by the nazi avalanche.'

There was considerable civilian opposition to nazism, centred on church leaders, civil servants, trade unionists and social democrats, and some coordination existed. However, the civilians felt that for any overt action they needed the military who possessed the hardware to make a coup stick. Among the military three groups could be distinguished: nazis (few), anti-nazis (slightly more) and non-nazis (most). The anti-nazis came up against the ancient oath of allegiance, to which their non-nazi brethren felt bound. They encountered further hesitations when victories were won against all expectations. Dohnanyi said that the hard-line anti-nazi military should first incapacitate Hitler. He felt sure that the soft-line non-nazis would follow. But this had to wait for the right opportunity. The royal efforts, however much appreciated, did not create such an opportunity, for queen and king could not give any further support.

After this depressing information little more could be done by queen and king than make a somewhat pathetic plea for neutrality to be respected. For although his talks confirmed Oster's warnings to the Dutch government, they also made it abundantly clear there would be no pressure to oust Hitler or make him change his mind from inside Germany. Elsewhere experiences proved equally sterile. In London the queen's personal emissary was reminded that Britain had not wanted the war in the first place. Twice more Alexander went to Berlin, to keep contact. This proved to be more useful in the future than was anticipated then.

In January 1940 it was my turn to be conscripted into the army and my world shrank to one of drill, rifle practice and barracks for four months.

Chapter Two

HOLLAND'S WAR
OF FIVE DAYS

The sirens woke us at dawn (4.05 am) on 10 May 1940. Light from a still hidden sun filtered between the buildings, beautiful but uncanny. Unaccustomed to real war, we jumped from our bunks and rushed outside, in our pyjamas. We watched ungainly planes roaring low overhead. Soldiers of all ranks joined us, all in nightdress rather than battledress. From all around us came a cacophony of sounds: shouts of 'English!' and 'Germans!', explosions of bombs, smoke rising into the pale blue sky, human cries of agony. Someone near me pointed at white specks in the sky a few miles away: parachutists floating down. There had been no warning nor even the politeness of a declaration of war.

In this untidy situation I heard a loud voice commanding everyone to get dressed 'bloody quick' It was Alexander, in battledress, on a horse. We all obeyed at once, the spell of utter amazement broken.

The modern barracks was built in the dunes just outside The Hague, Holland's seat of government though not its capital. It housed an artillery depot – to which I belonged – and an élite cavalry regiment, part of whose job it was to protect the queen. Within minutes Alexander led a large detachment of the royal regiment into town, presumably heading for the queen's palace. Other troopers went into the dunes to search for the parachutists, now confirmed to be German. I helped carry machine guns to the roof and we started shooting at two lonely

Junker planes. We found their range lamentably limited, but the firing gave us a sense of satisfaction.

We had been the target of a German assault aimed at capturing queen and government that day. The airborne attack on The Hague, far behind the lines, was a complete surprise. Luckily, the Dutch reserve army, stationed nearby, could be put into action. Luckily too, the airfields around the town could not cope with the heavy troop-carrying aircraft: most stuck in the soft soil. To add to their problems the German paras had dropped far more widely spread than planned. Most were found and taken prisoner; no more planes arrived; the Germans had used almost their entire airborne forces. Well over 3,000 landed around The Hague, many were killed, most captured. The Dutch lost some 300 in a battle that proved to be the only one won.

Our luck did not last. German victory could not be thwarted by one battle lost. (Its airborne commander, General Student, got his own back when *he* thwarted Allied airborne forces – on the ground – at Arnhem in 1944.) German victory in 1940 was quickly ensured by superior equipment, mastery of the air, the element of surprise and the occasional use of unethical methods such as German soldiers in Dutch uniform during the early stages. Five days later our army capitulated.

In our barracks the damage was severe, many horses slaughtered, some twenty soldiers killed and more wounded. We could not believe it. However, that was all the action I was involved in, bar the clearing up. We were a specialist unit without a proper role in such a messy war and consequently only used for bringing some order to the chaos caused by the bombs and thereby relieving troopers of the royal regiment for more active duties.

Not so Alexander. With his men, on horses and in two ancient armoured cars, he went to the royal palace, a mid-seventeenth-century gem in a wood on the outskirts of The Hague. He soon encountered another surprise element: the scare of fifth columnists. The term originated with General Mola, the falangist commander who had four military columns surrounding Madrid during the Spanish Civil War and claimed a fifth column inside the city. In our case they were supposed to be German civilian residents who would assist the German military invaders as spies and as snipers for killing top Dutchmen; briefly, the hidden enemy within. Although research after the war convincingly proved them to have been non-existent, they were then thought to be everywhere. These rumours aggravated the confusion and tied down troops, in The Hague as elsewhere. They also paralysed the town. To move around became almost impossible, and this seriously interfered with communication between cabinet and military. It is difficult to imagine a messier situation, though it had an aspect of comic opera in which Alexander got embroiled.

He found the palace guards in turmoil for fear of fifth columnists sheltering between the trees. Shortly after he arrived, a single plane flew low over the palace. Prince Bernhard, consort of the queen's only daughter and essential for the survival of the House of Orange, grabbed a machine gun and fired alongside Alexander's men. The petrol tank was hit and the plane crashed in a park near the centre of town. This provided the occasion for Alexander's first handshake with the prince.

However, jubilation soon gave way to anxiety about the safety of the royal household. They were bundled into an assortment of vehicles. Luggage was loaded too, though the queen insisted on carrying two bulky briefcases herself. Some soldiers were detailed to clear the wood, an easy task since there was no one there; others to clear the road into town, a job made hazardous by military patrols searching for elusive fifth columnists. It therefore took hours for the royal procession to reach its destination only three miles away. They settled in another mid-seventeeth-century gem of a palace, this one hemmed in by civilian buildings and vulnerable to mischief-makers. It had been the queen's favourite because she could go shopping nearby and often did. It was also less exposed to aerial attack and nearer government and military headquarters.

Soon after their arrival shots were heard which some thought came from neighbouring rooftops, apparent confirmation of the existence of fifth columnists. Again the prince rushed outside, machine gun in hand, to be met once again by Alexander, who stretched out his hand. They looked at each other, the prince grinned, then shook it, for the second time and not for the last. They doubted the existence of fifth columnists.

During the next few days the royal family stayed in the palace garden, near a bunker where they spent the nights. Communication with government and military proved complicated. The ministers sheltered in another bunker only a mile from the palace, but the telephone was suspect because of the fear of fifth columnists. Alexander was taken on as special royal courier – exchanging horse for motorcycle – and shuttled between the palace, ministerial bunker and military with messages, often verbal. The generals told Alexander they found the queen resolute if occasionally eccentric, but the cabinet hopelessly divided.

Meanwhile, at 6 am that first morning, two hours after The Hague had been bombed, the German ambassador had delivered a note from his masters to the Dutch minister for foreign affairs – Dr E. N. van Kleffens – with a demand not to resist German armed forces. The ambassador had vouched for Alexander the previous autumn, but was now in tears and unable to utter a word. In view of his silence van Kleffens wrote on the note in blue pencil that as a result of the unprovoked attack by the German army a state of war existed between the two countries. It had to be left to the Dutch to declare war!

Some hours later van Kleffens went to the beach and after a dangerous flight in an antiquated sea-biplane, arrived in London, shaken and haggard. In that condition he was received by Churchill, then First Lord of the Admiralty; an amazing courtesy, for a few hours later Churchill was called to his king and installed as prime minister.

Some years later, when I was working in his small department, Dr van Kleffens told me the gist of that talk.

Churchill could not help a scathing remark about the futility of a neutrality whose strict observance had prevented the Dutch from liaising with the British and coordinating plans for the very eventuality that had now arisen. The minister reminded Churchill of the existence of the North Sea, a formidable natural barrier for the protection of his country that

Holland lacked. Would the British have come to the rescue? Secret soundings by the queen's emissary the previous autumn had produced a lacklustre response. In those circumstances the only defence left to the Dutch had been to avoid upsetting Hitler and not present him with a pretext for invasion. Neutrality was not an act of faith but a pragmatic response in the absence of credible alternatives.

Churchill relented and confessed he appreciated the problem. He had himself been a lone voice for years. Even after taking office again at the very time of the secret Dutch approaches, his views were not always accepted. He had then argued that western Holland was essential for Britain's defence because German bombers could easily reach England from there. The reply to the queen's emissary had been non-committal because the Dutch prime minister was reported to be a weak and sentimental old man, in essence a defeatist. Even so, van Kleffens had retorted, the queen's efforts were supported by part of her cabinet, himself included. Their hands would have been immeasurably strengthened by a more positive reply. Churchill accepted this, and it is one of the reasons why the exiled Dutch government retained a 'special relationship' with the British throughout the war, unlike most other governments in exile.

In Holland the ministers felt overwhelmed by events. The prime minister argued that the German might was unbeatable and that an instant capitulation would be the only way to save Holland. Some supported him, others totally disagreed. Some agreed, but felt the government should continue the fight in exile; others disagreed but preferred to stay at home and resign. That made four conflicting views and there were more. No course of action surfaced from the ministerial bunker.

Alexander's courier job lasted all of 75 hours, mostly without sleep. On 12 May Crown Princess Juliana, with her daughters Beatrix and Irene, left for England. Alexander could do no more than salute them. They were escorted by a rebellious Prince Bernhard, who felt that as an active soldier he should be where the action occurred. No other soldiers were able to give preference to family interests. The queen, however, pointed out that he was also her ADC and ordered him to accompany the future queen, thereby assuring the succession. Alexander admired the prince's cool courage. Nor did his mother-in-law forget this display of loyalty from an ex-German with playboy tendencies. However, she continued to berate him for excessive zeal. He was, after all, the only male in a female royal household, for her two grandchildren were girls as well. No doubt the queen hoped for further offspring to be male. They were not.

Measures might be needed in Britain which only Prince Bernhard could take. Grudgingly, he conceded defeat and arrived in London the following day after an agonizing trip. He won the next round in this battle of wills though: a few days later he sneaked away to pay a brief visit to Dutch forces in the south-westernmost tip of Holland, a visit cut short by the advancing Germans.

On 13 May Alexander escorted the queen herself to the nearest port, where she embarked on a British frigate. She had not informed her cabinet. That was done by another ADC. Most ministers then left the safety of their bunker and also proceeded to the Hook of Holland, where they congregated in another bunker and continued their deliberations. By then the problem was reduced to one question: capitulate as a government or depart for Britain and leave it to the commander-in-chief to capitulate with the armed forces only.

The queen had sailed. With this her ministers had no quarrel. She had, however, taken some precautions unknown to them. One of these resided in the two briefcases which she had finally dropped in the gangway on board the frigate. They contained her personal documents. The other precaution was more subtle. Earlier that day the queen had sent Alexander to the two most vital officers of state with the request to join her. The presence of these two would give her exile the benefit of legality, even if she found herself without elected ministers. They were the vice-president of the Council of State and the director of the Royal Cabinet.

The Council of State is a permanent feature anchored in the Dutch constitution. Other democracies rely on a simple triangular division of power, the three estates: executive,

27

parliament, and a judiciary that is independent of both. Uniquely, Holland boasts a fourth estate, the Council of State, a vital further check on democracy. For the Council's approval is required for all legislation. Admittedly this came about as a result of historical forces rather than the ingenuity of constitutional experts. It was set up in 1531 by the Spaniards as a government for their distant possessions but developed into an advisory body after the Dutch monarchy turned from absolute to constitutional in 1848. The sovereign appoints its members and is president in name, the vice-president mostly in fact. Moreover, the vice-president acts as caretaker sovereign when the incumbent is incapacitated or dies without heir.

As the vice-president explained to Alexander: if he had stayed, the Germans might have claimed that the queen, having run away, was incapacitated, as indeed they did. Constitutionally the vice-president would then have had to act as sovereign. However, he would also have been hostage to the Germans. By taking him with her, Wilhelmina had effectively made government under German occupation legally impossible. The Royal Cabinet serves the sovereign in consultations with ministers and by taking its Director too, Wilhelmina was assured of continuity.

With the sovereign gone and with these two the key to the safe of constitutional Holland as well, Alexander had to shake off his tiredness and sense of loss, and tried to locate the cabinet. He found them by pure accident. The minister of justice, Professor Pieter Gerbrandy, was striding the ramparts of the old fort surrounding the bunker, in wild anger. Alexander learned from him that the prime minister was at his wit's end, desperate for a truce and capitulation as a government, insistent on a separate peace, yet equally desperate to preserve cabinet unity. Gerbrandy had feared coming to physical blows with his boss. He was only five feet tall and had an enormous moustache. When Alexander told him about the departure with the queen of her two chief councillors he threw up his arms, slapped his thighs and laughed loudly. He was delighted that his sovereign had cocked a snook at her prime minister.

All ministers embarked forthwith on a second British frigate, their arguments temporarily silenced by the news of the queen's departure. On the open sea they heard their sovereign announce from Buckingham Palace that her government had not capitulated and would continue the struggle against evil. It was a salutary lesson in the power of decisive action, at the right time and in the right way. Whatever one may think of their bickering, the cabinet did eventually go as a team, after due democratic process, and leaving their families behind.

The conflict between the two opposing views raged throughout the war, in high councils of state as in the minds of ordinary citizens. Even in Britain the foreign secretary, Halifax, considered approaching Mussolini to achieve an armistice, for Italy had not yet entered the war in those May days of 1940. Not surprisingly, Churchill vetoed it. Those who held the first view wanted to fight on until Germany had been subjugated, those who held the second accepted too easily the apparent superiority of arms or argument or both and wanted to avoid more bloodshed by capitulating. Wilhelmina abhorred political bickering that resulted in indecisive governments, compounded by partycracy, a word she had coined to express the excessive influence of parties and which briefly gained ground in England too. She tried to find strong people, within democracy not outside it, and desperately wanted changes made, to strengthen democracy rather than undermine it. She would never accept dictatorship of any kind, because she realized what it could lead to when in the hands of an evil manipulator. There was another, more basic motive: she was deeply religious and could not accept any human being as a replacement for God, neither the vicar nor the pope, and certainly not a politician.

One more event in those fateful days of May 1940 had a profound influence on the attitude of the Dutch. Their army had valiantly held out against strong attacks from German troops on both sides of the vital Meuse bridges which gave access to the second largest town, Rotterdam. By mid-morning on 14 May the German troops, tired of having their advance blocked, presented the local commander and the burgomaster with an ultimatum: capitulate or the town will be bombed. It bore no signature or name, only a typed 'commanding officer German forces'. Before its expiry a Dutch captain went through the lines to deliver a reply, asking for these missing details to prove its validity. The German general signed over his name and granted the Dutch another four hours to comply. At the moment that the Dutch captain recrossed the lines Rotterdam was bombed, its centre laid to ruin. Another breach of faith, another convention broken. For the target was not the military but the civilians of the city, who suffered great loss of life. The general's signal to stop the air raid had been overruled by Göring.

It was this mockery of accepted rules, of civilized behaviour, that stung. Many weeks passed before we believed the true story. Rumours persisted that blamed the commander-in-chief for acting too late. He had in fact acted swiftly. The Germans threatened to repeat the bombing on Holland's other major cities which were undefended and the army capitulated late that same afternoon. A precedent for nazi unscrupulousness was set. Some months afterwards, having failed to invade Britain, the frustrated Germans again used this tainted tactic, which they had, of course, initiated at Guernica during the Spanish Civil War. It produced a verb: Coventrying. Worse was to come, for it invited retaliation. Some years later when they were in a position to do so, the Allies relentlessly smashed German cities, culminating in the utter folly of Dresden's destruction. This escalation was even more doubtful: it gained little military advantage, nor did it achieve the intended loss of morale. But it did destroy culture and dent civilization. The increased reliance on intimidation of civilians instead of winning victories on the battlefield led to the use of the atom bomb, and initiated the proliferation of atomic weaponry which today threatens annihilation of people and plants alike, life itself.

These early incidents enraged us. The very indignation which Huizinga feared had been lost, was revived, a sense of outrage deep enough to survive the frustration of lacking an immediate outlet. Indignation fertilized the soil in which the people's resistance would eventually grow. Initially the Dutch felt betrayed by the flight of their queen. Within a few weeks their feelings were reversed. We soon realized the inestimable value of a fully legal government in exile and responded to the queen's firm resolve, shortly to be expressed in her regular radio broadcasts, to resist 'that man'.

To resist therefore. But how, when and where? There were no laws, no guidelines, no precedents to show the way. It was not like joining a church or a party or even a club. They all had rules and buildings. For resisting there were no rules and not even a skeleton of an organization. The term 'resistance' had not yet been coined. Then there was no simple word to describe a complex phenomenon, no neat label that nowadays glosses over its disparate nature. We felt like the bees of a bee colony deprived not only of their queen bee but also of their hive. Every individual had to decide for himself. Not a few found such decisions distressing; most decided to wait and see. The government had gone, the military were in captivity, parliament suspended, newspapers restricted. Consequently leadership was completely absent.

However, a small number of people knew what to do and they started to act, but without parliament and press they faced an uphill task in their endeavour to recreate leadership. It was this problem which occupied Wiardi Beckman – Uncle Stuuf – and a few others from across the political spectrum. It also touched Alexander and me, though in different ways.

Alexander stood in the Hook of Holland on the afternoon of 13 May without his bosses. With the departure first of the queen, then of the cabinet, he found himself jobless. He still wore the uniform of a first lieutenant with the badge of the royal regiment and the sash of an ADC to the queen. Somehow he should return to the regiment's base but he had lost track of them and they of him. To him the war was already lost. He sat down by the wayside, his motorbike propped up nearby. People moved along the road, some one way, some another. Among them were soldiers, but without apparent purpose. No one took any notice of him. He was alone. He felt drained, the purpose of his existence departed. Exhaustion and depression took their toll. Quietly Alexander cried. Nobody noticed.

31

Alexander raised himself with difficulty, tired and dazed, his eyes filled with tears. He went to the motorbike, automatically started the engine, straddled the machine, put it in gear and rode off, all without conscious thought. Shortly after, he touched a boulder, toppled over, struck his head and lay concussed on the road. Luckily, there were soldiers around who recognized his sash and quickly found an ambulance, which took him to a hospital in The Hague. Luckily too the damage to his body turned out to be less than feared. But he was an easy target for the Germans as an ADC to the reviled queen.

Three weeks after the capitulation the army was disbanded and the soldiers sent home. That included me, but not until I had assisted a few determined yet scared comrades in dumping rifles, pistols, ammunition and even some machine-guns into a nearby muddy ditch. This crazy exploit was intended to deprive our victors of their spoils, a first act of 'resistance', albeit a negative one. Little did I know that shortly afterwards I would be confronted with a more positive attitude to such arms caches.

Officers too returned to civilian life. save for a few, among them Alexander. Released from hospital and fully recovered, he was confined to barracks, closely guarded by Germans, then transported by train to an unknown destination. Alexander considered this to be against the rules, but found no support among his military fellow travellers and therefore kept silent. He brooded, though, for captivity would make him inactive. He noticed that the train was travelling towards Germany and looked for ways of escape. That night, as the train slowed down, he jumped out and ran into a wood, still in Holland, if only just. It was to be the first of several jumps to freedom.

Thus began his career as a freelance soldier.

Chapter Three

BUDDING RESISTANCE: THE APOSTLES

Amanda had waited for me, though not without an occasional dalliance as she later confessed. The six months of my military training had been broken only twice by short weekends at home. Written expressions of dedication tried to make up for the lack of physical ones: I was starved of female company. Although page for page Amanda's letters probably matched mine, I used large sheets and covered them with minute handwriting, she small sheets with huge scrawls. Judging from the few of my letters from this period that did survive – to my parents – they cannot have been much fun. These record the rather overexcited, sentimental outpourings of a youngster trying to express woolly thoughts poetically. I have often wondered what the Gestapo made of our love letters when they confiscated them later.

A week before my return home to pick up the pieces of a disrupted civilian life, Laura had contacted Amanda and introduced her to two more members of the little group she had told us about. They turned out to be friends of both of us but not of Alexander. The choice was made to limit complications, but it surprised us as we had thought everyone knew everyone else.

A codename was needed for the group as well as for each of its members. Laura felt that 'the Apostles' aptly depicted our pioneering role. The new boys were to be called Matthew and Luke, while I was re-christened Peter. In the absence of female apostles the girls were named Mary and Martha. Laura wanted to be Mary Magdalene rather than Mary of Bethany, Martha's sister, or Jesus' mother Mary, but a double name was too complicated. So she became simply Mary – which one was not clear – and Amanda had to make do with Martha.

When recounting this meeting Amanda giggled, then kissed me rapturously and wickedly because she was allowed to be herself and need not in real life conform to the biblical person who was rumoured to be virginal and rather bossy. Such was my somewhat puerile initiation into secret service for my country.

The day after Amanda had told me this story another friend – Eric – turned up with a splendid plan to whisk weapons away from the Germans. Ironic in view of my recent attempt to destroy them. Eric said that they were, after all, Dutch property. I agreed, unaware of the small print in the rules of war. Eric knew where some were hidden, not in mud but in caches. He had joined a recently formed paramilitary organization calling itself LOF (Legion Of ex-Frontline soldiers). I became quite excited but also bewildered. Having just been made an 'Apostle', this new approach to active resistance severely tested my intelligence. The first full meeting of the Apostles was five days away. I had not even been told the precise nature of my future activities. Nevertheless I felt that Eric should be encouraged, without, of course, informing him about the existence of the Apostles.

Still, I felt in a quandary and was keen for a talk to resolve it. The vow of silence weighed heavily on me. I had not told Eric about the Apostles. Could I now tell *them* about Eric? Clearly not. I hesitated about telling Amanda. She was younger than I and as a girl she should perhaps not be saddled with a purely male game of guns. This rational argument may well have concealed an emotional reason: I would be more completely enthralled than my infatuation already threatened if she were involved in all my veiled ventures. This would not help Amanda: she wanted a fairly strong – though not too strong – companion, not a reverential wet. Nor would it help me: I might lose my identity and the adored girl as well. A similar reason ruled out Laura who was even stronger and whose involvement might inflame the potential rivalry with Amanda which I sensed but could not fathom. Unfortunately the Paul brothers were not in town. Peter had returned to Delft University, having escaped military service as medically unfit, for some spurious reason. Alexander was reported to be in captivity.

That left my parents. They knew nothing of all this. Nor did I like dragging them into activities that might endanger their lives by proxy. My mother could be called sensible, her views uncomplicated, unencumbered by intellectual luggage, though sensitive. Indeed, she possessed that rare quality of being able to listen as well as talk, and to take what was said into account when expressing her own views. At 5'9", statuesque with clear blue eyes, wavy blond hair and a round face, she was an impressive woman. Only her upturned nose prevented her from being a real beauty. At best she was considered cute. We children called it a 'potato-nose'. My father, 5'10" tall, had a more positive nose and a long chin which some called strong and others weak. As both my parents were, like myself, a mixture of strong and weak I have long since given up trying to relate faces to character. I was considerably in awe of my father and more happy with my mother. Still, I needed advice and one's father seemed the obvious one to provide it. So I asked him for a talk, man to man.

As a filial duty I gravely reported that I was about to become involved in opposing the nazis, but could not, of course, divulge details. I hoped he would respond with questions which I would then not refuse to answer. Instead, my father, equally solemnly, approved my stance and gave me his blessing, but refrained from prying any further. I went to bed without the advice I had sought. That night I felt a failure, the first of many times when confronted with the conflict between the need for secrecy to maintain security and for openness in order to achieve something. I had, however, reckoned without my father's wisdom: the next day he advised me to consult Uncle Stuuf, who might provide more constructive help than he himself felt capable of giving in such circumstances. No doubt he feared as well that I might be dangerously irresponsible.

That same evening I went to see Uncle Stuuf in his hide-out.

35

The talk lasted a long evening and laid the foundations for much of what followed. He was fairly tall, very erect, with blond curls topping his head but the sides cut short in the prevailing fashion. He had a conspicuous mouth: the upper front teeth protruded from the stiff upper lip and the lower lip was very full and low. His mind was quick and incisive, he spoke fast with great assurance, clear thoughts well articulated yet not overbearing. Clear blue eyes beamed friendliness even when the words were fiery. His religion was not churchly but spontaneous, allied more to nature than dogma. Our rapport, built up over the next eighteen months, was based too on another similarity. We both tended to be reverential, though in his case it was more like deference, in mine like veneration. This could lead to contempt for those outside the chosen few as it occasionally did with Uncle Stuuf. Although his contempt related to opinions or lack of them and not to the individuals concerned, it sometimes led to problems. For some people found it difficult to distinguish between the two. In today's parlance he would be called an intellectual who lacked understanding for others not so equipped. Still, his mind focussed on practicalities as well.

Uncle Stuuf cherished a profound belief in people's good qualities, as I also do. He expressed it once as follows:

'Most feel and think as we do, most want to promote the beautiful and do good. Should we now look exclusively for their bad deeds and really believe their motives are villainous? That is arrogant for it implies that only we and a few of our friends strive for decency and all others are the devil's servants. Let us focus on the good. For the ultimate value of a person is not calculated on the basis of failures or bad behaviour but on the good achieved, the small bit contributed to the improvement of mankind.'

Some who knew him felt that this tendency to play down the ugly side reflected ignorance of the human character. However, most people were impressed by the combination of his talents, warts and all. He was authoritative, and no one doubted his commitment. He fought nazism from the day Holland was occupied. For all this he was revered.

That evening he sat in a straight-backed, padded Victorian

armchair in a medium-sized room on the first floor at the front of the semi-detached house. It had bay windows which enabled him to watch the street beyond the shallow front garden both ways for whatever hostile forces might descend upon him. The chair fitted the bay nicely, its high back to the main window, facing a large desk cluttered with papers and books. Escape would be by means of a balcony at the back, reached through a glass door at the end of the landing, whence a staircase led down into the back garden, which ended twenty yards on at a steepish bank, some fifteen feet high. This supported a rarely used railway track with more gardens and houses on the other side.

Uncle Stuuf's explanation of this ideal set-up gave me the first uncanny sense of what conspiracy involved. I learned an important lesson as well. I kept glancing nervously out of the window and contemplating the best way to climb the steep incline, whereas he did not seem to give it a thought. For him it was enough that the theory had been mapped out adequately. He did not lower his voice either, while I kept mine down to a conspirational murmur. When I mentioned the incongruity between meticulous planning and apparent lack of concern, he laughed.

'Both are necessary. Don't worry: the escape details are firmly planted in my mind. If I keep looking out of the window I can't look at these papers, can I? Life's full of dangers, but that shouldn't determine one's activities. I'll face fear when it presents itself.'

The room contained several more armchairs, a bed and a washbasin. It was well equipped for meetings, Uncle Stuuf explained, but rarely used for that purpose. More meetings were held in the offices of a friendly publisher, a few miles away in the centre of town, so that the hide-out would remain fairly secret.

The reason for the elaborate precautions so early on when few contemplated taking any, was that Dr H. B. Wiardi Beckman figured on a list of 100 prominent Dutchmen whom the Gestapo reputedly intended to intern as professed enemies of Hitler. However, at that time – late June – the immediate threat to his freedom had passed. A handful had been arrested, but the nazis could not possibly imprison all politicians and top civil servants. It would be counter-productive too. The civilian overlord or *Reichskommissar*, former Austrian chancellor Dr Arthur Seyss-Inquart, was trying to woo the Dutch with the idea of a 'Greater Germanic Realm'. He therefore needed as much support from the people and their rulers as he could muster. Putting the latter in jail would be unhelpful. Consequently, Uncle Stuuf returned to his home for much of the time to keep up appearances.

He harboured few illusions, however. For he was certain that the imposition of Seyss-Inquart to replace queen, cabinet, parliament and the rest of our cherished democratic institutions constituted a huge psychological error, as indeed it proved to be. Therefore he intended to retain this present hide-out as a safe-house from which to conduct covert activities and from where he could easily escape.

I was very impressed, but still nervous, and blurted everything out, about Laura's Apostles and Eric's weapon cache and LOF. Doubts surfaced too about the wisdom of involving myself in conspiracies that appeared to be beyond my rather carefree capacities. Uncle Stuuf had doubts neither about the need for the conspiracies nor about my qualifications.

'Nonsense, my boy. You're intelligent enough to understand the basic situation. You also love being active. Let's try to channel this. You're too young to indulge in destructive self-analysis. Be positive.'

'I've tried, but I can't see it any more.'

'One step at a time. First, I'd like to use you. That's why you're here and not at my home.'

'Marvellous. How?'

'By carrying my briefcase and bag from place to place, by delivering messages and so on.'

'OK. But what are you doing?'

'I'll tell you in a moment. Secondly, avoid mixing different activities for as long as possible. The risk incurred in the one will endanger the others. Some people can't help being involved in many things, but it should be left to the few, certainly not attempted by youngsters like you. Thirdly, if some want to use guns, fair enough.' He gave me the name of a reserve officer who coordinated such gun caches to pass on to Eric. 'If that's what you want as well, go ahead, but leave me out of it. And don't come back to me.'

'No, thank you. I'm not interested in playing at soldiers in the dark.'

'I thought you wouldn't be. You're not the military type. Therefore you must help in the main struggle, that of the mind.'

'I'd like that.' It sounded like an interview for a job, whatever the struggle of the mind entailed.

'Then don't touch guns, ever. They're more immediately dangerous than anything else, especially in the hands of excitable non-professionals. They might be tempted to shoot nazis at random. That will invite retaliation on the innocent population. After all, the army failed to stop them and individual sniping won't get them out.'

'What about the Apostles?'

'As I don't know their precise function I can only advise caution,' he replied, but added that I should continue with Laura.

'That may sound inconsistent but there's a reason,' he explained, 'Laura's father, Steven van Alblas, was in naval intelligence. Frankly, I'd like to know what she's doing without getting involved myself. There's an obvious advantage in using girls for these activities: they're less conspicuous. Laura's got a superb brain but she's also got a chip on her shoulder. Whatever she told you about sublimating her unusual physical appearance, she's highly sexed. Alexander used to be in love with her but apparently dropped her. There could be a residue of frustration which might erupt into irresponsible actions. Do your apostolics and report back to me.'

It all sounded rather devious.

'All right. What else can I do?'

'Well, you can listen, for a start. Let's begin with the Germans' misjudgement,' he said. 'Settle down. This will take a while.'

He then launched into a historical analysis that was not only fascinating but also turned out to be an uncannily accurate prediction. He spoke with the tongue of his mentor Huizinga and rode their shared hobby horse of national identity.

The Germans, he pointed out, claimed a common bond with the Dutch, racially, nationally and otherwise. That's why they had put in Seyss-Inquart as a civilian governor unlike Belgium and France, where they had installed generals as military ones. With subtlety they might achieve a lot of the desired cooperation. But nazis lack subtlety. Therefore they would press on with ill-conceived measures and the vast majority of the Dutch would come to see Seyss-Inquart as a tool for annexation.

'The people will have nothing of that! In their arrogance the nazis forget that as a nation-state Holland is three centuries older than Germany. Our struggle for independence started in 1568 and was maintained by a motley collection of regents. By that time we already had an identity and formed a spiritual and social unity. Hence the revolt. We were in fact a nation, consolidated soon after in a state. The regents chose William of Orange to lead the revolt, not as king but as first among equals. The Oranges have watched over Holland ever since, first as *stadholders*, lately as kings, a bond of four centuries.'

Now look at Germany, Uncle Stuuf went on. It consisted of kingdoms which quarrelled incessantly. The warring factions had only been unified in 1871, less than seventy years before. Although then a state, the people were not yet a nation. A king was imposed upon them and he proclaimed himself emperor, no doubt to keep up with Victoria of England and Franz Joseph of Austro-Hungary. Not surprisingly, his successor and grandson had been kicked out in 1918.

'And now they've got another big boss. That may well be necessary for them but is totally unacceptable to us.'

He drew a breath, then continued: 'There's another difference. Our spirit of independence permeated commerce and academia as well as politics. We never accepted politics as of prime importance. Politicians have always been our servants, however important, never our bosses. We may not have had vast armies but we did roam the seas in rickety ships and settled in New Amsterdam, the East Indies and elsewhere. We also produced eminent artists and scholars. When Leyden University was founded in 1575 it soon became a haven for controversial intellectuals from all over Europe, witness to tolerance. But the nazis don't understand the meaning of tolerance. To them it means weakness, avoiding conflict. It is, of course, the reverse. For beliefs must be held with passion to be accorded the accolade of a sincere search for truth. How else can those who hold opposite views be converted? Tolerance is the result of fierce battles of the mind, not of mindless prowess on the battlefield. For that reason usurpation of the queen's functions by an Austrian traitor will be seen as a sacrilege. And that will be the start of the real fight, for us and for the nazis.'

The details were familiar but our heritage had never been put in this context nor in such compelling terms. I asked what could be done about it.

'Simple in theory, difficult in practice and, most of all, time-consuming. Without parliament or press we can only work in small groups of reliable friends. Gradually the circle must be widened and a network created that embraces the most important of these groups. That would replace parliament in some way. It will be a long haul, for the participants have all got their own opinions. At the same time we desperately need a free press, to communicate, counteract the censored press, inform and guide the people. That too will start in a limited way and on a small scale.'

Completely absorbed, I failed to notice that daylight had passed through dusk to darkness and that the clock had moved beyond 10 pm. We had not looked out of the window for hours. Suddenly the door opened. I jumped. Two men enter-ed resolutely, neither of them Uncle Stuuf's host. For a moment I thought we had been ambushed. Unperturbed Uncle Stuuf introduced them. The first – in his mid-sixties – was Dr Scholten, professor of the philosophy of law at Amsterdam University, the other – in his late thirties – was Dr Telders, professor of international law at Leyden. Each of the three turned out to belong to a different party and to a different church. Religion nevertheless formed the basis of their friend-ship, in addition to mutual respect.

The two visitors had been expected. Instead of ringing the bell they had tapped the front door with the morse code for V for Victory: dot-dot-dot-dash. Already those symbols were equated with the opening bars of Beethoven's Fifth Symphony, used by the BBC to introduce its wartime radio news to the continent. They became as familiar as the by then prohibited national anthems.

The three formed the sort of group that Uncle Stuuf had talked about. A wide circle of friends guaranteed him access to several groups which had met in recent weeks, some openly, others less so. These two, for instance, had come to report on a large meeting of representatives from the main churches. Holland boasts even more christian denominations (sixty odd) than political parties (twenty or so), witness perhaps both to an independent mind and to tolerance. For no one church or party could dominate without taking the others into account. It had been agreed to set up a committee to coordinate reactions to nazist measures. Scholten would represent the largest protestant church on it. Although never very active, the Council of Churches was a major cooperative development in the struggle for moral sanity and in its quiet way became one of the pillars on which resistance eventually rested.

With Telders Uncle Stuuf also belonged to another group, less formal but more influential, which concentrated on planning postwar improvements to Holland's ailing democratic institutions. Their political interests made them a natural ally of the most formal group of all, the Political Convention. This started life soon after the army's capitulation as a committee of, initially, twelve members of the Lower House, two from each of the six main parties. With parliament prorogued and the cabinet in exile, they aimed to offer political guidance to the permanent secretaries of the departments of state, who now had to run the country without instructions other than from the nazis. The Convention survived throughout the war. Although as a body it studiously avoided involvement with illegal activities, some members did engage in them and thus formed links with other groups. While as members of the Upper House neither Uncle Stuuf nor Telders could join, both kept in close contact with the Convention.

With Scholten Uncle Stuuf attended yet another group, assembled around the director of the YMCA, the Rev. Dr J.

Eykman. The three had been involved in introducing Prince Bernhard into Dutch society, as previously reported, and formed the pivot for students and other young people who were inspired by religion, socially conscious, yet politically unattached.

Some months later this network of interests was to lead to the creation of the Great Civic Committee, bringing together the most active people from all these groups. The GCC represented the widest spectrum of opinions, more so than ever a parliament or government had done in peacetime. It became established as the most influential body of the resistance, recognized as such by those in the know, who eventually included the exiled government and, unfortunately, also the Gestapo. After twice being almost wiped out, its remnants revived to form the College of Confidants, who were able to avoid the Gestapo's clutches and act as an underground government on behalf of the exiled one during the last year of the war.

I have discarded chronology and looked ahead in order to indicate that these momentous developments had their origin in the web that was being spun that evening at Uncle Stuuf's hide-out. None of us then knew that nearly five more years of progressively tougher and more desperate nazi measures were to follow, which were to cost most of the initiators their lives.

Talk continued for hours, a harbinger of the future. For we talked a lot, particularly in the first eighteen months when we could afford the time. Meetings like the one that evening abounded, often a mixture of 'hard reality' and 'soft dreams'. Many ideas thus tested eventually found their way into one or another of the underground papers. Guidelines were coined for civil servants, from permanent secretaries to simple clerks, and passed on by word of mouth, as were instructions to the embattled, baffled and gradually embittered population. It did not, of course, work quite as smoothly as these few lines might suggest, but somehow it did work.

For me, at twenty, it was heady stuff. I remember the gist of the talk and some of the words because the same themes recurred again and again. Perhaps that explains why an element of elation could creep into the mood of disgust, distress and disaster. It lasted throughout the war, though practicalities loomed larger towards the end. Somehow we felt we were contributing to the brave new world that was bound to spring into being after the old one had passed. That was a prime motivation of old and young alike.

Of the discussion that evening I recall snippets, such as: 'Democracy is a great gift, next in importance to religion. In both strong brakes exist to contain the evil genius in all of us . . . Democracy harnesses the creative impulses of the many, whereas dictatorship throttles the human aspirations even of the few!' And more of the same followed, until it was past midnight and time for me to cycle home, in a euphoric mood.

Next I went to face the Apostles. This, our first real meeting, started in a bizarre way. We were to gather on the crowded beach. Laura was half submerged in the calm sea and at intervals each of us had to approach her individually to receive further instructions. The ploy was intended to divert attention from prying eyes, but only succeeded in attracting them. Other friends suspected that a party was being organized and kept on wanting to join in the fun. Eventually, though, we were all briefed. Matthew and Luke were told to take Laura's car to her home, Matthew returning alone to pick up Amanda and me, and again to collect Laura. He was the only one with a driving license and Laura's car was a two-seater sports coupé. An hour passed before we were all together for our first meeting as a team.

At this point in time the nazi occupation was only six weeks old, active opposition in its infancy and confined mainly to impatient individuals and their friends, most of them very young. The leaders were groping towards a coordinated assessment of the situation together with ways and means to deal with it. The hefty hand of nazi terror was still concealed. As with the leading elders, so with the guileless and guideless youngsters: all looked anxiously for support to the small circle of their immediate friends. Consequently the members of the Apostles came from the families of the professional intelligentsia. Matthew's family, for example, was a much respected notary public, Luke's a well-known lawyer.

Matthew was tall, dark and handsome, an undergraduate at Leyden University, where he read law. Luke was also tall, though almost bald with just a few blond hairs, attractive in a less conspicuous way; he studied medicine at the same university. I have since asked myself whether coincidence or choice made all Laura's male combatant companions turn out to be so tall, with me the shortest tall boy. Convenience perhaps? Matthew tended to haughtiness, Luke by contrast to gentleness. Matthew jumped to conclusions, Luke always queried. They represented opposite types of undergraduate. Yet they were bosom friends, in many ways complementary.

We assembled in a different room from the previous encounter, on the first floor, which, though smaller, was still large. Two walls were lined with books, very tidily arranged; an old oak desk stood at one end of the windowed third wall; the fourth accommodated numerous pictures, a few of them paintings, the remainder enlarged photographs, all with ships as their subject. A Louis XV chaise-longue, several lecterns with photographs and books and five comfortable armchairs with a less comfortable highbacked one behind the desk completed the contents of what had clearly been the study of Laura's father.

Laura explained the unusual procedure as a ruse to divert attention from an otherwise obvious meeting, insisted upon by her contact, who had also taught her to limit a cell to five people.

'A cell?' asked Luke. 'Isn't that a communist ploy?'

'It is. My contact happens to be a communist.'

That was a shock: to find wealthy baroness Laura in league with a communist.

A second shock followed. Her father had instructed her in some tricks for spying, or so she said. But she had not told him of her communist connection. That seemed devious in the extreme. We were, of course, political nincompoops, though Laura put on the air of an expert. We were flabbergasted.

'Are you a communist?' Matthew asked.

'A sympathizer,' Laura replied, clearly satisfied with the effect of her bombshells.

'Sympathy for what? With whom? The communists or their fantasies?' Luke asked.

'That's unfair,' replied Laura, quite relaxed. 'These fantasies, as you like to call them, are meant to solve real problems which neither socialists nor conservatives nor liberals have been able to solve.'

'What sort of problems?' Matthew crossed his legs and leaned back, as if he had scored a point.

'The underprivileged. Let's say the poor, both in mind and in kind. They never get a chance to improve their lot because they either lack the brains and the guts, which usually come from a privileged position, or they lack the money in what is euphemistically called "competitive society" but is in fact more like grab when you can.' Laura sounded triumphant and looked radiant.

'Isn't that rather inconsistent with *your* position?' I ventured.

'Not really. I can't help being born into money and position. Nor can I ignore my brains. I can use these advantages to redress the iniquities of the system. As the parable says: I must use my talents, not throw them away.'

Matthew laughed rather loudly. 'Well, well! Fancy our leader in the employ of one dictatorial state which is in league with another whom we are supposed to be fighting.'

Laura seemed subdued. 'Silly! If you want to fight the nazis, does it matter for what reason?'

Amanda sat upright, eyes flashing. 'Yes, I think it does. Whatever your motivation you've got to be straight. And to me it doesn't seem straight to get us here on the pretext of fighting the nazis when you really want to enlist us for communism. Nor is it straight to learn from your father, under false pretences, tricks that might harm or kill him.'

I took Amanda's cue: 'What are we here for anyway? Why introduce party politics into a simple fight against the nazis?'

'Sorry, but there is a rational explanation. Communist Russia and nazi Germany may be on the same side today, but it's an unnatural alliance and won't last, simply because Hitler obviously plays at power politics. Here communists are still suspect and the Germans will soon persecute them. Power's all right as long as it's used humanely. Also, I haven't said I support Russia or Stalin, only that I sympathize with com-

46

munist ideals. That's why I told you. Surely that can be called straight?' Laura now leant towards me with her tall figure.

Matthew shrugged: 'We all sympathize with the under-dog.'

Laura retorted: 'Do you?'

'I do!' Amanda interrupted, blazing. 'But sympathy can't be mixed with the fight against Hitler. We're in that right now. That's what we came to discuss.'

Luke had a pained expression. Looking at Laura, he said, piercingly: 'Are you in the employ of the communist party or Russia?'

Laura leant closer to me, as if for support, and said rather impressively: 'I'm not and never will be in the employ of anybody.'

'Thanks to your privileges,' said Luke.

'That's unfair.'

'Is it?' asked Amanda. 'You introduced the subject and invited the discussion.' Why this fierceness, I wondered, why this rivalry between the girls?

Laura, although subdued, was still very sure of herself. 'It's unfair because I mentioned something I haven't even told my father. And I told you because at least you now know my motives and my contact.'

I was beginning to understand. 'We don't know him yet. We trust you, of course, but it all sounds a bit unreal.'

'It's not unreal. It's a practical way to communicate with England. No one has any direct contact. My father has left, his intelligence colleagues of the army have left, all British agents have left. They were known to the Germans. Only one transmitter remains and the operator is a communist. It can't be found by direction finders because it sends long distance.'

'To Moscow?' asked Luke.

'Yes. But I got a promise that some messages with special codes will be passed on to my father in London,' replied Laura.

I remained practical: 'What messages? What are we expected to do?'

'Gather information. But I won't go into that today. You must all first promise complete silence about us. We must also trust each other completely. I've told you a lot already in confidence. Come back in a week's time and then tell me if you want to continue on that basis.'

'End of chapter one,' said Matthew.

'OK,' added Luke, 'but not with all that rigmarole to get here.'

'Right. Come here on your own, but at intervals of say five minutes. And put your bikes behind the garage.'

Laura took Amanda and me back to the beach to collect our bicycles. Matthew and Luke stayed. The end had come as unexpectedly as the beginning. Amanda and I pedalled home in silence. I wondered whether to tell her that I would be reporting to Uncle Stuuf, an obvious infringement of confidence.

When we arrived home, Amanda resisted my attempts at an embrace, furious with Laura. That solved the problem. I did not relish being at the centre of a budding rivalry. I told her about Uncle Stuuf. She then relaxed, as if grateful for the confidence, ready for my caresses.

Two days later I did report to Uncle Stuuf. He cautioned me but still advised me to continue with Laura and see what happened next. Amanda, he added, should excuse herself and not become involved with Laura. She was too young and too excitable. He had nothing against anyone fighting the nazis, communists included. However, one had to be careful, for a communist's allegiance was first and last to the party bosses. I could keep an eye on Laura, of whose dedication to the underprivileged he was sure, as he was about her common sense. But if she turned out to be gullible enough to think that the activities of the Apostles would be reported to her father in London via Moscow, she would be bitterly disappointed.

Almost casually he then added that he would try and get a message to Alexander, who was, he announced, in London. One wireless link with England had just been discovered, which was how he knew that Alexander had arrived there. This unexpected piece of information surprised me, but it delighted me even more. How had Alexander done it?

Chapter Four

ALEXANDER'S FIRST ESCAPE TO ENGLAND

According to Uncle Stuuf, Alexander had paddled the one hundred and fifty miles of North Sea to England in a dinghy. He had then established contact with some British secret service, which passed word of his safe arrival back to Holland. The news by itself was astonishing enough. But how had he done it? And how did Uncle Stuuf come to know? Why should Uncle Stuuf be interested in Alexander's fate at all? When I asked all these questions he did not give away much. Uncle Stuuf kept his cards close to his chest like a true professional and few if any are aware of all of his cards even today.

'We met at Professor Huizinga's last year,' he said, rather coolly. 'I needed someone young and intelligent for a delicate mission. Huizinga suggested Alexander and he fitted the bill. Don't ask too many questions. Just accept what I tell you. And don't tell Laura or anyone else.'

Only much later did I learn the details from Alexander himself.

Released from the army in mid-September 1939, Alexander had gone to Huizinga's home to discuss the thesis for his degree in history, an addition to the one in law he had just obtained. Towards the end of their session, Wiardi Beckman had entered unexpectedly – at least to Alexander – and changed his life. Alexander was asked to undertake the journeys to Berlin because no one would suspect him. The eyes and ears of the German nazis in The Hague were closely observing politicians and other eminent Dutchmen, though no one knew then quite how.

When, in early June 1940, Alexander had jumped from the train, he did not return home but contacted Uncle Stuuf instead and suggested that his presumed captivity might serve as cover for whatever secret operations were needed. He also mentioned that an officer friend – Charles Jonkers – had made promising progress with arrangements for a voyage to England. This inspired Uncle Stuuf to suggest that Alexander join Charles and establish contact with the British, then return. Charles had acquired a fairly solid dinghy with oars and an outboard engine, and had found a reliable skipper of a large fishing vessel with an equally reliable crew in Scheveningen harbour. The fishing boat would take them some way out into the North Sea before sending them on their way in the dinghy.

Charles Jonkers was a stocky 5'10" cavalry officer who sported a large blond moustache. He was the fourth generation in a family of military professionals. In the five days of war and the five weeks thereafter, Charles had shown qualities not usually associated with the product of so limited a background. On first acquaintance Alexander had considered Charles a pompous ass, but he soon detected underneath the intelligence that brought them together for their hazardous escape by dinghy.

The venture was a dangerous one. Similar attempts were to claim many lives later. The swell rocked their tiny craft relentlessly. Both Alexander and Charles were landlubbers. To combat sea sickness as well as to save petrol and keep anxiety at bay, they would occasionally turn off the engine and row. The vast expanse of a horizonless sea, without any other point of reference save that provided by their trusted compass, was overwhelming. But their luck held and the weather was kind. After more than two days they spotted the pebbly beaches and flat landscape of East Anglia, at which they both fell into an exhausted sleep, allowing the small craft to drift aimlessly.

Meanwhile a small crowd had gathered on the beach, puzzled by their strange behaviour. Only when the two awoke, warmed by the early morning sun, and Charles hoisted the

Dutch flag on one of the oars, did they react and wave a welcome. The landing itself was a triumph. Alexander and Charles stepped ashore to pints of beer and applause. They were not far from Lowestoft, a fishing port like Scheveningen, and the fishermen knew all about the treacherous North Sea. As Charles gulped down his pint, Alexander took a few careful sips, then reached into the dinghy and produced a stone bottle of genever. Amid cheers and laughter willing hands helped pull the dinghy up the pebbles and away from the water.

This happy scene was interrupted by a uniformed policeman who stepped quietly forward and congratulated them, and then, in a friendly but firm voice, asked to see their papers. Passports and military service books were proudly produced. The policeman and the crowd next accompanied the sailors into Lowestoft, everyone chatting excitedly.

At the police station things took a more serious turn. Alexander was allowed to phone the Dutch embassy in London, where he left a message for his uncle, naval captain Baron van Alblas. Then the police began to make phonecalls outside Alexander's hearing. As a result the police expressed their regrets but said that the two had to be escorted to the embassy for interrogation. Security regulations required proof of their bonafides. Germans had been known to infiltrate in all sorts of ways. Two friendly policemen accompanied them on the train and to the embassy in London.

There the interrogation, conducted by a moustached British man in civilian clothes but of distinctly military bearing and in the presence of a Dutch official, started pleasantly enough. Gradually, however, it turned nasty. Suggestions were made that they had been happy to get rid of the queen, that their crossing could as well have been for the glory of the Führer as for hers.

Then, more subtly, the Englishman − Lieu.-Commander Crane − continued: 'So a trawler took you out of Scheveningen harbour and some thirty miles out into the North Sea. Your boat was then lowered, complete with engine, petrol, oars and a Dutch flag. The skipper and crew watched this operation. Well, well, how nice. D'you expect me to believe that fairy tale? Why would the skipper risk his ship, his life and his crew? Why not continue to Lowestoft? More likely the Germans dropped you off.'

Alexander's answer was so simple he knew it sounded unconvincing. The skipper planned to assist more people across the North Sea. Patriotic skippers wanted to help, not become helpless exiles.

The interrogation was making Charles increasingly angry. His voice rising, he pointed out to the Dutch official that their papers proved them to be officers of the royal regiment. If that were not enough, what would be? 'Where's the ambassador? Where's the queen? They can vouch for us.'

Meanwhile Alexander had begun to enjoy the situation. They were after all in luxurious surroundings rather than in prison. And he remembered that Crane had been introduced as an officer from naval intelligence, like his uncle. When Charles lost his temper, he decided to intervene.

'Did you contact Captain van Alblas?' The quiet question stopped Charles by its unexpectedness. It did not ruffle the Englishman.

'Of course.'

Charles, his anger returning, could not resist interrupting. 'Then you must know that Baron van Alblas is Mr Paul's uncle.'

'I know about Mr Paul, Sir, but I don't know him personally. We've never met before.'

Charles did not let go. 'You could've asked Captain van Alblas to vouch for us at the start, couldn't you?'

Crane said teasingly: 'I'm afraid that's up to me to decide.'

Alexander now prodded Charles. 'Don't be a fool, Charles. The commander wants all the information he can get out of us before losing us to the Dutch.'

'Mr Paul is right, Sir. If you promise to cooperate I'll ask Captain van Alblas to join us now. He's been waiting long enough and you must be starved and sleepy. That is,' he added mischievously, 'if your story is true.'

At last Charles laughed. 'We'll soon know, won't we?'

At that moment van Alblas entered.

'Alexander, my boy! Welcome. Charles! Well done,' he said with much shaking of hands and patting of shoulders.

'Uncle Steve! You've been listening!'

'Have indeed. Next door.'

Charles became indignant again. 'But, Sir, with respect, why all this grilling and snooping?'

'Good question. Should really be addressed to Bruce Crane. We're in his country, though formally on Dutch territory.' Van Alblas spoke in clipped sentences, a habit which he had acquired when commanding a destroyer and found useful to impress subordinates and superiors alike. He was tall, like most of Alexander's relatives, well over six feet, with an aquiline nose, a high forehead and what would have been a mass of curly dark hair had it not been cut short according to military practice. Contrary to the impression his bearing and speech conveyed, he was a kind man as well as an intelligent one.

Crane explained that Charles and Alexander had arrived in an unorthodox way. Regulations required him to establish their identity. That was the easy part, for Captain van Alblas, while still hidden from their view, had instantly recognized them, of course.

'My other concern,' Crane went on, 'was to make sure you didn't have any connection with the Germans that might, shall we say, endanger British security. That was less easy in view of Mr Paul's activities during our phony war.'

Alexander reacted quickly: 'So that's it. Charles is aware of my trips to Berlin, though he knows little about the details. Uncle Steve is, of course, fully informed. Go ahead, Mr Crane, and reveal all.'

'Thank you, Sir. You'll appreciate that I'm interested to know who your contacts were.'

'Could you explain why?' Alexander stalled for time, intrigued by this unexpected development.

'If they were with the Abwehr our military people would obviously be interested.'

'Come off it, Mr Crane. I'm sure you've guessed who my contacts were.'

'Guessing isn't the same as knowing.'

The two were well matched, neither giving anything away until sure it was safe to do so.

'I'm quite prepared to say more, but I'm still puzzled by your approach. Unless it is to establish that the people I met in Berlin didn't bribe me into spying for the Abwehr.' Alexander smiled.

'You've got it, Sir. That possibility crossed my mind, or something like it. You see, we happen to know that some Abwehr people are anti-nazi, even at the top. What they might've done is to recruit you to establish a link with us, in their commendable attempt to frustrate or overthrow Hitler. If that's what they want.'

'Right, Mr Crane, that is indeed what they want. But I can assure you that they haven't "recruited" me.' He went on to remind Crane that German resistance was a delicate matter, as British intelligence had reason to know: in the autumn of 1939 two senior British agents – Payne-Best and Stevens – had met a supposed anti-nazi German officer near Venlo, on Dutch soil, a few miles from the German border. They were kidnapped by the Gestapo.

'True, Sir. Most unfortunate. It's made us rather hesitant. We don't distrust the motives of these Germans, but we don't know who they are, whether they can deliver and if so, what. And what can we do about it? Would it help if we got involved? Would it help us? Perhaps the Gestapo would just infiltrate and wipe out the lot.'

Charles was clearly relieved: 'So that's what the grilling was all about.'

Van Alblas took over: 'Yes, Charles. Sorry. Wondered how best to use you two. And Alexander's contacts. Grilling to test you. And convince Bruce Crane you're the tough boys I told him. Teach you to cope with Gestapo. Much tougher, no comfortable chairs. Ha, ha! Thought Alexander might escape. Lowestoft police phoned. Contacted Bruce Crane at once. Made some plans. Tell you later. Too late now. You deserve a meal. It's ready. Beds also made. Temporary arrangement, of course. Embassy doesn't normally cater for mad Dutchmen. Bruce Crane and I want to keep you away from society. You'll soon see why.'

They did. At noon the next day van Alblas took them to Eaton Square, where the queen and her small staff occupied a huge house, put at their disposal by King George VI. Later, for

reasons of thrift, the queen moved her home first to Roe-
hampton, then to Maidenhead, and her office to a smaller
house in Chester Square. She disdained grandeur. The queen
had been informed of Alexander's role in the abortive peace
attempts. They were to meet Her Majesty, after lunch, but
would first see her private secretary, François van 't Sant.

Van Alblas cautioned Alexander and Charles to be discreet,
for van 't Sant was a controversial figure. As well as being the
queen's secretary, he also headed a small Dutch intelligence
unit with the rank of major-general. But four years earlier he
had resigned as chief constable of The Hague after being
accused of embezzlement. Later an official government enquiry
merely reported not having found any proof of guilt, a
conclusion some saw as less than a complete exoneration. The
truth remained hidden until 1979, with the unfortunate result
that during the war the resistance suspected him of duplicity,
even of treason. That it took so long for the facts to be known
was due to the queen's sense of propriety and loyalty. She was
born in 1880 and brought up to adhere to the strict virtues
then prevalent. At the age of four the last of her brothers died
prematurely, followed at the age of ten by her father,
whereupon she found herself queen, albeit under her mother's
tutelage. That ended in 1898 and at eighteen Wilhelmina was
on her own as well as the sole survivor of the House of Orange.
Her lonely existence combined with the need to perpetuate the
Oranges demanded strong nerves and degree of luck in the
choice of a royal consort. In that she was less lucky than
Victoria of England. Having married a minor German princeling
– Henry of Mecklenburg – in 1901, the succession was not
assured until 1909 with the birth of their only child, Juliana.
Affairs of state weighed heavily on the marriage. Prince Henry
started playing around and needed protection from blackmail
over possible illegitimate offspring. The then chief constable,
van 't Sant, fulfilled this role admirably. In one case the money
for a pay-off led to the accusation of embezzlement and to
van 't Sant's subsequent resignation. The crown could not be
dragged into this shabby affair. Mutual loyalty and respect
dictated a conspiracy of silence, while rumours continued to
haunt van 't Sant. Hence van Alblas' warning.

The meeting over a sober lunch was a great success, for van't Sant was a charming man. Charles took to him immediately, a liking equally quickly reciprocated. Alexander, more reticent, always remained slightly sceptical, though he was prepared to give him the benefit of the doubt.

Alexander and Charles had a two-hour meeting with Queen Wilhelmina in private. She cherished privacy and confidentiality. The two would have preferred the presence of familiar faces to help them avoid pitfalls, but their initial nervousness was soon dispelled. I know how they felt from my own experience later. When Alexander recalled the meeting I felt again the extraordinary sensation of being put at ease by this little rotund lady without ever forgetting her majesty. That often caused an awkward moment at departure: one felt inclined to look *up* to majesty instead of down to the lady who embodied it.

Next day the two were collected from their small hotel near Marble Arch and taken to a pretty old house in Queen Anne's Gate off St James's Park. After numerous checks they were greeted by Bruce Crane and a middle-aged gentleman. They never came to know his name for certain until long after the war, but at the time guessed – correctly – that he was Sir Stewart Menzies, in charge of intelligence, with direct access to the Chief of Staff and Churchill himself.

After expressing approval of their escape, the gentleman surprised them by asking: 'Would you like to join us?'

Both looked at van Alblas, then at Crane, and, astonished at their own audacity, replied in unison: 'Yes, Sir, thank you.' Only then did Alexander ask for an explanation.

'Well now.' A pause, during which the gentleman looked out of the window. 'You seem to be sure of yourselves. That's good for our purposes, as long as it doesn't lead to over-confidence. Captain van Alblas and Mr Crane speak highly of you. It looks as if we've been lucky in getting two intelligent, inventive youngsters to help us with some quite tricky problems. We have to assess what the enemy is up to, his strengths and his weaknesses.' He paused again, then came to the point. 'We don't have enough agents on the continent. Would you mind returning?'

Charles hesitated, but Alexander replied quickly: 'Of course not, Sir.' To him it sounded almost too good to be true, precisely what Wiardi Beckman had wanted.

Bruce Crane amplified: 'Regular personal reports, that's what we need.'

'Mr Crane and Captain van Alblas have suggested certain plans which I endorse,' added the gentleman. 'They will shortly explain the details. I just wanted to meet you and make sure of your dedication to our cause and willingness to serve it.'

At last Charles spoke: 'Of my dedication to our queen you can be assured, Sir. Any job she asks me to do I'll execute to the best of my ability. But may I point out that my abilities are different from Mr Paul's?'

'We've been aware of that,' said Crane, rather nastily.

Van Alblas stepped in, gently. 'Different in what respect, Charles?'

'Well, Alexander studied law whereas I'm a professional soldier.'

'Yes, Charles. Appreciated. Does that affect the present issue?'

'It may not, Sir. But then it might. After all, we don't know yet what's in store for us. Returning to Holland will involve stealth and secrecy, but of a different kind than in battle.'

Alexander nodded encouragingly, glad that Charles had avoided belittling himself – as he often did to Alexander – and that he had shown an awareness of the problem.

Van Alblas replied: 'Could have different tasks.'

Charles reacted enthusiastically: 'Thank you, Sir. It'll be a great honour.'

The gentleman got up. 'Well, gentlemen, if you'll forgive me.' And, almost as an aside: 'Incidentally, Mr Jonkers can set his mind at rest about his queen.' Charles' subtle distinction between his crown and the British cause had not gone unnoticed. 'Mr van 't Sant, whom I greatly admire, has confirmed that Her Majesty approves.' For Alexander that settled van 't Sant's credibility. 'Thank you for coming. Good luck. See you again before long.'

Such polite behaviour – very English to Dutchmen – was

most comforting. Alexander and Charles felt they were in good hands. It was left for Crane to explain their assignments. Alexander was to re-establish contact with Dr Hans von Dohnanyi in Berlin, Charles to assist the lone British agent left in Holland with setting up units to gather military intelligence.

A few days later they recovered their dinghy from Lowestoft, a delightful interlude. They stayed with the fisherman who had supplied them with beer. A party was thrown that evening in a pub, attended by police and civilians alike. It became very lively. Charles absorbed endless drinks without getting drunk, told increasingly salacious stories, much to the delight of the ladies present, and danced with young and old alike. The crowd loved him.

Alexander felt happy to let Charles steal the show. He was having success of his own and attracted the attention of several ladies of varying ages. As the evening wore on, kisses were showered on him to which he responded in a less cavalier way than Charles.

At one point he found himself in a dark corner with a very pretty young girl who started using her tongue as well as her lips. She wore a low-cut dress that only half covered her distinctive breasts. She felt they merited more approval and took one out of its hiding for Alexander to savour. He obliged by planting a kiss on it. Not satisfied with this galantry she pressed his hand around it and began to draw him towards the landlord's parlour.

A struggle ensued between mind and body. Alexander was in England and free, also of the restraints that occupied Europe would soon enforce. Above all, he was sorely tempted. But doubt kept him back. The bell for closing time gave him an excuse for escape. He kissed the nipple gently, whispered that she was lovely and very desirable, but closing time prevented consummation.

She clung to him, then restored the breast to its rightful place. 'My husband will be disappointed,' she giggled. 'He had great expectations of you.'

Her husband? He turned out to be one of the nice policemen who had escorted them to London. She maintained that he would have been honoured. He said a quick prayer of thanks, for he did not want to leave Lowestoft at the mercy of gossip, with the policeman's permission or without it. However, virtue brought little reward. The Lowestoft beauty bragged about her conquest regardless and no one minded either way.

Back in London they met Prince Bernhard, a happy reunion. The queen had informed him of their planned return to Holland and he wanted to assure them of royal support. But he added a request of his own. He revealed that the queen had decided on a change of prime minister and would like to strengthen her cabinet with a few ministers from occupied Holland. Could they make enquiries? Charles sadly pointed out that his task was of a military nature, but Alexander promised to pass the message on.

Training was concentrated but limited. For a couple of weeks they were taught parachute jumping, the rudiments of signalling, security and how to act when caught. Crane stressed that both missions were to be brief, exploratory, to appraise the situation. They would be dropped into Holland together in early August. The transmitter in their luggage was intended as a reserve for the British agent whom Charles was to assist in communication. Alexander's was the more complex job, for he had to obtain reliable false papers before venturing into Germany. Crane could not supply these. Both should return before winter set in to discuss their findings and devise ways for improved liaison and communication. Charles would be collected from a lake in Friesland by seaplane in early October, Alexander a little later by motor gun boat (MGB) from one of the islands of Zeeland province.

Chapter Five

HOLLAND'S PHONY PEACE

What next? No one knew what would happen and most did not want to know. The calamity had not yet touched daily life. The anxiety of the first two months of nazi occupation wore off and the drudgery of everyday existence reasserted itself. July and August were traditional holiday months, yet they brought uncertainty: whether to go away and where, as if by going one might let the side down. My friends and I wanted things to happen to which we could react with firm purpose, but on the face of it little did happen. To most people it all seemed strangely normal.

The nazis were, of course, preparing the next stages of their scheme to envelop us. But for some time we remained unaware of them. Although most people displayed what seemed to be an acceptance of the inevitable, it masked consternation and frustration. Stories of atrocities committed in Germany were shrugged off as rumours and balanced by stories of efficiency. After all, Germans were civilized people, we reminded each other: great musicians, authors, painters, philosophers, historians, scientists, even one or two statesmen. They would never tolerate truly uncivilized behaviour. Discipline had been needed to aid recovery from defeat in World War I. And authority. Hitler provided both. Authority and discipline would contain any excesses of bullying. And so on, despite Huizinga's warning of a crazy world where accepted values would be reversed or stood on their head.

Amanda had joined her parents on holiday. So, a week later, I accompanied my parents, brother and sister on ours, to a rented cottage in the dunes some thirty miles north of Haarlem, a couple of miles from the beach and a similar distance from a sleepy village. There was no telephone, nor a radio. The few letters we might receive and the occasional newspaper had to be collected from the village postmaster, who doubled as the policeman. I felt unhappy and impatient and showed it. My brother – two years younger than me – and sister – then eleven – romped among the dunes, on the beach and in the sea, sensibly ignoring my brooding presence.

My father tried to reason me out of my depression: 'The nazis haven't done anything nasty.'

'Yet,' I retorted grumpily.

'Well, then wait. And relax.'

My mother said nothing about my grumpiness. Instead she sent me off shopping and urged my father to do something more positive than arguing. So he began to take me along on visits to artist friends. Most were painters, generally content to let the world take care of itself as long as it took note of their work. Politicians and generals would eventually settle their differences, one way or another, they contended. None could unsettle their idyllic surroundings nor their artistic aspirations. Their discontent focussed on the presumed lack of support for their painstaking efforts to create something beyond bread, butter and bombs. Their arguments may sound platitudinous, even trite, but they had an unexpected practical consequence after the war.

We also met frequently with Adri Roland Holst, a revered poet a few years older than my father. He was a gentleman of independent means with an Oxford degree in Celtic mythology, a bachelor with an eye for women but without any of the outward trappings with which convention adorns artists. His only concession was a bow tie, but it went with a smart suit.

'Art belongs to culture, itself part of civilization,' he said. 'And civilization survives death and destruction. It inspires people. It's the yeast that leavens the bread.'

He agreed with the painters' judgement and pointed out that as an architect my father was in an incomparable position to put it into practice. My father responded eagerly. He rarely used his hands while talking, but when excited his high forehead wrinkled and his eyebrows went up and down. He explored the idea.

'Yes, yes,' he said. 'The great buildings of the past owe their splendour, and their survival, to the dedication of craftsmen and patrons alike, to honour the great and the good and give pleasure to future generations. Often anonymously.'

The poet nodded, then added: 'And they do give pleasure, don't they? The extra dimension lifts them above mere utility and efficiency. And lifts creators and spectators above their daily worries.'

When my father became chief state architect just after the war he persuaded the cabinet to agree to a unique experiment, set in train during that summer holiday: to introduce a statutory requirement that added two percent to any public building's costs for purely artistic purposes – paintings, sculptures, mosaics, leaded windows, tapestries, and such like. It was introduced even though it placed another burden on the public purse, which at that time also had to finance the repair of extensive war damage. More than forty years hence, in more affluent circumstances, the guardians of the public purse reduced the percentage to one and a half. But the statute still stands, a constant stimulus for the principals to support contemporary art and for the taxpayers to appreciate it.

I listened to these discussions – for the themes recurred on many occasions – with increasing fascination. Would not this spirit also imbue Uncle Stuuf and his friends when they wanted to shape something politically stable from the disasters of war? The poet was convinced that the nazis would fail to kill such human aspirations. So were the politicans. More than that: in their different ways poet and politician both felt that it would focus attention on them.

The poet was a man of contemplation, not action. 'So am I,' my father said, 'but others aren't.' And he looked significantly in my direction. I felt horrified, all the careful reticence spoiled. Still, I suddenly realized that he looked upon me as an alter-ego, a youthful extension of himself who would act where he felt inhibited. There was a silence. Then the poet, appreciating both the hint and its potential awkwardness, said:

'Good luck, young man. If God can't help you, perhaps He'll bless you.' I remember his words well: it happened to be my twentieth birthday.

Amanda returned before we did. How would she feel towards me after nearly six weeks of separation? She was known to switch partners fairly easily. A break then, vaguely feared, would have crushed my new-found confidence.

The first morning after our return I cycled to her home in brilliant sunshine. In the presence of her stern but otherwise friendly father decorum was preserved, but when we went over to my almost empty home she left me in no doubt. Nothing had been lost. Far too quickly I rushed into an account of Uncle Stuuf's advice that she should renounce her apostleship and keep clear of Laura.

At once the mood changed. My words unleashed Amanda's fury and in me a flurry of conflicting emotions that left me floundering.

'Who does your precious uncle think I am?' she shot at me. 'A poor, innocent little girl? He's not even your real uncle.'

I was taken aback by this sharp retort and replied rather meekly: 'I'm sorry. You're right. Still, he specifically told me to warn you.'

'Against what? Against whom? That overblown cousin of Alexander's? I don't much like her anyway. Nor her sexual overtures.'

'That's all right then,' I said, relieved that she had opened a way out of the dilemma, though more in hope than out of conviction.

'Perhaps it is. And Matthew and Luke are dispensable too.'

I still do not quite understand the way women suddenly switch. But confusion turned to gratitude when Amanda added mischievously: 'I'm perfectly satisfied with you, even though they're much more handsome.'

'What a rotten compliment.'

'It isn't a compliment, simply a fact. At least for the present.'

Was this a threat? Or could there be another explanation? I raised my eyebrows but kept silent.

A pause ensued before Amanda continued: 'Don't be tempted by Laura. For your own protection.' That rivalry again. Could she be jealous?

So I replied: 'Thanks for the compliment. Don't you trust me?'

'Not really, no. Not where Laura is concerned. She's a magician.'

'So are you.' And I tried to kiss her again. After all, Amanda had just demonstrated her spiritual as well as physical loyalty. She turned her head away.

'Thanks. I'm not talking about the sex, silly, but about her dominance. You're too weak to stand up to her.' Amanda has always been very perceptive.

Again I had no immediate reply. Then Amanda switched tack once more.

'Wouldn't it be much more useful if I helped you with your dear uncle's work than if I spied for the communists?'

I was lost. She did not know any details of 'Uncle's work', nor was it Laura's intention to spy for Moscow. Amanda continued to explain that she did not take Laura's communism seriously. I did not interrupt to tell her that I did. Amanda also felt that Laura's spying activities sounded too vague and too inconsequential. That seemed correct, at least for the moment. Though Amanda had never met Wiardi Beckman she nevertheless sensed that his approach to resistance would be more immediately valid. After all, he was a member of the Upper House of parliament and my 'uncle' consequently a close friend of my father.

Could it be the struggle against nazism that so motivated Amanda, or her attachment to me, or the excitement that covert action promised? The answer, presumably, was a mixture of all three. The motives for active resistance at that early stage were as varied as the individuals involved: spiritual, political or merely frivolous. As for Amanda, she was undubitably attached to me at the time. Also, though young and not very interested in politics, she fully appreciated the issues at stake and, having started to play her part with conviction, she persevered throughout. Still, she possessed that rare and lovable addiction to life's wonderful qualities and therefore responded easily to the promise of excitement and, later, to the excitement itself. She is still like that.

Next I reported back to Uncle Stuuf, this time at his home. He possessed the rare ability to make complex problems seem simple. While this served him well in his dealings with people of different views, it had its drawbacks. Thus it led to an unhappy misunderstanding when he did not turn up at his newspaper after being demobilized in June. He felt that no respectable newspaper could be produced under nazi tutelage – rightly so – but he did not warn his journalists, who looked for guidance. To those who complained privately, Uncle Stuuf pointed out that if he had made a speech at the newspaper openly setting out his position, it would have been reported to the nazis and invited retaliation. His demonstrative absence should have been guidance enough. Right again, but awkward and insensitive.

A different tactic was used by the social-democratic party. Uncle Stuuf belonged to the leadership of the party who at the end of July advised all members to leave the party. They did, and the party therefore ceased to exist officially, a shrewd move. Unofficially executives and party stalwarts continued to function, creating an underground network. This impelled party leaders to travel widely and talk much, which Uncle Stuuf did with alacrity and devotion, in addition to all his other activities.

At our post-holiday meeting I could, of course, contribute little more than the artists' sentiments and my father's resolution to translate them into practicalities. He laughed uproariously.

'That's the spirit! The artists are right and I'm sure that your father will produce a laudable result. But in politics things are more complicated; more people involved, more diverse and divisive opinions to contend with. In politics we deal with such esoteric subjects as happiness, fairness, and efficiency on the one hand, and on the other it's: why can my neighbour afford a washing machine and I can't?'

I felt taken aback but ventured: 'But it's the spirit not the details.'

Uncle Stuuf patted me on the shoulder: 'Of course. But don't get too excited. A building serves a clear purpose, in politics, as I said, it's less straightforward. Politicians belong to parties and parties have programmes for action. These are usually the result of endless discussions and then attain the stature of dogmas. It's difficult to dislodge such dogmas and get to the real aspirations. Not surprisingly most politicians ultimately aim at happiness and fairness. As the nazis have effectively suspended all political programmes, we've got a chance to discard them for the moment and concentrate on coordinating our attitude towards the nazis. My job is to build bridges across the divides. Hopefully these bridges will one day serve to revise the programmes!'

Uncle Stuuf went on to list some nazi measures that revealed the meaning behind recent events.

'Look,' he said. 'On 24 June Seyss-Inquart prorogues Parliament and the Council of State. On 4 July he prohibits listening to the BBC. On 14 July he introduces food rationing. All clearly related to the war and perceived as fair. But on 16 July he appoints a nazi administrator to run the unions, a few days later another one to run my paper. Nothing to do with the war. On 20 July he outlaws the communist party. Why only that party? Because few will cry over it and it creates the right atmosphere for dealing with other parties. Then on 31 July he sneaks in the first still innocuous anti-Jewish measure by the backdoor: ritual animal slaughter prohibited. All this quite openly. But on 28 August he reveals his plans in a secret meeting, where he tells the permanent secretaries in private that Jews can't be appointed any more nor promoted.'

It would be the task of an underground press to report all this. The regular press had, of course, given full publicity to Seyss-Inquart's inaugural speech of 29 May, four days after his arrival as *Reichskommissar*. His soothing words encapsulated the promise of non-interference with Holland's traditional values and laws. Most people were taken in and wanted to believe it. A reliable underground press was becoming essential to counteract such propaganda. A few individuals had already started 'subversive' letters, with Bernard Ijzerdraad the pioneer on 15 May, the day after the army had capitulated and

Rotterdam had been reduced to rubble. None of these early efforts – handwritten and copied by hand to begin with, later typed and stencilled – had access to information more reliable than rumours. None were made by journalists until on 25 July professional journalist Frans Goedhart typed his first Newsletter under the pen-name Pieter 't Hoen. Uncle Stuuf had just made contact with him. Thus we became involved in the preparation, and later the publication, of *Het Parool*.

At this point in our discussion we were joined by a party stalwart, who turned out to be a union leader as well, a massive middle-aged man with dark stubble, flashing brown eyes and a frightful accent. The disparity between the neatly dressed patrician sitting erect in his chair and the shabby plebeian slumped in his was striking. The contrast extended to their speech but not to their understanding. The unkempt hulk soon showed his intelligence, not crafty shrewdness but straightforward sound simplicity, similar to Uncle Stuuf's approach. Notwithstanding Uncle Stuuf's shyness and his awkwardness in the presence of those other than his intellectual equals, they clearly felt deeply for each other.

The party stalwart reported on the sensible wait-and-see attitude of his mates, who would not throw away their livelihood unless provoked. The might of the nazis was too overwhelming for pinpricks like strikes to produce any effect. These would only result in exemplary arrests or worse.

'We'll just ignore the bastards,' he growled. 'They need us and won't touch us.'

Sturdily perseverant in organizing his workmates and party members, he became an early victim of the very first strike, in February 1941, reported below.

A week later I cycled to an Apostolic meeting alone. How could I explain Amanda's absence convincingly?

Matthew and Luke had already arrived at Laura's immense home and were talking rather loudly in the vast drawing room. Matthew languished on a sofa, pontificating, his legs stretched to their full length along its seat, his body reclining against one end, his arm across it. Luke sat deeply ensconced in one of the armchairs, with a smile that somehow conveyed both admiration and scepticism. Laura went to a more upright armchair while I dropped onto another sofa. We drank some fruit juice. Titillation turned out to be off the agenda. Laura had herself well in hand and was deadly serious.

I explained Amanda's absence by pleading protection for a schoolgirl. This inevitably evoked grins from the boys. Matthew mumbled something about Amanda being mature for a schoolgirl. But they accepted Laura's argument that maturity in bed does not necessarily imply maturity for 'acts of sabotage against the German war machine.'

This was the first indication of our future activities. Matthew reacted in his languorous way: 'Snipe at the almighty Wehrmacht? Is that what we're supposed to do?'

Laura remained cool. 'Sabotage in a general sense, not literally. But before I explain you'll have to answer first whether you promise complete silence and complete trust in each other.'

Luke was the first to do so, pulling himself upright out of the depth of his chair. 'I'm afraid I can't, at least not yet. It's all a bit too ambiguous for me. I dislike communism just as much as nazism. And Stalin doesn't seem any less evil than Hitler. You used the word "cell" to describe us. That's communist jargon. You mentioned a communist who transmits to Moscow. Where's your professed independence?'

Unperturbed Laura replied: 'Fair enough. You attach too little weight to the practical argument. Communism is a human ideal which I happen to support. Nazism and fascism have nothing to do with ideals. They're systems for organizing the state. With evil methods full of racist claptrap, with contempt for all non-nazis, in fact for all people as individuals and for their lives. Such systems, those methods I happen to detest, as I'm sure you do. Dictatorships may be all right for some nations, but surely not for us. Run by an evil genius it's simply abhorrent. Salazar, Franco and Mussolini seem to be fairly civilized men enthralled by a stupid system. Hitler is evil. The nazis are here, the Portuguese, Spanish, Italians, Russians are not. All else is irrelevant in practical terms.'

I had come under her spell, so had Matthew, but not Luke. He remained unconvinced. 'Aren't you being rather gullible?

In Russia communism is a dictatorship, not of the proletariat –
a fatuous term – but of Stalin. As repressive as the nazis. The
Russians proclaim the need for world revolution. Their leaders
seem quite capable of promoting it too. I accept your
motivations, of course. I might even support your ideals. But I
think consorting with communists invites disaster.'

I was fascinated. Luke's arguments reflected Uncle Stuuf's,
yet my sympathies were with Laura.

She now leant forward and became slightly tense. Then she
delivered what was clearly intended as the coup de grace:
'You'll remember I said I'm not in anybody's employ. That
means I'm a free agent. When undue pressures occur I'll opt
out. When what we're asked to do stops serving the purpose of
sabotaging the nazis I'll opt out too.'

Luke had moved to the edge of his seat as well. He refused to
concede. 'My point is: will you be able to? Are you really the
free agent you think you are?'

'I am and always will be. The communist organization can't
do anything to control me in nazi-occupied Holland. Not even
stop me from opting out.'

'A determined young lady,' Matthew interrupted without
moving.

Laura was incensed. 'You should know me by now.'

'Not all of you, my dear, at least not yet.'

'Shut up,' I broke in, surprised by my vehemence. 'Don't be
vulgar.'

Matthew did not really want a fight. He was surprised that
his quip had backfired, and relented.

Luke had by now relaxed, though not quite into the depths
of his soft cushions. 'Look, Laura, I'm still a long way from
being convinced. Your arguments are persuasive. You're
obviously sincere. But I doubt the wisdom of the course you're
taking. In the circumstances it's unfair for me to hear more
about your plans only to opt out later. Rather like spying on
you.'

That was awkward. Was I not supposed to do just that? For
the best of motives, of course, to protect Laura. Who now
protected whom? Had Amanda been right? Had I fallen for
Laura's magic? I did not feel equipped to act as a sort of double

agent, as we both intended to work on the same side towards the same goal.

Laura, subdued now, leant back in her chair. She had made a decision. 'All right,' she said with quiet dignity. 'I'm sorry that my admission of communist sympathies upset you. I'm grateful for your honesty. Please keep all this absolutely confidential. I'm sure you realise what would happen if you didn't.'

Luke got up to leave. 'Of course I do and of course I promise to keep it under my hat.' He clearly meant what he said.

Laura, with a quiet smile said: 'Thanks. See you some time. Give me a kiss.'

Luke obliged and left, visibly depressed. I had a premonition that we would see him again.

After Luke's departure Matthew remarked: 'And then there were three.' He took two cigars, lit both, offered one to Laura and added: 'Relax, little one. Tell us.' He stretched out on the sofa.

Silence prevailed for some time. No more promises were exacted or even mentioned. Our very presence seemed to satisfy Laura. The discussion with Luke had taken its toll, however, for she looked exhausted and pulled on her cigar absentmindedly.

Matthew broke the silence. 'Buck up, little one. Three are better than five.'

Then Laura broke down and wept, though not for long, nor in loud spasms, but in gentle hiccups. It dawned on me that her distress was caused less by the arguments themselves – which she must have expected – than by her failure to convince. To Laura three were not as good as five. Perhaps she realized too the failure to enlist us for what she clearly saw as the ideal double cause. She had tackled it in the wrong way, sincerely but too emotionally.

After a few minutes she recovered her poise and motioned Matthew to the sofa on which I sat and put herself between us. In a more confident mood she puffed at her cigar, pensively, and leant back, though without putting her arms around us as I had expected. We waited.

Laura then casually explained what we were supposed to do.

It proved to be an anti-climax. Had she decided to slow down for fear of losing more of her apostles? Or had Luke's arguments sapped her own conviction? She wanted us to conduct espionage, not sabotage: report on military objects, troop movements, where officers billeted, all without giving any idea of where to find these or how to recognize them.

What a magnificent person, I thought. Her long legs, high-heeled sandals, the cigar between fingers ending in long nails, her tall, taut body – it all seemed far removed from the world of espionage. I enjoyed just looking at her, without feeling tempted, even when she turned and looked at me in what can only be described as a 'significant way'. For I was sure that glance was a cry for support, not an invitation to bed.

I left, relieved, and whistled as I cycled home, where I found Amanda uncharacteristically concerned.

After telling her what had happened, I suddenly became really afraid, for the first time. What had I let myself in for? I felt uncertain and inadequate. Resistance was proving to be different than I had expected, much more complicated, involving emotions that distracted from the simple resolve to fight the nazis. Any grandiose visions that I might have cherished disappeared as I fumbled to get a grip on reality. Loyalties to both Amanda and Laura jeopardized, spying on Laura for Uncle Stuuf – it was all far removed from effective opposition to nazism.

Uncle Stuuf solved my dilemma a few days later by ignoring it. When I reported to him, he waved my anxiety away in one sentence – 'Good, obviously Laura accepts the protective role I advised you to play' – and then went on to outline my future tasks. I was to be used more regularly as a courier, carrying written and verbal messages which he preferred not to pass on by telephone. I was also to sit in on meetings as well as helping to raise finance and distribution for the planned underground paper. It would be very professional, he said, an enlargement of superior quality of the newsletter which Frans Goedhart had started. It would be called *Het Parool* – parole, watchword – the paper with a message as well as with news. Resistance became a lot simpler after that, also because events were overtaken by the unexpected arrival of Alexander.

Chapter Six

ALEXANDER'S FIRST RETURN

Their training for the projected drop completed by early August, Alexander and Charles had to wait another three weeks before a suitable plane was found. Not until more than a year later did the flying facilities come to match the dropping demands. The Battle of Britain raged all over northern England, though not yet over London. The Luftwaffe concentrated on ports and airfields in preparation for the landing of troops, a massive military bombing campaign and not yet an operation to soften up the civilian population. The papers reported huge enemy losses. London was tense but the people calmly went about their daily business.

Waiting turned out to be one of the most frustrating side aspects of the war. In those weeks Alexander and Charles found themselves virtually in quarantine. Although their small hotel near Hyde Park was comfortable, security prevented them from meeting anyone. They came to know Hyde Park well. Bruce Crane relieved the boredom a few times by taking them to dinner to a quiet, select restaurant. Van Alblas did the same twice. The second time he turned up accompanied by Adrian Pelt, the Dutch government's information officer, previously press chief of the League of Nations in Geneva. An amiable, short man with a round belly and a bald dome, he was to play an important part in Alexander's life after the war. His presence was intended as a diversion, not to discuss details of their missions, presumed to be secret. Or were they? For, the exquisite meal almost finished, Adrian Pelt in an aside to

Alexander unexpectedly gave vent to his horror at finding the Dutch cabinet so crushingly indecisive at crucial moments.

'The prime minister wallows in self-pity, can't live without his wife. He argues for peace overtures to be made and fails to provide any lead. What a difference with the queen! I'm sure she won't stand him much longer. And that goes for some of the other ministers too.'

Alexander remained silent, already anticipating what Pelt would say next: 'Very sad that few capable candidates to replace them are available outside Holland.'

That corresponded so neatly with Prince Bernhard's earlier plea that Alexander smelled collusion. Again he waited, fearing what now seemed bound to follow.

'Are you going back to Holland?' Pelt asked.

'Did anyone tell you that?'

Fortunately the conversation became general again and the moment of danger passed. Alexander had not told a lie, nor disclosed the secret truth. But the episode strengthened his resolve to approach Wiardi Beckman.

Finally, on 28 August they parachuted down into some bulb fields north of The Hague. A smooth enough landing, with their bags dropping neatly beside them instead of getting entangled with their legs, a risk that caused unpleasant landings and a few tragic accidents later on. They buried their parachutes in the sandy soil of the empty field and made their way quietly to a nearby hut where they hid the bags, one with the ponderous transmitter. They then started on the six-mile trek to Wassenaar – the villa village bordering The Hague – avoiding main roads, sometimes hiding when they saw something suspicious, and at 2 am knocked on the door of their first safe-house.

Some time elapsed before their unsuspecting host – Doctor Fleming – opened a little window in the door, recognized Charles and let them in. With his wife he provided sandwiches and drinks, took them to a spare room, made up beds for them and left them to sleep. They did so, until noon.

Doctor Fleming was the father of Charles' closest friend, Michael, whom Charles hoped to enlist. Michael was away, however, and his mother was rather frightened. The news of

Charles' escape had filtered through, though not his safe arrival in Britain. His return to occupied Holland barely two months afterwards stunned them. It also drew admiring remarks about the efficient organization. So far all had indeed gone smoothly and neither Charles nor Alexander had reason to dampen such optimism. Efficiency was hardly the correct word, however. It would take three years and many disasters before genuine efficiency prevailed.

After lunch Doctor Fleming drove them to the bulb field to retrieve their bags. That evening an intense and prolonged discussion followed. Arthur Fleming was a jovial man in his mid-fifties, small in comparison to the towering Alexander but also smaller than his wife, Gertrude. He was very active, with a mass of curly dark-brown hair and what can only be described as mischievous eyes: his glance revealed a jocular twinkle and a slight roguishness. Gertrude's hair was immaculately coiffed and artificially coloured, a subdued blond. Her make-up tended towards the excessive, her nails too long for ordinary household work, her dress rather exuberant, all clearly designed to impress men, which slightly disturbed Alexander. Gertrude flirted openly with her handsome young guest.

Yet they were made quite comfortable. Both Flemings helped eagerly and without complaint, though also with care. There was a risk of unexpected arrivals: their daughter from The Hague, a domestic servant about to return from holiday, occasional patients. Hence places of concealment had to be devised, even though at this early stage the dangers were not all that great and the house contained several unused rooms on its two floors. Guarded phonecalls resulted in Charles' departure the next day with the transmitter. Alexander was then asked to stay for as long as he liked — under his assumed name — as the son of friends living abroad.

The arrangement soon proved its value. Alexander contacted Wiardi Beckman, whom the Flemings knew of but had never met. Thrilled at the prospect of meeting him, they suggested that Alexander invite him to come and stay the night. That would facilitate their discussions and alleviate the dreariness of Alexander's enforced idleness. So one evening Uncle Stuuf slipped discreetly into the house. Although from another part of the political spectrum, the Flemings were easily charmed by him and during dinner he made converts of people who would not even have listened to him in normal times.

The visit stimulated Gertrude into voluble pleasantries. These did not embarrass husband Arthur; far from it – his eyes beamed approval. As he explained to Alexander in the days that followed, his wife's flirtatious behaviour excited him, for he knew that in the end he would be the beneficiary. In the early days of their marriage her behaviour had caused him a lot of worry, until he came to understand that it represented two sides of the same coin. Gertrude was very much a woman and relished male adoration. She also abhorred infidelity. As a result she had developed a technique that satisfied both her romantic cravings as a desirable woman and her equally romantic marital loyalty.

Alexander and Uncle Stuuf shared a bedroom and spent many hours discussing all the aspects of his double mission. Eventually this led to the first wartime link between Alexander and myself. All had gone according to plan so far but Alexander felt less certain about the next steps. Wiardi Beckman pointed out that crossing into Germany with a Dutch passport would entail an almost unacceptable risk. (The Dutch embassy in London had provided Alexander with a genuine one in an assumed name.)

'Why not try and get German papers?' suggested Uncle Stuuf. 'Cross the frontier on foot in the north-east and pick up a train on the German side. I know a party member who'll be glad to help with the crossing.'

'How do I get German papers? It's what they suggested in England as well.'

'No idea. Also, I wonder how keen Dohnanyi and Oster will be to cooperate. The war has progressed beyond the joke it was when you last saw them. The situation is damned serious. Why not see Rudolf Smend first, to test the water?' Smend was the renowned professor of law at Berlin University.

'That makes sense. In London they thought it would all be easy, that Canaris and his lot would be desperate to stop the madman. He probably is. But he's also an admiral and a very able intelligence chief.'

'Is he part of the conspiracy?'

'That's what I've got to find out. The trouble is I've come to like Hans von Dohnanyi a lot. And I don't want to expose him to more danger than he can cope with.'

'Then don't press him too hard. Time's on their side.' It never was.

A pause ensued, both deep in thought, until Alexander changed the subject: 'Are you all right?'

'My health is excellent. Otherwise no, not quite. It's all rather frustrating. Various discussion groups have been set up. The atmosphere is harmonious. Most agree to weed out weaknesses in the political system. And yet . . . there's no way of communicating with more than a handful of party members. That may seem an advantage: no encumbrances, no jockeying for position, no politicking, if that's the right word in this context. But it carries a danger. Innovations will only stick and last with public support and that needs a sound underground press. Also, there are still too many political skeletons in too many party cupboards. If the situation does last a long time and gets rough, those skeletons will come out again.'

'I'm sorry.' Alexander judged this to be the moment to spring his surprise: 'Would you like to go to London and be rid of it?'

Wiardi Beckman did not immediately grasp the implications of what Alexander was saying. 'Certainly not. Rid of what? I know what's got to be done. It needs time and patience and a lot of perseverance. That's my job.' He paused. 'Hey, why d'you ask? What would I do over there?'

Whereupon Alexander reported on his talks with Prince Bernhard and Adrian Pelt. In London the queen had meanwhile forced the prime minister to resign and had replaced him with the fighting little minister of justice. Otherwise the cabinet remained unchanged. The BBC had announced it.

'Well now. That's different. I'll have to think about it, sound out others.' He waited a while, then said: 'I'll need time to balance the pros and cons. This is not indecisiveness but stark realism. Renewal has to come from here, not from a small clique over there.'

They both paused. Uncle Stuuf got up and paced the room.

Alexander broke the silence: 'You don't really want to go, do you?'

'My instinct tells me no. But I appreciate the problem in London.' He sat down again and looked at Alexander before springing his surprise: 'There's something else. Your cousin is in contact with a communist network.'

'Laura? A communist?'

'She's set up a cell of five called the Apostles and reports to a communist operator with a transmitter to Moscow.'

'You must be joking!'

'I'm afraid not. It doesn't look very serious yet, but Laura is a very determined young lady, as you well know. I think you've got to do something.'

'Why? And why me? How awkward. She'll report my presence to Moscow, even if I don't tell her why I'm here.'

'It's a risk but worth taking. She would be a good catch if she could be persuaded to cooperate with London. Didn't you have a special relationship with her?'

'What are you suggesting?'

'Sorry, but it's a rather unusual situation. I can't afford to get mixed up with espionage. Would you mind telling me what happened?'

'Well, we had a little fling, but she was rather possessive and we're both too young for serious entanglements. At least that's how I feel. There's been no break. We're good friends as well as cousins.'

'Are you sure there's not more to it on her part?'

'I don't know. There isn't on mine.'

'Can't you approach her? If she's still got a crush on you she might reveal the communist operator and how serious her involvement is. You'd also be better placed to woo her our way. Herman Friedhoff is my informant and a member of these Apostles. At my suggestion he keeps an eye on her. He can't do more than report and if she's serious will have to opt out anyhow. Don't get me wrong. I've nothing against fighting the nazis alongside communists. But their subversive tactics could do endless harm after the war if not during it.'

Alexander chuckled. All of a sudden he saw an intriguing development. Often attractive ladies are used to lure male agents; now here was an opportunity to reverse the roles. Could he do it? 'It's rather unfair on dear Laura,' he said, 'And tricky, for I can't jeopardize my present mission.'

'You don't have to.'

'All right. I'll see what I can do.' It would after all be a family affair and was not meant to harm her

The next morning Charles phoned to announce his imminent arrival with what he called 'interesting news'. After Wiardi Beckman had left for an important meeting he sneaked in by a side door. He had set up his transmitter and two nights hence would send his first message. He was also on the trail of the British agent.

Michael arrived a little later. He resembled his mother more than his father from whom he had nevertheless inherited the eyes, almost as sparkling. He was elegant, blond, with those dark eyes, and as ebullient as his mother. He had happened to visit the same people whom Charles had been to see and was instantly ready to join as well. Moreover, he already formed part of a small group which boasted the inestimable asset of a German connection, an anti-nazi captain in one of the SD departments who was having an affair with the sister of one of their group. This had enabled them to obtain German papers. Charles had assumed a connection with Alexander's previous visits to Berlin and guessed that German papers might be of help. Various documents were in preparation. They now needed passport photographs and Alexander's signature in the name of Günther Franck, undercover official of the SD. His second adopted personality.

During a further period of waiting, Alexander phoned a farmer – a staunch supporter of Wiardi Beckman – whose property bordered the German frontier near Enschedé in the north-east of Holland. The farmer promised to guide him across the frontier and also provide him with essential German currency.

Alexander also phoned Laura, one of his most difficult tasks yet. He could not see her face to gauge her reaction, nor did he know the strength of her attachment to the communist cause. Inevitably she was stunned, having heard of his escape from

Scheveningen. Fortunately the ploy worked: before he could offer an explanation she proposed a meeting in a tone that clearly suggested a renewal of their old personal relationship. A not unnatural reaction, for why else should he ring her up? He consented happily enough to a meeting, then explained that his flight had been aborted but that, having been spotted, he should remain in hiding.

'But I'm on to another possibility. We might even work together. I'll ring you again later on.'

'When?'

'Don't quite know. In a week or so.'

'Hurry up, darling Alexander. It's so marvellous. I can't wait.'

'Don't do anything foolish. Don't tell anyone that I'm in Holland. If you did it would be too dangerous to meet.'

'What d'you think I am? A blabbermouth? And risk losing you again?'

'OK, OK.' And Alexander hung up, rather pleased with himself for having avoided any commitment. He did not yet know what mixture of pleasure and work was needed to succeed, nor what the work would entail, nor even his own attitude towards entanglements of a more intimate nature.

Laura was still aglow when she met me the next evening and blabbed.

A few days later Wiardi Beckman reported a mixed reception from his political friends. He had suggested that in view of what looked like a serious cabinet crisis following the resignation of the prime minister, two or three of them should attempt to strengthen it. Some considered the dangers involved in the journey to England forbidding; one felt it to be presumptuous for them to impose themselves on a legitimate cabinet; another was nervous about making what amounted to a vote of no confidence. The consensus was that the nazi action would occur in Holland, where guidance would consequently be most needed. Still, Uncle Stuuf felt concern for the queen and wanted to reconsider. He was very impressed by the queen, though he called her a 'confused personality'. She had done all the right things and possessed political wisdom in excess of most around her. But she must have led a very unsatisfactory emotional life, he felt. However, she had clearly pointed her head towards the future and was caring as well as astute. Therefore he could consider all options. And time was available. Alexander would be on his way to Germany and could hardly report on this issue until the other one had been dealt with.

Alexander agreed: 'We'll keep it simmering, as I've kept Laura simmering.'

'Splendid. If only these women would sort themselves out!'

Alexander took a train to Enschedé, carrying a briefcase large enough to accommodate pyjamas, shaving gear, toothbrush, two unmarked shirts, some SD folders and two German books. He wondered nervously what papers to use if he were stopped. He was not Alexander Paul any more, nor yet Günther Franck. To the farmer he would be Uncle Stuuf's 'young man'. During the journey he tried to adjust to this confusion of personalities, a problem that was to increase as the war dragged on and those who wished to avoid the Gestapo's clutches would have to use increasing numbers of different personae, sometimes several at a time.

Alexander's various papers were not put to the test and he found the farmer waiting at the station. He was driven to the farm, stepped out of the car, but was not invited into the house in order to avoid complications. The farmer led him away on foot along fields, then into a wood. It was pitch black. In his dark grey mackintosh he merged with the trees, and a strong wind drowned any sound they might have made. After a couple of hours of walking in eerie silence the farmer whispered that they were now in Germany. It had been as simple as that. He showed Alexander the direction. It was ten o'clock and if Alexander found the road without losing his way he should catch the last bus to Rheine and arrive there just before midnight. With his SD papers, the farmer said, Alexander would not encounter any problems at the hotel. Rheine had a rail link with Hannover where he should change for Berlin.

'I don't know what you're up to, young man, and I don't want to know,' the farmer concluded, shaking his hand warmly. 'But Germany is an awkward place for a Dutchman to be in right now. Good luck.'

Alexander was on his own, in alien surroundings and on

enemy soil. For the first time he also felt very lonely. Although crossing the North Sea had been a frightening experience, loneliness had not crept up on him as it did now. Charles had been with him and they had been busy rowing. While walking at a brisk pace he wondered whether to take the bus. His German was rusty and grammatically most imperfect. On a late night bus, probably with few passengers, talk might be difficult to avoid and his accent might betray him.

The trees gave way to open fields and soon he touched the deserted road. A sign pointed to Rheine via Bad Bentheim, only three kilometres further on. He decided to walk there and trust to luck rather than risk the bus. The wind blew more fiercely and the long threatened rain burst upon him. At that moment a bus overtook him, stopping a little further on. The driver must have noticed him and halted out of pity or curiosity. Alexander could see that the driver was alone. What should he do? The open fields offered no hiding place. No doubt the driver would report the mysterious pedestrian if he were to refuse so considerate a gesture. Still, the driver would surely also want to talk.

Alexander did not really see any alternative but to brave it out. He might as well get it over with and test his adopted personality as well as his German. He climbed the steep steps into the bus, coughing heavily, pointed at his throat, mumbled something in a hoarse voice about his car having broken down, took out a ten-mark note and asked the Rheine.

The driver was most sympathetic, handed him a ticket and some coins for change and got the rattling bus going again. He drove at great speed and chatted throughout the forty-five minutes to Rheine, with little chance for Alexander to say much. The driver was obviously happy with any company in the nasty night.

He stopped in front of the hotel at 11.30 pm. The front door was closed but a light was still on. He hooted his horn until it was opened, shook hands with Alexander and drove off.

Alexander showed one of his papers, most impressive with a large 'SD' printed on it, and was taken to a sizeable upstairs room. When almost undressed the door opened without a knock. The large lady in slippers and dressing gown who had let him in had brought a generous mug of hot chocolate. The ordeal was over, the first hurdle taken. Relieved, Alexander was able to relax.

The next morning he shook hands and said goodbye in a less croaky voice. The lady was obviously happy about this improvement and advised him to drink more hot chocolate. She did not seem to have detected anything wrong with his German.

The train journey turned out to be long and tedious. His papers were checked twice and proved valid. Alexander had by now become accustomed to his new personality, whose credentials appeared to impress.

At around seven that evening he descended from the train and entered Berlin. He took a cab and arrived safely at the home of Professor Dr Jur Rudolf Smend. A servant opened the door, but Smend happened to be crossing the hall, saw him, stretched out both arms and without showing any surprise said: 'I knew you would return one day! Welcome!'

Chapter Seven

MY FIRST VENTURE OUTSIDE HOLLAND

September had arrived without any decision on my future being taken. Amanda now attended a college for arts and crafts which was supposed to teach her needle and copper work, tapestry and pottery. Incongruously, it also included a course on typing. This would keep her occupied in a vaguely useful way. Women undergraduates were still exceedingly rare, careers for girls almost inconceivable. Girls were assumed to be potential wives and mothers. Exceptions like Laura were only accepted as just that: exceptions.

Amanda did not class herself with Laura. She had no need to prove anything by obtaining a degree nor did she have to earn a living. Her future was clear to her: marriage, not in order to settle down to beatific boredom but to realize her potential for pleasure. There would be a number of men in her life – in sequence not concurrently. She would also have children, not for the supposed pleasure of giving birth and weaning but for the sake of creating new individuals, moulding them and taking pride in their achievements.

As a male, however, I would have to earn a living and join the rat race. When the nazi occupation prevented my planned departure for Oxford University, my parents strongly recommended a Dutch alternative. I then made the even more quixotic decision not to go to university at all but to dedicate myself to whatever the resistance might require of my time and energy. The gaps could be filled in by reading up on a few favourite subjects like philosophy, history and international relations. My parents were only half convinced. They feared that what I presented as the chance of a lifetime would turn out to be a chance missed for a lifetime. We compromised on private tuition. This proved most satisfactory and unwittingly shrewd, for the university closed shortly after.

I cycled to the next meeting of what remained of the Apostles at Laura's home. Rain pelted down, but I rode along whistling, looking forward to the comfort and the company.

Laura was in high spirits, due to her contact with Alexander. She mentioned the phonecall casually and in confidence, but still against Alexander's express wish. She hoped that his unexpected surfacing would influence our course of action. Matthew looked glum and did not display his usual breezy demeanour. He must have taken advantage of Alexander's absence and Laura's excessive desire. Although he had not met Alexander, Matthew sensed that his monopolistic relationship with Laura, so recently established, was in jeopardy. Some inconsequential information of a military nature had been gathered. Laura seemed pleased. I suspect she held back on her own researches.

She next proposed that we enlarge our field of enquiries to include political activities. Matthew looked sceptical and stayed silent, still sulking.

I did not understand. 'Spying on Seyss-Inquart or the Dutch nazis? I don't know any of them.'

Laura laughed. 'You could try.'

'Ingratiate myself with the nazis? They wouldn't believe me.' Future events in the life of the Apostles were to remind me of this innocent remark.

Laura continued laughing. 'You're right, they wouldn't. But what are our own politicians up to?'

'What d'you want to know that for?'

'Well, they might have information that we could pass on. Aren't you a friend of Wiardi Beckman?'

I felt shock and a twinge of guilt and confusion. Did Laura have some inkling of my devious role? Or had she been asked by her communist contact? I had not told her about Uncle Stuuf, nor ever did. Nor did Alexander, as he had recently confirmed. Laura did not press the matter and the meeting ended without a decision.

Still, it had to be reported to Uncle Stuuf. He reacted with a shrug. When I mentioned Laura's telephone contact with Alexander he just smiled. So I switched to the slow and laborious work of collecting money for the planned underground paper. But he seemed satisfied. He told me about some recent talks but nothing about Alexander. I had to deliver some messages and carry out other jobs, which kept me fairly busy until our next meeting ten days hence. He mentioned that the secret instructions given to the permanent secretaries on 28 August by Seyss-Inquart would soon be implemented.

As indeed they were. On 7 October civil servants received a questionnaire about their ancestry which could confirm them as Aryans. Whoever Aryans might be, they were certainly not Jewish in the convoluted sense the nazis attached to it. Essentially one had to declare the number of one's Jewish grandparents. The next phase, just a month later, demanded the dismissal of all civil servants with three or four Jewish grandparents, curiously leaving out those with two and one.

Civil servants included those employed in education, among them university teachers. When on Friday 22 November their sacking was announced, the undergraduates of all faculties at the technical university of Delft decided to attend the regular Saturday lecture of the Jewish professor of law. They found the door to the auditorium locked, whereupon they proclaimed a boycott of all lectures for the following Monday and Tuesday. It was observed by everyone. On the Wednesday the nazis closed the university and prohibited the students from enrolling elsewhere.

Meanwhile at Leyden University the dean of the faculty of law, Professor Cleveringa, let it be known that he would replace his Jewish colleague, Professor Meyers, at his regular lecture. Consequently on Tuesday 26 November he gave an address that extolled Meyers' great learning and personal virtues. To a student audience that overflowed into other halls and onto the street, where loudspeakers relayed the address, Cleveringa pointed out that his dismissal violated the law of the land which guaranteed equal rights to all citizens irrespective of race or religion. While the international law of war permitted an occupying power to protect itself from dangerous elements, his elderly humane colleague hardly qualified as such. Furthermore, Cleveringa concluded, Seyss-Inquart had promised to respect Dutch law.

Afterwards a massive demonstration took place. Leyden University too was instantly closed and Cleveringa arrested. (He was released eight months later, which enabled him to play a covert and most important part as a member of the College of Confidants.) Both Matthew and Luke were present and became enthusiastically involved in typing out copies of the address and distributing them.

Two and a half months went by before public protests erupted again on a significant scale, this time in a different and more frightening way. In mid-February 1941, encouraged by the Germans, Dutch nazi thugs started to smash up Jewish shops in Amsterdam. A protection group was hastily formed, mainly from non-Jewish dockworkers. On 19 February the street fights resulted in the death of a Dutch nazi, by accident not by design. German police raided the district on 22 February and arrested 400 Jews who became the first to be deported from Holland to camps.

This time the people's protest took another form. The students had openly reacted to the German measures, now the workers did so. The city's employees were called out on strike. This was completely observed: on 25 February Amsterdam was a dead city.

The question of who called them out has been a bone of contention ever since. Communists were prominent, of course. A myth has grown up that communists controlled all continental resistance. They never did in Holland. Thousands of them lost their lives like any other patriots, and the survivors never posed a threat even to our monarchy. Dutch communists were dedicated anti-nazis, in contrast then to their Russian comrades, whatever the revolutionary prattle in private. They were also more disciplined and active and hence promoted the strike. But they neither controlled it nor initiated it, for the strike was a spontaneous protest of blue- and white-collar and itinerant workers. Whoever suggested the strike first touched a patriotic chord.

My next meeting with Uncle Stuuf occurred in October 1940. This time it was arranged in the publisher's office, situated in one of the narrow streets of the old city that wind their way to the central square. I cycled past the pretty gabled houses that were once homes for old people whose regents Frans Hals portrayed and which are now used as a museum named after him.

A surprise awaited me: Alexander was present. He was on his way back from Berlin, though he did not tell me this. He just wanted me to keep an eye on Laura until he returned, though he did not say where he was going or when he would be back. The Apostles were not really a serious group, he said, but he had a high regard for Laura herself. Whereupon he departed, leaving me puzzled.

Uncle Stuuf went on to discuss ways of raising money for the underground press. Surreptitiously he slipped in the desirability of opening up a route to Switzerland. I could not connect this with his own possible departure and interpreted his words as an attempt to establish an alternative means for communication with the exiled government. Only slightly surprised, I nodded, pleased to have been presented with another challenge and a clear purpose.

The search for a route out of occupied Holland by land made little progress for several months until a chance encounter that winter brought help. It came from a young Roman Catholic who boasted a connection with a monastery close to the border with Belgium. He had already adopted a fictitious name: Frans Maas, the Dutch name for the river Meuse which traversed his hometown of Rotterdam. It was a subtle device to remember his pseudonym, for when it surfaced his real name turned out to be Frans van Rijn, after Holland's other major river, the Rhine. We were to cross the frontier between Breda in the south of Holland and Antwerp in the north of Belgium, from where we would sort out the next stages. My objective was merely exploratory, Frans intended to reach England. It turned out to be my first failure, at least in personal terms.

In early January 1941 we left Rotterdam by train, alighted at Breda and took a bus to Wernhout, a mile or so inside the Dutch border. It was freezing hard and the ground was covered with snow. In the twilight of dusk we walked on the crackling snow to the monastery, where monks in brown habits welcomed us with broad smiles though few words. They gave us a generous hot meal and an equally generous supply of wine. They also gave us instructions about the way to behave once we were across the border and what transport to take. We were warned as well to make sure of reaching our destination before the ten o'clock curfew. We did not know about a curfew, none having yet been declared in Holland.

'Ah well. Some German soldiers were molested by drunken Belgians a few nights ago.'

One of the monks guided us across the invisible frontier through an all too sparsely wooded countryside to Wuustwezel, the first village in Belgium, where we arrived in time to catch the eight o'clock tram to Antwerp. I did not have a Belgian identity card, carrying only my Dutch passport. As it had not been stamped at the frontier, it could be awkward if I were stopped, for no stamp meant illegal entry. I began to shiver, not primarily as a result of the cold weather. For the first time I was far from the protection provided by my family, Amanda, Uncle Stuuf, Laura, all the cosy familiarity of my home environment. I was on my own, utterly and frighteningly so.

Everyone on the rattling tram looked like a potential enemy. I felt certain everyone could see that I was trespassing. Some-one would surely denounce me. Frans, however, appeared unperturbed and happy. That did not help either. Gradually a fear such as I have never known crept into me. In following years situations occurred that warranted more fear. By then I was used to danger. This was my first real experience of fear and physically painful. Fear is irrational. It still occasionally erupts today. When it does I can invariably trace it to those winter hours. Perhaps no one is ever fearless. It certainly strengthened my resolve to keep out of the Gestapo's clutches, for fear weakens resistance to torture.

The tram took nearly an hour to reach Antwerp. It was crowded but none of the passengers showed any interest in us.

They chatted happily, even rowdily, and gave me no comfort. Nor did Frans, who still appeared unaffected. Casually he mentioned the people we were due to meet in Antwerp's suburb Hoboken. 'I'm told they're marvellous people,' he said with a grin.

'Don't you know them?'

'Never met them.'

This unexpected confession increased my fear another notch. Although the train was comfortably warm, I shivered.

More terror awaited me. We alighted at the terminal and started walking along streets that rapidly emptied, the ten o'clock curfew creeping nearer. Frans led the way confidently. At one point I summoned up the courage to ask him how much longer it would take to reach our goal.

Frans replied merrily: 'No idea. Can't be far.'

'But you know the address and where we are now?'

'Sorry, I don't. I've forgotten. Don't worry, I've just remembered their names.'

Such casualness about a matter I had come to regard as one of life and death caused me a further shock. Fear turned into panic. Ten o'clock struck from a nearby church. The town was deserted. We could not ask our way, nor look in a telephone directory, for there was no telephone box to be seen.

Now Frans too became worried. 'I'm afraid I've no idea any more where to go.'

At ten thirty he stopped and looked at me puzzled. To my utter astonishment he suddenly went down on his knees, folded his hands, fondled a rosary, closed his eyes and mumbled a prayer. It lasted no more than a few seconds after which he got up, put his hand on my shoulder and pushed me along for two blocks, straight to a house wth a bright green door where he rang the bell.

'The Lord provideth,' he said cheerfully while waiting for what to me had become the door to heaven itself to open.

The door came fractionally ajar. Frans mentioned the name remembered and elicited a smile from a young man. It was the right place, though his parents had moved across the road to stay the night with his married sister and her baby girl in the absence of her husband. Swiftly we crossed the street, rang the bell at a bright yellow door and waited what seemed an interminable time before being welcomed by an elderly man. He admitted us hurriedly while listening to Frans' story. They lacked a spare bed at his daughter's and he accompanied us back to his own house with the green door and the smiling son, where we ended up in the parents' double bed. The Lord *had* provided, somehow. I report the incident as it happened. It was one of those events I have never forgotten.

The night passed slowly, frustratingly so. I shivered throughout, much to Frans' disgust. He was a lot smaller and lighter than me and often had to struggle to avoid being pushed out. He got up early and somehow found a thermometer, which confirmed his suspicion that I had run up a temperature. It worried him but caused a deep sense of relief in me. To Frans it explained my strange behaviour. But I knew better. The fear, now dissolving as my temperature increased, had been worse than any cold.

The trip served its purpose nonetheless. During the four days I spent in bed in Hoboken a Belgian identity card was fixed, a friendship established and a safe-house assured. My hosts were to prove their hospitality again on future occasions, providing shelter, false papers and much besides. Frans continued his journey and in due course reached England.

Later, when I reported what I regarded as my cowardice to Uncle Stuuf, he complimented me on a very sound admission of my own limitations, a quality he called essential for survival. He may have been right. I accepted it as a lesson for the future. Fear, I saw, was a figment of the imagination. All I had to do was to train myself to conjure up other imaginings and blow fear away. From then on my attempts to do this may well have contributed to my survival.

Meanwhile the closure of Delft and Leyden Universities focussed attention on the jewish question. Reappraisals were set in motion, numerous discussions held. Even the intelligentsia were baffled. There never had been a jewish problem in Holland, not even when some 16,000 Jews flooded into our country prior to the outbreak of war.

When the problem forced itself upon them, the Dutch lacked mental preparation and therefore a basis for effective resistance. Holland's Jews themselves felt that they were Dutch, as did the Roman Catholics, and all Dutchmen are equal before the law regardless of religion and race. This was not merely a doctrine, not just a clause of the constitution, but self-evident, an ingrained fact of life that had never before been questioned or tested. For centuries Holland had offered a haven for those persecuted elsewhere. The victims had been accepted as refugees, people under threat for some silly reason. They included Jews from various countries but also Catholics from the south at the height of our struggle for independence in the sixteenth century. That was after all a protestant revolt against institutional catholic intolerance. Jews, Catholics and other 'aliens' had long since become an inalienable part of the nation.

Indeed, Holland in 1940 was more overtly anti-catholic than covertly anti-semitic. Like many, my father refused to buy from shops owned by Catholics. Not because he disliked Catholics – some of his best friends were Catholics – but because he feared institutional influence from the Roman Curia, a threat to the tolerance that lay at the foundation of our society. The threat was not totally imagined either. Catholics then formed forty percent of the population and with their high birth rate might soon attain a majority, whereas the Jews formed less than two percent. Whatever influence the Jews had stemmed from individuals, not institutions. Catholics had their own schools, trade union, political party, various associations right down to such things as hockey clubs, each one supervised by a priest on behalf of the Church. The Jews had none of these.

Confusion existed too about the vexed question of whether Jews constituted a race or a religion. Hitler decreed them to be a race – and an inferior one – with a pernicious religion. The professional experts waved this away; to them Jews were 'just a group of people racially mixed but linked by a common history and religion', not unlike Christians of many skin colours. Such reasoning suggested a disturbing thought: once these small 'alien elements in the pure German body' had been

91

subdued, Hitler might attack the larger Catholic and Protestant Churches.

Few believed he would be so impractical, for it would divert manpower and resources from the more sensible aims of nazism. No one suspected his true intentions. Even the few like Wiardi Beckman who remembered the *Kristallnacht* of November 1938 and guessed something of its evil, did not really believe its ultimate purpose: *Endlösung*, the Final Solution. Nor had anyone outside our country. Hitler was regarded as a bully, a nasty one, not a stupid madman intent on killing millions.

Today, of course, we know what happened and this colours our perception. At the time no one could have known about the holocaust. It had not even started. Although concentration camps came into being soon after Hitler's ascent to power the early ones were intended to educate opponents, not to exterminate them. The change to wholesale slaughter was not decided until the Wannsee conference at the end of January 1942 and sanctioned by Hitler in early February. It remained a closely guarded secret. Ordinary Germans knew little of it, the Jews knew nothing. The Dutch Jewish Council – like their counterparts elsewhere – cooperated by registering all Jews and eventually bringing about their despatch to 'camps'. The official historian of Dutch Jewry – a Jew himself – after painstaking research, concluded they did not know. All of us failed to detect the ultimate horrors, a failure we share with almost everyone else in the world.

We did not need stronger incentives to resist than the dismissal of Jews and their later despatch to camps. They were then called 'labour camps' and accepted as such. Many non-Jews were sent there as well. That was horrible enough. We simply acted in defence of human values that surpassed religious or political disagreements. This explains why our resistance concentrated on helping individuals rather than on a massive uprising.

We were unprepared for so convoluted a nazi idea as the victimization of Jews. The Jewish President of the High Court of Justice counselled against obstructing nazi measures, if only for fear of making matters worse. The dismissal of civil servants was seen as misguided and a sad infringement of Dutch laws and values. But there was a war on. It was not the only infringement either. Nor were the nazis the only infringers and the Jews the only victims. What else could ordinary citizens do but accept such inconveniences. It would all blow over, one day the war would end, Holland would return to normality and those who had suffered, including Jews, would participate in the community as before. This is not postwar reflection but a truthful resumé of the discussions held during the winter of 1940/1.

Unhappily, there was no way such thoughts could be discussed openly. No leader could make his views known or exert influence on more than a handful of others. To those with clear views like Wiardi Beckman it meant agonizing frustration.

For Amanda it meant something different. Just before Christmas and before my trip to Antwerp we had the rare opportunity of spending an entire night together. She guided me into a long session of lovemaking, spurred on no doubt by the scarcity of such occasions, its consequent novelty and our youth. I flatter myself with the thought that I responded reasonably, but I shudder to think what might have happened if nature had been allowed its normal course: preventive measures were unknown to us. The morning after, however, she asked me unexpectedly what I proposed to do about the growing oppression of the Jews.

'I haven't a clue. Why d'you ask anyway?'

'I've dug up a great grandmother who was Jewish. That makes me one eighth Jewish, my father even a quarter.'

'That must prove a point, though I'm not sure what. Don't worry, the nazis only go for wholes and three-quarters, not even for halves, let alone quarters.'

'Don't mock. I'm serious.'

'I'll protect you.'

'How?'

'Well, we don't know what protection you need yet, do we?'

'Why don't you find a way to escape to England?'

That was awkward. Also, the presence of the Junoesque

Amanda weakened my earlier resolve to keep my planned trip to Antwerp a secret for reasons of security. So I told her about it.

'I'll join you!' she said eagerly. 'If you want to return, I'll go on.'

'We can't take a girl to a male monastery,' I protested.

That did not work. 'Nonsense. I'll dress as a man.' She would have too.

'Listen. There's no rush. You're in no danger. I'll be back, hopefully with a route opened up. My job is to explore and I can't chicken out.'

'You don't want me to go, do you?'

'You bet I don't. Not now. What about your father who's a quarter Jewish?'

'All right,' she said sullenly. 'I'll wait I'm sure we'll go some time.'

Chapter Eight

ALEXANDER GOES TO BERLIN

It was almost a year since Professor Smend and Alexander had first met in late September 1939 and six months since their last meeting. Outside the house circumstances had changed dramatically. Inside nothing had: the large hall with the monumental staircase disappearing into nowhere; the impressive chandelier; the half-moon mahogany table underneath the carved mirror; the uniformed maid who took Alexander's coat and hat and stowed them carefully away in the cloakroom underneath the stairs: all evidence of subdued opulence and peaceful constancy.

Rudolf Smend, in his early sixties, was of medium height with a high-domed bald head and a long straight nose. The nose supported half-spectacles which emphasized his extraordinary blue eyes. The eyes alternated between moments of sparkling exuberance and a disconcerting dullness when his interest flagged. They sparkled as he took Alexander's elbow and led him to the library, a vast room with a high ceiling, most of the walls covered by books arranged in regimental order, with a stepladder to reach the top shelves. Thick carpets and curtains in a quaintly harmonious mixture of soft brown and soft red flowers made Alexander feel in another world from the war.

'Alexander, my fellow, how did you manage it?' Smend asked in precise English with a slight but distinctive accent, as if his tongue relished every word.

'Not Alexander. I'm Günther Franck of the SD.'

'Herr Franck of the SD? Very clever. Tell me more.'

'I went to London, in a dinghy across the North Sea, with a friend.'

'Ha, ha! You have achieved vhat our army failed to do: *fahren gegen England*!'

Alexander recounted the sea saga and his subsequent contacts with secret service people. 'Apparently their contacts with your resistance are at a low ebb, for they asked me to patch them up.'

'Vell, vhat experiences. Vhy did you not first go to Dohnanyi?'

'Because Dr Wiardi Beckman thought Hans wouldn't feel very happy at the moment and that you might inform me about the situation before I saw him.'

'Yes, Hans keeps a low profile these days. So does Oster. Ve all do. But ve have not given up and vill never give up. Vhy this interest from the Englanders?'

'I don't really know. They never tell you more than necessary. Probably just to re-establish a line of communication.'

'Let us have a glass of vine first. I varn Emily to have a bed prepared and lay another plate. Dinner is in half an hour. After dinner ve talk about details.'

Over a glass of Würzburg Steinwein, one of Alexander's favourite bocksbeutels, Smend described the situation, resorting at last to German.

'Our Führer has become impossible. Everything he touches continues to succeed. It's difficult for anti-nazis to do anything just now. The non-nazis wouldn't want to support any overt action. The Fatherland can't be betrayed at the hour of glory. The country of Goethe and Heine, of Kant, Schubert and Schumann is now addicted to guns and conquests, like the ancient Huns whom we're accused of aping. Of course, the Führer lost his chance when the army didn't cross the Channel at once. Somehow Göring convinced him that the Luftwaffe could force England to its knees. Ha ha! But it is losing the air battle: our Stukas are too slow, our fighters fly lower than the British. And the weather prevents the army from crossing the sea until next summer. England will have rebuilt its army. If the Führer has second sight, as reported, he'll soon realize the impossibility of invading England.'

'So what will he do next?'

'Of course, second sight is nonsense. He is just very clever and very lucky. But he still makes mistakes. Naturally he'll prepare for more adventures and tighten his grip on Europe. He needs to: the German economy is in tatters. It means a long war, more destruction, more murders. D'you know what Hans Oster said when Poland was invaded? *Finis Germaniae*. He was right. German culture will be destroyed along with its cities. The trouble is that it reduces the chance of keeping the Russian bear in his lair. That's what we fear most. Hitler thought his pact with Russia would do the trick and avoid fighting on two fronts. But the Russians are re-arming furiously. When the Führer starts more adventures – and who knows what they'll be – he'll end up fighting on more than two fronts. The whole world will be against him, including America. Everyone shudders in fear of our armies, but that won't last. After all, tanks can't swim. More of his own people will turn against him. And he'll lose the heart of the German nation.'

Smend refilled their glasses and paced up and down the room, one hand in the pocket of his jacket, the other around his glass, gesticulating gently. He had discarded his spectacles, placing them neatly on the desk.

'It's doom all around. Wagnerian. Still, I see the end of the tunnel. One can't take on the whole world and ignore Christ's teachings at the same time. The Führer was foolish to start the war in the first place. He didn't need half of Poland. But that was a political error that could be rectified. He'll lose because he tramples on Christian ethics. When the armies gain more victories – as they may well do – he increases the scale of his problems and more trampling on ethics will occur. Whatever else our resistance does, its ultimate function is to shift the heart of our people – and their pride – away from military and material successes back to cultural and ethical achievements.'

A gong sounded.

'Don't mention why you're here. I don't want to involve Emily just yet. She probably has a shrewd idea anyhow. I'll tell her later. Say that Leyden is becoming a bore and you're

97

investigating what courses Berlin University offers. Perhaps a course with me?' He laughed. It would not not be such a bad idea either.

They had an excellent meal with more Franken wine at a mahogany table that could accommodate twelve and probably often did. Emily Smend was petite, mostly very quiet, but also highly intelligent and at times eloquent. A lot of silvery grey hair, once black, a severe dark-green dress that suited both her small figure and the abundant hair, and, incongruously, rather long slim fingers with a huge turquoise ring on one. She never asked why Alexander had come, nor how long he intended to stay. Instead she praised the wonderful way in which Huizinga had described their predicament. How difficult, she opined, to put Christian values in a modern context. When Alexander pointed out that Huizinga had not written a religious tract but a cultural one wrapped up in a historical context, Emily Smend laughed.

'That's the point, dear Alexander. Listen: the church expresses itself in biblical language. That's as it should be inside the church. But outside it has lost its immediacy, its relevance, its appeal. And the Christian message is heard more clearly from laymen like Dohnanyi.' A pause. 'And Rudolf, of course,' she added, with a wave of the hand to her husband, the massive ring emphasizing the gesture.

Smend interrupted and said: 'Laymen don't have to worry about scriptural purity.'

Alexander returned to Emily's theme. 'Why have the Christian churches lost their clout?'

'The answer is simple, but also depressing. A church is a house of prayer and introspection where we as individuals can repent and derive inner strength to face the world outside. Once the outside world is brought inside, the standards of the world are introduced into the church.'

'D'you mean that the church should remain silent on some of the most important issues of the time? Such as the persecution of the Jews?'

'Not at all,' Emily went on. 'Don't confuse the pastor as shepherd with the church as an institution, which includes specialists and laymen. They should, of course, speak up.'

'But don't we need the shepherd's support?' Alexander asked.

'Of course. But you'll get more support from the pastor who concentrates on Christ's message than from the one who talks politics. Imagine yourself in church. You've just sung psalms, you've prayed and you're trying to communicate with God. And then the pastor expostulates about the world outside, takes you back outside. Your mind is taken away from God, starts arguing. Man takes over and God is lost.'

Smend interrupted: 'Careful, darling Emily. What about your adored Martin Niemöller? And the Catholic Bishop of Munster, Cardinal Count von Galen?' Like a few, von Galen had spoken up.

'They are the exceptions that prove the rule. The specialists I referred to are church leaders. Unfortunately the church institutions are too uncertain about their role in the modern world. If lawyers must point out misuses of the law, church leaders must point out misuses of human values.'

Alexander had to be satisfied with that, a view as unexpected as it was challenging. It confirmed the ethical nature of German resistance, which stressed the importance of methods used and values abused. Quite a few religious leaders had initially been tempted by the clear path that Hitler appeared to offer out of the weakness of previous governments. But, like Martin Niemöller, they soon revised their opinion. Unfortunately after having voted Hitler into power.

It was not until several days later that Dohnanyi arrived, with his wife, for dinner. And not until after the meal, when the men had left the women for Smend's library, did they discuss Alexander's mission. Although both wives were aware of their husbands' conspiratorial activities, they kept away at that stage for security reasons. Dohnanyi's face had a tense expression, made more severe by thin metal-rimmed glasses. Hans was one of several civilians enlisted by Canaris for the Abwehr – military intelligence – ostensibly for his sharp legal mind, in reality to serve as an umbrella for anti-nazi activities. He was wonderfully incisive, with an unbelievably wide range of knowledge, which he used almost casually. Smend later called him the intellectual head of the conspiracy, a judgement with which the Gestapo, after the bomb plot of July 1944, agreed.

Dohnanyi pointed out that Alexander's presence in Berlin was dangerous and would progressively become more so as the war went on. He could easily run into one of the random checks. His Günther Franck papers might be genuine, but Günther Franck himself was not. His accent might arouse suspicion too. Taken into custody for verification, the Gestapo would soon discover that there was no such person in the SD. Briefly, he was not the right person to act as agent or courier.

There was another problem. Their conspiracy concentrated on internal German resistance, not on supplying Britain with military intelligence, which the British would surely prefer. Britain, however, could do little to assist German resistance in any overt action. When successful there would be little difficulty in establishing contact. Frequent contacts were therefore superfluous and increased the danger of leaks. They could also be counterproductive. Every failed attempt at overthrowing the hated regime would tend to increase British scepticism.

Though taken aback by such arguments, Alexander retorted that he had an open mission without specific instructions. He hoped other approaches could be found. Hans admitted the value of a sympathetic and reliable contact on the other side and promised to confer with some colleagues.

The result was surprising. Two days later Dohnanyi returned at dark, not with his wife but with a girl of Alexander's age. She was of medium height with an angular jaw, that gave her a square face without detracting from the delicacy of her features. A mass of chestnut hair, deep brown eyes and a Junoesque stature turned distinction into unusual beauty. Her name was Irena Schweichert, of Polish descent but German nationality. She was an assistant to Admiral Canaris, who as head of the Abwehr was also the boss of both Oster and Dohnanyi, and had been of her previous superior, Hans Bernd Gisevius.

Irena turned out to be a distant relative of Colonel Antoni Szymanski, head of the German desk of Polish intelligence and military attaché at its Berlin embassy when Germany invaded Poland. Szymanski had been arrested and removed to Helsinki. However, his wife and three young children were escorted to Switzerland by Irena at the request of Canaris. That much came out in the course of the evening. It was only recently that Alexander discovered that Mme Szymanska's presence in Switzerland contributed to one of the most amazing stories of World War II.

Although it has been said of Canaris that his wife 'was the only woman ever known to figure romantically in his life,' the admiral's relationship with Mme Szymanska must have been more than mere friendship. The Polish lady had been introduced to British intelligence in Switzerland by her compatriots. A British case officer was appointed who reported direct to the head of MI6, Menzies, the same man who had sent Alexander on his mission. Whenever he could, Canaris visited Mme Szymanska and supplied her with increasingly important intelligence. Gisevius was sent to Switzerland as vice-consul in Zürich, a cover intended to facilitate this communication. Canaris also contrived meetings with her in Paris and Rome, until his dismissal early in 1944. The admiral was eventually executed.

Dohnanyi must have been aware of this amazing link between the heads of opposing intelligence services, but he never mentioned it. He said instead:

'Irena will act as courier. Switzerland would suit us best. She'll be able to go there fairly easily. Could you arrange to meet her there?' Unaware of the background, the question struck Alexander as rather abrupt and unexpected.

Alexander quickly glanced at Irena, then replied carefully: 'Sounds like a good idea. But I'll have to consult London.'

'Of course. Irena's brother happens to be stationed in Holland for the Abwehr. He is one of us, in the conspiracy. When you're back in Holland you'll no doubt contact London. Then report the result to him. He'll let us know and Irena will travel to Holland at once for the two of you to arrange a date and a place.'

'You've got it all worked out, Hans, haven't you? What made you change your mind?'

'You did.' Dohnanyi laughed, then continued: 'Your personality not your argument.'

'Why such flattery?'

'We've always wanted a line of communication with England separate from military intelligence. But we've had many disappointments. Some of our friends tried to interest the English government before the war, to warn them and also to tell them that there is another Germany. But they met with scepticism in London and never got through to a minister, and only one of them saw Churchill.'

'And you want *me* to succeed where *they* failed?' Alexander now laughed. 'When I was interrogated on my arrival in England they suggested I might have been recruited by you. They appear to be right.'

Dohnanyi laughed again: 'Interesting. But no, sadly. The situation is now different. The threat of war has become the reality of war. There's a new government with Churchill. Perhaps our friends did not use the right arguments. We too have grown up. I understand British scepticism. I realize too that the onus is on us. We'll have to establish our credibility gradually. That will take time. We don't want an ambassador to plead our cause. So we're not recruiting you. But we do need someone who is sympathetic and can evaluate our information properly without bias. Perhaps someone who can be their ambassador to us?'

Alexander paused before replying: 'And you think I can do that?'

'I've talked to Smend and Oster and a few others. We agree: yes, you can. But we'll have to supply you with facts, a few at a time, to cement credibility both ways. Hence Switzerland and Irena. Hence also the need to separate our resistance objectives from military considerations.'

'I see your point. But England won't like that separation.'

'We insist, because otherwise we run the risk of the one compromising the other. Military matters will somehow find their way. Admiral Canaris agrees to the use of Irena.'

It made sense. They relaxed and Alexander looked at Irena in a different way. He needed all his equanimity to retain his composure at the sight of her. He wondered whether only males reacted in such a primitive way. His eyes must have betrayed him, for when the evening came to an end Irena smiled rather mischievously. 'Here we go again,' he thought. He was getting mixed up with a procession of attractive women. As an ordinary impressionable young man his physical loyalties sometimes conflicted with loyalties of a more ethical nature. Alexander remembers twisting in his bed that night, banging his fists on the blankets and bemoaning: 'Damn, damn! Why can't these women be plain?'

Alexander returned to Holland by the same route and arrived back in Wassenaar to a warm welcome from the Flemings less than a fortnight after having left them. During Alexander's absence Charles had established regular if erratic contact with London. He was restricted to transmitting for no longer than a few minutes at a time to avoid being caught by an enemy direction finder. This meant sending and receiving brief, condensed messages, demanding a linguistic skill he did not possess.

Michael Fleming had meanwhile assisted Charles in setting up espionage units. They pondered a long time over the phraseology of the message to be transmitted. This was complicated by Alexander's reticence in telling the others more than that he had been in Berlin. They finally decided on: 'Talks went well stop Future talks in Geneva stop Please agree I travel there urgent stop Walter'. Berlin had been left out to confuse nazis monitoring transmissions. The reply came the next day: 'Pick up 20th as agreed stop Well done'. Why no reference to Geneva? In any event, it left him only a fortnight in which to arrange a meeting with Irena, see Wiardi Beckman and come face to face with Laura.

Meanwhile with moment had arrived for Charles's return to England. He would be collected as planned by seaplane from one of the larger lakes in Friesland on 11 October. Michael Fleming had taken over the transmitter and was already familiar with its workings.

Events now moved swiftly towards disaster.

The seaplane could accommodate several people and Charles had agreed to take a few passengers he considered important for Britain. They rented a boat, ostensibly for late-night birdwatching on the lake. On the night of the 11th, however, fog prevented the seaplane from landing. Instead it circled over the lake making an excruciating noise before finally pulling away. The party of presumed ornithologists tried again, repeating their boat trip the following night. But by now the Germans had been alerted, and the noise of the plane roaring in to land drew heavy fire. Again the plane pulled away. Charles and his party were arrested by the Gestapo. The documents found on Charles incriminated him beyond any doubt and he was subsequently shot. The other members of his party were sent to camps.

News of the disaster arrived a few days after. The Flemings were not immediately told as Michael did not want complications from worried parents. Alexander was deeply shocked. He had lost a companion and friend, the first of many. Alexander also felt depressed because the rescue had been badly bungled and he became worried about his own collection. This was to be at a remote spot near the tip of the most northern island of Zeeland. He asked Michael to radio a request to cancel it. The reply was brief: 'Sorry about mishap but war goes on stop Pick up at time agreed'. There was no alternative but to obey. He had already met Wiardi Beckman and arranged meetings with both Irena and Laura.

Uncle Stuuf asked him to convey to the queen his genuine anguish at her predicament but to explain that in the prevailing circumstances it would be wrong for him to leave Holland. However, the priorities would look different, say, in a year, when greater consensus about postwar reconstruction might have been achieved.

Alexander went next to the van Alblas home under cover of darkness. He did not carry a bag for he intended to leave without staying the night. Forewarned, Laura let him in by a side door, to avoid servants and her brother. She briefly pressed herself against him, then led him to her father's study, where he found his aunt sitting behind her husband's desk. Lady Rosemary van Alblas gave him an affectionate welcome and came and sat down next to him on the sofa.

Aunt Rosemary chatted amiably. She felt distressed by the

absence of her husband, always a tower of strength. She was ready to face the deprivations of war but suffered from the lack of support from her adored strongman. She did have Laura, of course, and Laura had proved a great help. She then expressed the hope that Alexander would not disappear again, for both now had to rely on him. With this ambiguous statement and a light kiss on his forehead she left, with Alexander bewildered and not a little unhappy about the false position he found himself forced into. It was hard not to divulge his meeting in London with her husband, Uncle Steve, and to persist in the cover story of a failed escape attempt.

Laura sat opposite him. Gradually he felt the full impact of her steady gaze. The prospect of what might happen next made him nervous. Initially nothing happened. Laura stayed in her chair, smoked her cigar and mentioned her contact with the communist operator. This disarmed Alexander completely. He would not have to use any wiles to extract information about Laura's curious contacts. His original idea of himself as a sexy male imposter infiltrating an alien network evaporated. He relaxed. That was fatal for his determination to avoid amorous entanglements.

Laura got up, filled two glasses with wine, but returned to her chair, not to the sofa as he had expected. She calmly asked his opinion about the communist connection. Alexander's guard dropped further. Again it was her personality and her acute intelligence that attracted him first, not her physical attributes, nor her excessive verve. Yet, he began to notice her shapely legs, her exquisite hands, her breasts. Later he realized she had shown a better understanding of his personality than he did of hers. A frontal assault would have repulsed him.

At last she moved out of her chair to the sofa, though without touching him. She offered her cigar, at which he dutifully puffed before putting it in an ashtray. The first touch came from her high heel, a little nudge, as if to say 'wake up'. By now he felt ready to respond. He took one breast out of her blouse, fondled it and planted a kiss on its nipple. Events moved swiftly from then on. Laura undid the blouse, then had second thoughts, stood up and almost dragged Alexander along the passage to her room.

Leaving the van Alblas house the next morning Alexander felt worried. He was afraid of having created expectations that could not be fulfilled. He loved Laura again and deeply, but marriage would have to wait. He had not mentioned his immediate departure either and felt a coward. His luck had held, but would it always?

It certainly did a few days later when he phoned Laura to tell her that another escape route had been found and he would be leaving. She said she understood and, surprisingly, added she was sure he would return and looked forward to sheltering him then. 'Give my love to my father,' she added, 'and tell him to send you back quickly.'

The day before he was due to be picked up Alexander travelled to Doorn in the centre of Holland to meet Irena and her brother. They lunched in a restaurant in the tranquility of a wood, not far from the Abwehr office where young Schweichert worked. When Alexander showed them the messages sent and received, Schweichert smiled: the Abwehr had intercepted them. His colleagues could not make hear or tail of the contents, though, never having heard of Walter, but they had successfully tied up the 'mishap' to the arrest of Charles. Irena agreed to go to Geneva and suggested they meet the day after Christmas. Once in London Charles should send a message to whoever had transmitted the earlier ones and address it as before to Walter. The Abwehr would intercept it and Irena would be informed by her brother. They hoped the message would arrive within the next week, as Irena had to make arrangements for her trip without attracting attention.

Alexander left his few belongings at the Flemings as a gesture of confidence that he would one day return. But he took his various identity papers, if only to avoid suspicion should the doctor's house be searched by the Gestapo. He told Arthur and Gertrude merely that he was on his way back to England to report. Gertrude, embracing him, cried a little on his shoulder and clung to him for a while, but then laughed and both wished him good luck.

To reach the pick-up point they had chosen in London Alexander made his way first to Zierikzee, the main town on the island, and from there by bus to Renesse, a tiny village. He then walked a few miles into the dunes and hid comfortably in a hut on the beach near the pre-arranged spot. The only sound came from the strong wind and the breakers which threw up more foam than he relished. It was going to be a rough passage.

Towards 11 pm he walked another mile further up the beach, hugging the dunes while staring out to sea for the agreed flashlight. He had to wait a while before it came. He flashed back with his torch. To his great surprise his own dinghy, the one Charles and he had sailed to Lowestoft, was beached soon after and two men jumped out. One whispered in Dutch that it had been damned rough and disappeared into the dunes with a heavy rucksack. The other turned out to be a British naval lieutenant who complimented him on the quality of his dinghy but cursed the wind and the waves. He had brought waterproof clothes and boots.

They pushed the dinghy through the breakers, then started rowing over the foaming rollers. It took them almost an hour to reach the MGB, a journey that in calmer waters might have taken half that time. They climbed up and hoisted the dinghy aboard. The lieutenant manned the machine gun. The MGB moved away from the coast, slowly to keep the engine noise down and without lights.

Suddenly a roar announced the arrival of an enemy speed boat. The MGB revved up and dug its bow into the waves. Bullets whistled through the air, some overhead. A flare went up, exposing them and their pursuer to a harsh light. As the flare flickered out in the seething sea, a heavy shell skimmed across the deck. A second shell struck home, blowing a hole in the deck and wounding the lieutenant and a rating. Alexander quickly took the lieutenant's place at the machine gun. That turned out to be a tricky operation: he had never handled one before and the bumping of the ship made accuracy virtually impossible. More shells from the enemy boat flew overhead. Alexander continued to fire, however. The MGB pulled away and lost the enemy boat in the darkness. The damage was limited, the wounds not serious though Alexander's dinghy had been shot to pieces when the shell struck. It had served its purpose twice and probably prevented worse damage to their MGB.

As they headed out into the North Sea – and safety – the captain yelled praise for Alexander's wild firing. 'I saw you hit it!' he shouted, holding up his night binoculars. 'It slowed down.' Better than that: a day later the agent who had been landed radioed that the German E-boat had sunk. All in all it had been 'quite satisfactory', as Alexander said on landing in Harwich, having acquired something of the legendary British phlegm himself. However, this ideal spot for pick-ups and landings on the Dutch coast would have to be written off: the nazis would strengthen their watch in the area.

Alexander reported to Uncle Steve, starting with Laura and their unofficial engagement. Baron van Alblas shook his nephew's hand warmly, then looked at him seriously.

'What is this nonsense about Geneva?'

Chapter Nine

THE UNDERGROUND PRESS
COMES OF AGE

Tuesday 11 February saw a celebration at my home. A crazy idea, for apart from birthdays and scholastic achievements there was little to celebrate. In our underground war no battles could be won, only dignity and lives lost. Yet that day we celebrated and jubilantly too. Which is why the exact date can so easily be recalled.

Most dates of that period in my life have faded, fallen like dead leaves in the undergrowth of memory. The few still remembered mostly relate to unpleasant events. This one was pleasant and spontaneous at that. For I did not expect to share my contentment with my family. They were not supposed to know any details of our shadowy activities. Nor did they, mostly. Fortunately, or they would not have survived. But a rare coincidence produced a rare response. It was even rarer that subsequent events over the next four years should have vindicated this celebration and the elation. They can still be vindicated in retrospect.

That morning I had gone out on my trusted bicycle to collect the first issue of the underground newspaper that had been so long gestating: *Het Parool*, proudly dated 10 February 1941, the day before. The parcel was large and weighty. I whistled happily while pedalling through the quiet wood bordering our home, arrived at our equally quiet suburban road and got off the bike at the entrance to our house. A high hedge protects the front from inquisitive eyes and is followed by some five yards of lawn to provide a sense of space. Carved wooden pillars flank each side of a gap in the evergreen hedge. A drive-way leads along the north wall to the front door and the garage.

I saw to my horror three animated faces behind the wide window that occupies much of the ground-floor frontage. Arms shot up and hands waved. I stared, stunned to find three unexpected witnesses – my parents and Amanda – to what had been a carefully planned secret operation. And why were they so excited?

It was simple enough. My father had come home for lunch, which was unusual. My mother had not gone shopping as she had intended. My brother and sister were at school. Amanda, who knew what I was doing, had played truant from her crafts college to join me in distributing the paper. She knew, of course, of its appearance that morning. Unable to contain her excitement, she had spilled the beans. She also needed an excuse for her unforeseen arrival.

Lacking the heart to be cross with her, I opened the parcel. Amanda grabbed a copy and ceremoniously handed it to my parents. My father opened the only bottle of champagne left, which he had been carefully preserving for my parents' silver wedding anniversary, three years ahead.

'But before that occasion arrives,' said my father, toasting me rather formally, 'we shall rout the Krauts, thanks to your successful slog!'

'Yes! To *Het Parool*!' Amanda responded. 'And to Uncle Stuuf for reminding us that the pen is mightier than the sword.'

It sounds silly, but at the time that platitude inspired us.

The occasion delighted me because it was the first opportunity to show my parents one result of our covert actions. It was worthwhile for another reason as well, entirely unknown at the time. The underground press turned out to be a pheno-menon of unique significance. Over the next four years it would counter nazi propaganda, undermine the effectiveness of nazi measures, warn against traitors, report BBC news, caution some of the time but stimulate most of the time. In its immense variety there was yet a unity of purpose and a historic significance. It succeeded in replacing not only the regular press but also parliament and government, to a degree.

After the war the Dutch Institute of War Documentation

counted 1,193 illegal papers, many shortlived, many with a circulation of tens rather than thousands, and of varying quality. The Institute estimates that between one and two hundred people read each copy, with many reading more than one paper. Eventually the vast majority of the Dutch read the underground press and most acted upon its guidelines, silently, passively, actively or otherwise. Holland's resistance differs in this respect from that in most other countries. The French underground press informed, but the Dutch also inspired to action. The French claim a readership at its apex of two million, the Dutch of four million – twice the number in France, with a fifth of France's population, therefore ten times France's penetration. France also has more space: its population density is one quarter of that of Holland. In Luxemburg too the underground press blossomed and had the same purpose, but it remained restricted to pamphlets, due to the small size of both the country and the population. Such distinctions are not intended to be judgements, but to highlight the vital role of the underground press in Holland. France, of course, had its maquis, which Holland lacked.

I still feel grateful for having been involved – even if only at the beginning – in what became one of the most potent forces of the Dutch resistance.

Satisfying it may have been, but it was not easy. In those early months, during my rounds to collect money for *Het Parool*, I discovered that few people were ready to back sympathetic words with hard cash. I started with intimate friends of the family, sensible because I would be certain of a friendly audience and in no danger of betrayal. They passed me on to their intimate friends, who in turn introduced me to less intimate friends, and finally to acquaintances, a dubious practice that offered little security, as some unlucky ones were to discover.

All these people were friendly enough, though few were willing to part with even the small amounts needed at this stage. As in the biblical story, the less well-off parted more easily with their limited earthly goods than the better-off. I became frustrated and at times rebellious, most uncharacteristic for me at the time. Some feared reprisals, others doubted the efficacy of an 'illegal' paper, yet others were kindly concerned about my safety. But then, nazi measures had still only been fairly innocuous. I did not have a sample either. Yet, in spite of these drawbacks the four months leading up to the publication of the first issue provided cash enough for fifteen issues. Or so we thought.

The date for the first issue had to be postponed twice until it finally appeared as a thousand stencilled copies. Amanda and I went on our delivery rounds in high spirits, no doubt rather carelessly. The response from the recipients was warm and pleasing. February 1941 was the month of the workers' revolt in Amsterdam. The one thousand copies proved totally inadequate and stencilling most impractical. From 11 August that year the issues were printed, the first underground paper to do so. Initially the print-run was 8,000. It grew steadily to 12,000, then 15,000, rising to 50,000 in 1942, before reaching its maximum of 60,000 shortly after. It was reckoned that 250,000 would have been welcomed, but such huge quantities presented logistical problems – printing-time, the supply of scarce paper, distribution – that might endanger even more lives.

By then other underground papers had become successful. This gave rise to a remarkable co-operative effort. Underground newspapers were not rivals for the same audience nor were they in any sense commercial. Clashes did occur, though rarely, and they were not caused by any envy but by differences in the personalities of the leaders and in the opinions about postwar reconstruction. Clashes were the exceptions that proved the rule: anyone able to publish was regarded as a recruit to the same cause.

By modern standards the system was anarchic. Copyright did not exist. Articles in one were copied in others, with or without acknowledgement. The reason was simple. Finance, distribution and information depended on accidental contacts. There was no publicity, and even word-of-mouth recommendation was restricted, although surprisingly successful. Groups of like-minded people, in churches, political parties, and various clubs formed the nuclei for distribution. All were united by their sense of purpose: to fight the enemy and counter nazi propaganda.

The money so painstakingly collected was to pay for paper and printing only, not for remunerating editors and reporters, not even to re-imburse distributors. No clear system of finance had yet been devised, nor could there be advertisements. We simply begged for money to support a good cause. It was a never ending task: success contained the seeds of disaster, for a five or tenfold increase in the print run incurred a corresponding increase in costs.

Ironically, the threat of disaster stimulated the dodgers. The style and contents of the first issue impressed the waverers. When rumours spread that no more copies were available and that even reprints might not satisfy demand, some saw the need for a different approach and offered their services. They pointed out that finance and distribution were too intricately interwoven. To drop a paper through a letter box was simple, took little time and could be staggered. The recipient could deny having asked for it. But to collect money at the same time increased the risks. The recipient had to be at home, would then want to discuss the situation, might have second thoughts or might not have the cash to hand. The money received had to be accounted for, requiring lists with names and addresses.

My talks with members of the silent majority – potential readers and supporters – often lasted long evenings. They provided an opportunity to assess the nature of the nazi occupation, its impact, and the chances of war. Few doubted the outcome. Most – including myself – expected an Allied victory if not in 1941 then surely in 1942. I talked volubly, like an insider. I had no inside information, of course, only a strong conviction. The nazi measures were meanwhile opening the eyes of most. Slowly people came to pay more.

Eventually the financial burden began to be eased when one of my initial supporters came out of his shell. Robert Peereboom had been in the newspaper trade all his life and was then joint owner with his brother Piet of *Haarlems Dagblad*, the respected local daily. It prided itself on being the oldest newspaper in the world still in existence, as it does today, proudly displaying the date of its foundation: 1656.

Robert acted as editor, Piet as manager. Both were in their forties, but that was about all they had in common. Robert was a sporting type, square and solid, Piet slim and polished; Robert ebullient, extrovert, slightly arrogant and easily excited, Piet quiet and reserved, more introvert. It was Robert who came to the rescue.

Robert had resigned as editor of *Haarlems Dagblad*, in protest against nazi interference, leaving his brother to protect the family business. Robert, respected for his principled stand, was already involved in resistance activities of which I knew nothing. I introduced him to Uncle Stuuf. Soon after my role changed. They would obtain large amounts of money from just a few people – a role for which I was ill-equipped – and the issues were to be distributed free to those who wanted them. Incidental gifts remained welcome and continued throughout the war. Later finance was further eased. A secret fund was set up by bankers for a variety of resistance activities and guaranteed by the Dutch government in exile.

(*Het Parool* flourished and still does, as a national paper. Frans Goedhart, the originator of the Newsletter as Pieter 't Hoen, was arrested in mid January 1942, escaped eighteen months later after having been sentenced to death, and survived other hair-raising experiences to become a rebellious though much respected member of the postwar parliament. All editorials, however, continued to be signed 'Pieter 't Hoen.')

Like many, I tended to forget that the silent majority regarded life and survival as too important to throw away wantonly and that most people were in no position to do anything, certainly not in the first eighteen months of the occupation. When nazi measures started to bite, fences came down, the uncommitted became committed. As the number of our copies and the number of underground papers grew, the contents came to wield an influence that no peacetime newspaper can ever achieve.

Many tens of thousands were actively engaged in editing, producing and distributing underground newspapers, to serve many hundreds of thousands of passive recipients and millions of readers, inevitably including nazis. Many thousands died, among them a few whose only crime was the possession of copies. Among the eighteen shot in March 1941 – of which details follow in chapter eleven – was the first newspaperman,

114

Bernard Ijzerdraad. They were commemorated in a simple yet profound poem, printed in various papers, which became and remains to this day a national literary monument.

THE SONG OF THE EIGHTEEN DEAD

by Jan Campert*

A cell is just two metres long
And scarcely two wide,
But smaller still's the plot of land,
As yet unknown to me,
Where I shall nameless lie,
My comrades by my side.
Eighteen we were in all
And none shall see the night.

O sweetness of the sky and soil
Of Holland's once free coast!
When conquered by the foe
I could not find an hour's rest.
What can a man, sincere and true,
Do else in such a time
But kiss his child and kiss his wife
And join the futile fight?

I knew the task that I began
Would be awash with pains.
But yet the heart could not resist:
It never shuns whatever risk.
It knows that in these parts
Once freedom had prevailed,
Before his cursed hand
Decreed it otherwise.

Remember, you who read those words,
My comrades in distress,
And most of all their dearest ones,
Forever suffering adversity.
As we have given thought
To country and compatriots.
A day will follow every night
And every cloud blows past.

* My transation follows the rhythm not the rhyme.

I can now see the rays of dawn
That linger through high window bars.
My God, please ease my dying.
Whenever I have failed,
As everyone can fail sometime,
Grant me Your grace,
That I may leave this earth a man
And stand erect before the guns.

One member of the silent majority of readers, an exposed and normally careful civil servant, wrote ecstatically in his diary for April 1942:

'. . . the new issue, in a word: priceless! It is impossible to overestimate the value of these grey and undistinguished leaflets in this total war. How many waverers are given solid backing, how much confidence to faint hearts, how much rapture and insight and awareness. My hat off to you, anonymous editors: God's blessing be upon your work. I have to force myself to pass the issues on. One would like to read them again and again. But that is not right, for they must be handed on and quickly while still topical.'

Our intentions of a year earlier, however, did more than create and sustain morale during the war. They made a vital contribution to postwar European development. The spirit of resistance, as revealed in the underground press, laid the foundations for international reconstruction. As one example out of many, *Het Parool* of 12 December 1942; wrote:

'In our continent peace cannot be permanent when it is based on contempt and oppression. Nationalism, however healthy, can easily turn into mortal danger. This war should be seen as the ultimate crisis of the sovereign state. If the fighting is not to be in vain, the war must result in a European co-operation between states that are ready to cede part of their sovereignty to secure collective sovereignty. A new super-organ must follow – whether a European directorate or a federation – with the power to enforce the collective will and ensure peace. Not a super-organ that dictates all life in Europe from one central point as the nazis would like to do, but one that leaves the continental national units sufficient autonomy and self-determination. This solution would guarantee the German people a place in the European community and at the same time restrain them.'

This was written at the height of nazi oppression, yet it reads like part of a blue-print for the Common Market. At the time hate and the desire for revenge predominated. Moreover, on the day it appeared twenty-three of its staff faced a nazi court, including the editor Frans Goedhart. He escaped, but seventeen were executed and five more died as a result in camps.

The three Apostles had met at irregular intervals with little substance to boast of. But a significant meeting took place shortly after these first large-scale executions in March 1941. The news was sobering and shocking! There but for the Grace of God . . . Memories of the fear that gripped me on my first cross-border venture to Antwerp surfaced. But what I felt now was different. Everyone had talked loosely about the dangers attached to our work, including that of losing one's life. But it had been like talk of death on the road: it would not happen to us. Now we knew it might. Strangely, this knowledge reduced the fear, which lost its grip on us. The reality of death reinforced a sense of duty and renewed our determination to banish fear to the fringes of consciousness. Instead the mind focussed on the practical issue of avoiding capture. We were on our way to becoming professionals.

I was taken off collecting money although continued to distribute copies of *Het Parool* and later also of another paper, *Vrij Nederland* (Free Netherland). I was also asked to gather facts and supply information for the editors. As will be seen, this coincided nicely with a change of direction of the Apostles. All this led inexorably to the very mixture of activities against which Uncle Stuuf had warned. No one minded, for in the first year it could hardly be avoided, nor was it as dangerous as it became later on. Individual initiative was all. There were no professional agents to guide us, nor experience, nor precedents.

Just as well, for combining different activities was an essential preparation for resistance as it developed later.

Once again we were four. Luke returned to the fold after a telephone call from Laura, in its turn a result of Alexander's second return to Holland, as I will recount in the next chapter. Luke did not apologize; he did not say much at all. Matthew looked distinctly uneasy, which I attributed to Laura's rebuff of his amorous attentions.

Laura, on the other hand, appeared confident, even radiant. She was also quite brusque and eager for us to leave as quickly as possible, for reasons of security, she said. The regularity of our meetings – the same day of the week at the same time, in the same house for the same length of time – benefited us because it provided a familiar pivot, like meal and bed times. But the same regularity would also benefit the Gestapo if they ever came to harbour suspicions. It sounded eminently sensible.

As did the change of tactics Laura now announced. No more military intelligence, for which we had proved to be singularly ill equipped. We were now to collect reliable information about all aspects of life in occupied Holland and pass it on to the government in exile. No more chasing shadowy Germans, but scanning newsprint – including nazi publications – and listening to the BBC for specific items. These would be used to compile reports about the situation, to provide the Allies with a clearer picture.

Laura did not mention Russia, nor did she indicate by what means the reports would be transmitted. She did not even say who would write the reports. This again turned out to be the result of Alexander's still secret presence. At the time I did not give it a thought.

No date or place for our next meeting was fixed. Instead, Laura would contact each one of us in the near future. And why not? I saw nothing sinister in all these proposals, for Laura's instructions fitted admirably with Uncle Stuuf's ones. As we left I patted the gloomy Matthew on his shoulder: 'You ought to find yourself a girl!' I said cheerily. His smile was noticeably wry. I cycled back home in a happy enough mood.

Reading newspapers was no problem. Never before had so

many dailies, weeklies, monthlies and sundry printed matter seen their way into my home nor have they since. My parents were both surprised and uneasy. I merely explained that the papers would be a perfect alibi if the Gestapo ever entered our house, and detract attention from more 'compromising material', which I avoided specifying, feeling clever. My father doubted whether the Gestapo would be deceived, though they might be confused. My mother added that this nazi material was so obviously alien to the family's stance that no one would be taken in, unless we started lying, 'which God forbid'.

Amanda was her shrewd self. When I faithfully reported on the Apostles' meeting she at once sensed a conspiracy.

'Conspiracy? By whom against whom?' I asked not unnaturally.

I was sitting rather uncomfortably on a straight-backed wooden chair in her small bedroom. We were allowed there for only brief periods, to preserve decorum. Rather hypocritical, for amorous dallyings were not the great unknown in her family that they seemed in mine, where the subject never arose. We would shortly descend to greater comfort in the drawing room for tea and biscuits with her father and stepmother. In Holland tea is an evening addiction, not an elaborate afternoon break.

Amanda was somewhat impatient and a trifle irritable: 'I don't know. But why was Laura in such a hurry? Why was Luke so silent? Why was Matthew uneasy?'

'No idea. Is it important? What she told us to do seems quite sensible.'

'Of course it's important. Either they wanted you out of the way or something happened to upset Laura. Could it have something to do with Matthew? He's rather a weak character.'

'We three men left together, so it can't be me.'

'It's Matthew, I know it.' She turned out to be right, intuitively and uncannily right, though she had no facts to go on.

We went down and drank tea, and chatted amicably with her parents. Her father was a charming and handsome man in his forties with a neatly trimmed black moustache, balding on top with some greying crops of hair. Her mother had died when Amanda was eight and remained irreplaceable in her affections. On some large framed photographs, conspicuously exhibited, she looked angelic. That is exactly what she meant to Amanda – presumably still does – an other-worldly angel, ethereal, who became real only when attempts were made to replace her. The stepmother had joined the family a few years before, long after the mother's death, obviously more as a permanent plaything to replace the shifting population of less constant female companions than as a replacement for Amanda's mother. Her undoubted physical attractions were fading, her mental abilities restricted to 'gosh' and gossip and clothes. She was, however, wise enough to leave most of the talking to us.

All the way home and for part of the night I racked my brain to unravel the riddle suggested by Amanda's suspicions. I was rather gullible – still am if it comes to that – and my efforts remained unrewarded until several evenings later, when Laura phoned and came to see me.

I sat on my bed, Laura in a comfortable desk chair of my father's design. Although Laura must have sensed my admiring glances, no amorous contacts occurred. The situation was too serious for frivolity and both of us were basically loyal. My parents never raised any objections to my entertaining girls in my room, though I always politely informed them in advance. My mother occasionally brought us a cup of tea.

Laura was unusually excited: 'Matthew has been spotted in the company of notorious nazis. I don't trust him any more.'

I was flabbergasted. 'Matthew? Spotted by whom?'

'By Luke. And not just once but regularly.'

'He must have been trying to seek solace in someone else.'

'Don't be frivolous. Luke heard from a friend that Matthew went to see Professor van Dam in Leyden on several occasions.'

'So what? Van Dam's subject is early Dutch history. He's a nationalist and bound to have sympathies for national socialism. But he's a decent man, not a traitor.'

'Agreed. But wait. Van Dam took him to a party where Matthew clung to an ostentatious beauty whose father is a notorious nazi, one of Mussert's cronies who tries to ingratiate himself with the Germans.' Mussert being the pathetic leader of the Dutch nazi party.

Only a week previously I had told Matthew to find himself a girl. But Laura was describing much earlier events. Matthew's wry smile took on a different meaning.

She continued: 'Most other people at the party were nazis, except Luke's friend, who left as soon as he realised his mistake.'

'Then how does he know what Matthew did except cavort with a girl?'

'Because, after he'd kissed her, Matthew stood bragging in his usual way to some male undergraduates, all of them nazis whom we always avoided like the plague. That woke Luke's friend up. After leaving he hid outside to see what would happen. Matthew walked out, not with the girl but with the nazis.'

'Well?'

'The friend told Luke, who then started keeping an eye on Matthew. He saw Matthew more often in the presence of the nazi boys as well as the girl.'

'Luke spying on a friend?'

'There's a war on. But it wasn't like that. Luke was perfectly straight, simply surprised at Matthew's recklessness. And sad. He told Matthew what he had seen and demanded an explanation. Matthew laughed it off. He said he had found himself a gorgeous girl and that her entourage might interest the Apostles.'

'Sounds reasonable.' But I could not quite believe this any more.

'Agreed, and I would have been happy for his sake. But what shocked me is that this happened four months ago. Luke asked Matthew over a month ago whether he'd informed me or the Apostles. We've had several meetings since then and I've met Matthew twice alone. And he never mentioned anything.'

'Did you make love?'

'Certainly not. He tried, but I told him off.'

'Bravo.'

'So,' she asked, after a pause, 'what do we do?'

'Hold another meeting in your house and confront him.'

'Luke's done that already. He won't like going through the agony again.'

'Why did Luke turn up at our last meeting? There must be more to it.'

'There is. But keep this absolutely to yourself. Don't even mention it to Luke. It's Alexander. He's back again. When I told him the story he suggested I get Luke to return because we need more people – strong, reliable ones.' Her tone was very serious now. 'Matthew should be dropped.'

'Alexander in Holland?' I said, surprised. 'Why not ask him how to drop Matthew?'

'He told me how.' She looked at me in a peculiar way that made me feel uneasy. Her look became a stare. I felt my pulse started to race.

'So, what did Alexander advise?'

'Shoot him.'

My heart skipped a beat. Shooting did not figure in our copybook. I had heard of traitors being eliminated, but this hardly qualified as treachery. Only later did we learn that the nazis used V-men, confidence tricksters, who all too successfully infiltrated resistance groups. I swallowed and made a pretence of coolness.

'That's rather excessive, don't you think? And presumptuous. Taking the law into our own hands without giving the victim a chance to defend himself. Isn't that what we object to in nazism?'

'Of course. I said something similar, but Alexander pointed out that in this sort of war self-preservation prevails over sentimentality. He offered to supply a gun.' She paused, then: 'Will you shoot Matthew?'

I blinked. I could not even contemplate it. 'I don't like it. It's wrong,' I said, desperately playing for time, searching for reasons to evade the issue. 'The evidence is not conclusive. Amanda always said Matthew was weak. Perhaps he's not a traitor, just easily led. Never a gun.' I added emphatically.

'It's the weak who are tempted to turn traitor. Hey,' her face clouded, 'what does Amanda know about this anyway?'

'Nothing,' I replied quickly. 'Only, she smells potential dangers long before I do. She has a sound sense of people too.'

There followed a pause. Laura's suspicions seemed to die and she returned to the problem. 'I don't like it either, nor does Alexander. But how else do we protect ourselves and our work?'

I hesitated. Then, at last, I found the courage of my convictions: 'I don't ever want to kill anyone, except perhaps in self-defence. I don't carry a gun and won't carry anyone else's.'

'I see.' Laura gave a shrug of resignation. 'I don't particularly like to use one either. Still, this is after all self-defence.'

'Sure, we've got to protect ourselves,' I said, having regained my self-assurance. 'But I would call it murder if we shot Matthew in the present circumstances.' I paused and suddenly saw how I could get out of this dilemma. 'Would Alexander join me in confronting Matthew? The two of us?'

Chapter Ten

ALEXANDER'S SWISS WINDOW ON GERMAN RESISTANCE

Alexander realized he had a fight on his hands when van Alblas pointedly asked about Geneva. He had expected a probe, not a prosecution. Having survived the ordeal of his 'battle of the North Sea' in the MGB he felt relaxed in the relative serenity of wartime London. People went about their daily tasks unaffected by the psychological pressure prevalent on the occupied continent. Air raids, of course, dominated much of their visible activities: firefighting, debris clearing and ambulances galore. But these were considered part of the game and tackled with quiet resolve. He was therefore unprepared for the severity of his uncle's question, though still able to keep his cool.

'Did you see my cable?' asked Alexander.

'Sure. Rather brief. Not much to go on.' Uncle Steve now acted very much the boss rather than the prospective father-in-law.

'The Germans were listening in.'

'Thought as much. Very careful of you.' It sounded sarcastic.

'So why couldn't they have let me go to Geneva first and report afterwards?'

Uncle Steve now softened his steely approach. 'Far too delicate to touch without knowing what we think. Besides, we don't know what happened in Berlin. Sensible to hear your full story first. On a practical level, the journey to Switzerland

124

is more easily arranged from here than through occupied Europe,' he said, more at ease. 'Less dangerous too. Ha, ha!'

Van Alblas wanted to hear his nephew's story but not until he had rested. Alexander stayed the night at his uncle's flat, slept soundly and woke strengthened. Towards seven that evening Crane arrived with his boss Menzies, a pleasant surprise. The three elders nursed whiskies, smoked, and listened to Alexander's account without once interrupting. In the beginning this made him nervous, for he would have preferred the cut and thrust of question and answer rather than the staid delivery of what sounded like a lecture. However, he had used the afternoon to make some notes and, with his audience attentive, gradually relaxed. After he had finished, silence reigned. It was broken by Menzies, whose glass of whisky rested untouched in his hand.

'We've let you do the talking for two reasons,' he said in a friendly way, taking his pipe from his mouth. 'The first is probably obvious: we couldn't react until we'd heard the whole story. The second may sound uncomplimentary but is really a precaution: we needed to test your ability to report. Full marks, young man. For clarity as well as compassion.'

Alexander felt a little alarmed by the use of the word 'compassion'.

Bruce Crane drew on his cigarette. 'Do you trust the people you met?'

Alexander winced. The answer should have been obvious from his account. And why had Crane's boss introduced compassion? He waited a while before replying. Menzies took a first sip of whisky. His uncle remained silent, though he threw him an encouraging glance.

'I do and I don't,' Alexander replied at last. 'They're absolutely sincere, if that's what you mean.'

'It's not what I mean,' Crane retorted. 'We take sincerity for granted. But what do they want and what can they deliver?' The question was rather unfair, for they had sent Alexander to Berlin without requesting him to bring back such specific information.

'They want to get rid of Hitler, as we do. They also seem to be in a better position to do so than we. But they haven't got any

125

pretentions and don't underestimate the scale of the task. Nor did they give any indication of when they can deliver or how.' Alexander now felt on surer ground.

'That's the point!' Bruce Crane was triumphant and rather too quick.

'Not all of it.' Menzies put his glass down and relit his pipe. 'You see, we've had emissaries before. Ewald von Kleist and Adam von Trott zu Solz in 1938, Fabian von Schlabrendorff in spring 1939. There have recently been messages through the Vatican. All from respectable sincere anti-nazis.'

Alexander winced again. So what then did they need him for?

'The trouble with all these approaches can best be put in the words of Schlabrendorff. He introduced himself to Mr Churchill – then only an MP – by saying "I'm not a nazi but a good patriot," to which Mr Churchill apparently replied "Me too". They are sincere in their abhorrence of Hitler and equally sincere in their patriotism. Trouble is, they want to have their cake and eat it. In other words, to have Hitler out of the way but his conquests confirmed. What Mr Crane meant is, to put it crudely: if they want us to pull their chestnuts out of the fire for them, why haven't they acted before? Why don't they act now? How widespread is their conspiracy and how strong their support?'

Alexander was worried now. 'I can't answer any of that, Sir, except to say that they didn't seem to be fools. But I might find out more in Geneva. Dohnanyi told me that one plan to eliminate Hitler had been aborted by the Munich accord. Hitler was to have been arrested on entering Czechoslovakia. But then Britain and France sanctioned his action. I got the impression from the way he told me that some of the conspirators felt relieved, though Dohnanyi himself was definitely not. Whether this points to inefficiency or lack of resolve I don't know. It's not easy to organize a revolt against Hitler *and* his henchmen *and* his Gestapo.'

Menzies said gently: 'Agreed. Still, when Hitler has been eliminated the question still remains: what next?' Another pause ensued. He puffed at his pipe, Bruce Crane took a good swig at his whisky.

Van Alblas broke the silence: 'The question now: should Alexander go to Geneva? If so, what instructions does he get?'

Menzies: 'That's a tricky one. On balance I'd like to recommend it. Your nephew is a little young, but I've come to appreciate his sense of proportion. Also a senior person wouldn't do at this stage. It would give too much weight to what is after all only a recce. Didn't you say, Mr Paul, that your Germans wanted someone who sympathized and could interpret their position?'

'That's correct, Sir.'

'I'll have to consult the prime minister, of course. The trouble with Mr Churchill is that he's all for unorthodox adventures. He'll like it even more when I tell him that the captain of the MGB has recommended Mr Paul for a DSO.' This unexpected piece of information must have been kept to the last on purpose. Bruce Crane frowned, his uncle raised his eyebrows. They had not known either.

For once Alexander was lost for words. 'I don't really deserve that, Sir. I only did what had to be done, my duty . . .'

'That's it, young man. You did your duty. As far as I've gathered you did it in circumstances where few would have acted: in a rough sea, without being familiar with the gun, after the tensions of a dicey trip to Berlin. But you haven't got it yet.' He wagged a finger in mock warning, and everyone laughed. 'And, while we're on the subject: I appreciate your compassion, which your German friends no doubt do as well. But keep as cool a head as you did on the MGB.' Menzies and Crane solemnly shook Alexander's hand, whilst his uncle beamed approval.

It was a week before Alexander received confirmation as well as formal instructions, and the promised DSO. He felt the decoration was intended more as an encouragement for his new venture than an acknowledgement of services rendered. A cable had been sent to Walter in Holland. Now receipt was confirmed by 'Walter and partner', clearly a reference to young Schweichert of the Abwehr in Holland and his sister in Berlin.

Alexander was not allowed to contact anyone else, not even van 't Sant or Prince Bernhard, an understandable precaution but irritating nonetheless. He would have liked to report verbally on Wiardi Beckman's opinion about prospective government ministers to be collected from occupied Holland. Instead, his uncle asked him to put it in writing, a task that took much of Alexander's time. Van Alblas would then communicate the contents, though not the paper itself, to the prince and queen, to avoid speculation about the way the information had been obtained.

After being allowed out to buy what were called 'diplomatic clothes' — with the compliments, and the money, of the British — Alexander received his instructions. They were brief and blandly ambiguous. He was to listen, not to commit any government. He was to report to a special agent of MI6, Count Frederick Vanden Heuvel, the Dutch name of a British subject with a Roman peerage, who acted as personal representative of Menzies in Switzerland and later became head of the MI6 station in Bern. On no account should Alexander contact either the British embassy or the Dutch legation. His mission had to remain secret, both for the benefit of his German friends and to preserve room for manoeuvre.

He was to travel by train from Portugal through Spain and France to Switzerland. For his journey to Portugal he was made a British diplomat, in Spain and unoccupied France he would be an American one, and British again in Switzerland. It would be tricky only in the unlikely event of passport control being done jointly by border guards of both countries.

Alexander was curious about the reason for such VIP treatment. Did it imply a strong wish on the part of Britain to end the war or did the British merely want to score a point, undoubtedly a major one? He had not raised the matter, nor had any of his three elders. He never found out the answer. By piecing together scraps of information during the decades that followed he came to the conclusion that there may be one Britain but it holds many British and quite a few conflicting opinions.

The existing link between Canaris and Menzies through Mme Szymanska went by way of Vanden Heuvel. She reported to him and he in turn reported only to Menzies. That link was so astonishing and unique that independent confirmation of its reliability became of the utmost importance. They did not doubt Mme Szymanska's sincerity, but both Menzies and Churchill wondered about the motivation of her source, Admiral Canaris – as many have done since his execution, with wildly varied judgements, from vilification to adoration. Menzies had to make checks, to obtain both a correct evaluation of the often cryptic military messages which this unorthodox link provided, and an assessment of the future treatment of Germany. Hence Alexander's mission was not military – to spy on spies – but political – to appraise the German resistance.

Alexander flew to Lisbon, took a train to Madrid, another one to Barcelona, then to Marseilles and thence via Grenoble to Bern. The frontier crossings went by without hiccups. He became accustomed to impersonating a multitude of personalities without losing his own. On the day after Christmas he travelled to Geneva, where he was to meet Irena Schweichert in the station.

When she came, Irena was not alone. An elderly lady, more than a head smaller than her, and with beautiful grey hair, accompanied her. Both were wrapped in elaborate fur coats, though their abundant hair was uncovered. When he came closer, to his surprise and delight Alexander recognized Emily Smend, though he wondered about her role in all this. On their walk to a car neither of the women offered an explanation. Instead, they chatted inconsequentially about the freezing weather, with Irena turning round to see whether they were being followed. Neutral Switzerland, like Spain and Portugal, was then a hive of espionage, bustling with agents, sub-agents and informers of all warring states. She seemed satisfied that they were not.

On the road Irena explained. They were staying with her uncle and aunt in their immense villa near Lausanne. He would be introduced as a distant relative from England. Yet another personality with another cover story. He need not worry for her uncle and aunt were old, rather deaf, and therefore more interested in talking than listening. A library would give an opportunity for privacy.

The family reunion was the pretext for Irena's brief

Christmas holiday outside Germany. Emily Smend's presence was explained as that of a friendly companion substituting for Irena's dead parents and incidentally acting as chaperone during a long, perhaps hazardous journey through wartime Germany. In reality Emily represented the civilian resistance because her husband Rudolf had felt that *his* absence might alert the Gestapo. Irena and Emily had to return to Berlin the coming Saturday morning. This left them two nights and a full day.

Irena's uncle and aunt proved charming, entirely unassuming, undemanding, seemingly unaware of and unconcerned about hidden motives for this reunion. The uncle was a Pole who had moved to Switzerland in the previous century as a young banker. He had married a Swiss-German girl and settled contentedly in this mecca of banking and neutrality. He took Swiss nationality before World War I and retired as a wealthy man just before World War II He had the same square face and delicate bone structure as his great niece. Irena was the much loved granddaughter of his brother and one of his few relatives, his only son having died a bachelor. A devout Catholic of respectable but not aristocratic parentage he abhorred extremism, whether the fragmented variety of his native country or the singular one of Germany, which frightened him. On the other hand, the absence of extremism in his adopted country invited complacency. 'The Swiss,' he said mischieviously, 'shit in their trousers for fear the nazis enter.' He had chosen his English words carefully but pronounced them almost unintelligibly.

The old man talked virtually non-stop, with Emily attempting to shout the occasional interruption. Alexander, reduced to bemused silence, gradually noticed that Irena was glancing at him. At first he thought she was just being sympathetic. As the evening wore on and the frequency of the glances increased, he wondered whether they meant more than sympathy. Certainly her aunt noticed them and smiled.

After supper the aunt and uncle retired and Irena and Emily showed Alexander the impressive library. Some pleasant patter followed, as did more glances from Irena until they departed, leaving him sipping a disgustingly sweet pear liquor. He looked absentmindedly at the books, prints and statuettes for a while before climbing the stairs to his room. Tired and slightly puzzled by Irena's suggestive looks he slowly undressed and quickly fell asleep.

Shortly afterwards he woke abruptly. The door had opened and closed. He made out Irena's silhouette against the window in faint moonlight. When he stirred she laughed softly.

'Asleep?' she chided him. 'That's not very complimentary to me.'

'No offence meant. I wasn't expecting you,' he replied, fully awake now and sitting upright.

'Well, we couldn't talk downstairs.' That was disingenuous, for she could not possibly be there just to talk.

To avoid misunderstanding he told her he was engaged and would have been married but for the war.

She turned to face him. 'So am I. Does it matter? We get so few opportunities.' Then she sat down on the bed and leaned against his shoulder. 'My husband-to-be is in Poland and hates it.'

He stroked her hair. 'My wife-to-be is in Holland and hates your army being there.'

'It's nice to know that you and I are on the same side,' she said, nestling into his arm. 'Perhaps we can do something together to end this mad war.' Whereupon Irena took his free hand and placed it on a very full breast that had somehow slipped out of her dressing gown and nightdress.

The next morning business started at nine in the library, where the three were left alone. Emily handed Alexander a letter from Dohnanyi but asked him to read it later, nervously slipping the huge turquoise ring he had noticed when they first met in Berlin on and off her finger. She explained that Hans was involved mainly in civilian resistance, like her husband, but unlike Canaris, who was 'just a military man'. She went on to point out the differences between military and civilian considerations. Military intelligence might be more important at the time but the resistance had to think beyond the war. Franz Canaris felt too old to take action and was anyway too much of an oldfashioned sailor and patriot. He was, of course, happy to allow his Abwehr to be used for the support of the resistance and to shield Oster, Dohnanyi, Bonhoeffer and others.

'Surely he does much more?' Irena said, calmly, not realizing how close she was to the truth. Today it is known that Canaris did act, not in organizing or even orchestrating the resistance, but carefully and cryptically in his field of intelligence.

Alexander was fascinated, not just by the subject but by the circumstances: two attractive women of varying age and background discussing major issues of war.

'Darling! There's no blame,' Emily replied with some vigour. 'Franz Canaris simply can't do anything else in his exposed position. He has to remain the military expert if he is to retain Hitler's trust. He also has to prevent Himmler from infiltrating dim-witted SS-men into the Abwehr, or, worse, taking it over. Where would the resistance be then? Franz is well aware of the limitations this imposes on him and the image it creates for the outside world. He has few ambitions beyond protecting resisters and saving the honour of the fatherland. There now,' she ended triumphantly, 'does that satisfy you?'

Emily's fieriness confirmed Alexander's feeling that the German spymaster was sincere in his attempt to sail between the devil and the deep blue sea, that he would consequently be an ally in the struggle against nazism, regardless of his own nationalistic preferences. Most commentators fail to appreciate the consistency and logic in what appears to be Canaris's behaviour. As spymaster in a ruthless dictatorship he could hardly leave memoirs. Menzies, his opposite number in democratic Britain – who died a natural death in retirement – did not either.

But the ladies had still not provided answers to Crane's blunt questions: what did German resistance want apart from erasing nazism? And what could they deliver?

They continued to talk. Irena, consulting some shorthand notes, reported that Canaris would find his own way to supply military information. Clearly she had no idea about the link to Menzies. She also mentioned that Canaris was interested in preserving German dignity, the main motivation for most German resisters.

Emily next reported at considerable length on the resistance, as much for Alexander's benefit as for Irena's. In future Irena would be the only messenger as her relatives provided an alibi for travel abroad. Resistance was difficult to organize in Germany because Hitler had disrupted society's structures as well as normal human relations. The danger came as much from ordinary people as from the Gestapo. They were the informers, often unintentionally though intentionally as well. They protected their jobs and their skin. Hitler had poisoned the whole atmosphere of human relations. That explained Canaris's predicament and was also what made resistance so dangerous.

Alexander was utterly absorbed, his eyes fixed on Emily's ring, his mind fully on his words.

The German resistance lacked a large pool of reliable non-nazis, Emily went on. The communists with their disciplined organization had already been decimated. The social democrats, less strong on organization, were quite tempted by the comforts of life. Unions suffered the same fate. Academics by their nature avoided organization, so did members of the intelligentsia like writers, musicians, painters, journalists, actors, publishers, even lawyers. No local club offered safety. Only the churches held together.

Still, diverse anti-nazi groups did exist. They were primarily concerned with the future, which meant getting rid of Hitler. But not only of him, for he had many ensconced acolytes. That demanded careful planning. An alternative government would have to be ready to take over instantly, with guidelines for policy and for the vital international relations. All this demanded substantial precoup preparation.

Here two weaknesses occurred: there would be too many people with too many conflicting ideas and too great a tendency to perfection. Many people would have to be involved to prevent the nazis from regrouping, most of whom fulfilled important functions. Sifting out reliable non-nazis took infinite patience in addition to running the risk of betrayal.

'And once you set lawyers to construct blueprints for a postwar ideal state they're apt to forget the people for whom it is intended.'

133

She laughed at her own audacity in implicating her lawyer husband. Emily had been in full flow for a long time. Now she was exhausted. 'Much depends on the British attitude and the nature of their support,' she ended and slumped back in her chair.

Alexander had been fascinated, but Emily's analysis also depressed him. Her spirited apologia for her countrymen incidentally explained British scepticism. If the Germans failed to deal with their own predicament, what could Britain do? He pondered how to phrase these doubts without hurting two proud patriots.

Emily gulped the glass of wine Irena had poured her. Soon she recovered and joked about her 'litany'. She also diverted attention by taking off her ring and handing it to Alexander for inspection. Laughingly she said: 'You've concentrated more on the turquoise than on the tragedy.'

Alexander smiled. 'It's a well known fact that when one concentrates on an important issue the eyes tend to focus on an object. When it's beautiful too it's an aid to relaxation.'

Irena intercepted the ring as it was being passed back, put it on her finger, contemplated its suitability there and, satisfied, gave it back to Emily.

The long afternoon session produced no solutions and no answers to the questions dominating Alexander's mind. German resistance seemed substantial but lacked mass support. It was also curiously ineffective. No single explanation fitted this failure. It could hardly be blamed on the individuals involved. Emily and Irena had named quite a few from all strata of society.

Finally Alexander felt sufficiently emboldened to mention British scepticism: an assassination orchestrated by Britain would boomerang, even if it were feasible; Germans would resurrect the myth of the stab in the back, thus creating antagonism instead of a co-operative spirit.

Emily agreed. The same problem caused conflicts amongst resisters. 'Some want Hitler killed, others insist upon his arrest and trial for all the world to see his crimes,' she remarked. 'Legally condemned, he can hang legally.'

'Killing him is the only solution,' Irena interrupted emphatically. 'An arrest won't deter his acolytes nor dispose of his charisma. There's far too much preoccupation with perfect preparation instead of concentrating on eliminating the culprit. There are enough honourable people to fill any government. Wouldn't the British hail such a great achievement?' Her reaction exactly matched Alexander's feelings and presumably those of his British employers. But he did not say so.

Emily retorted: 'But England will demand the return of Austria, Bohemia and all the other gains that have re-established German pride.'

'Nationalism, pride, all the old shibboleths,' Irena replied contemptuously. 'That's not dignity. They led to this war and the terror.'

'I was only being ironic.' Emily turned to Alexander: 'Just ignore me,' she said softly.

But Alexander could hardly do that and still report honestly on his talks. 'What d'you think?' he asked. 'How many prefer an enlarged Germany to an early peace? Are they in a strong position? Or will the ethical argument prevail over the political pride of the ultra-nationalists?'

All too rapidly both ladies agreed that ethics would prevail, as Hans von Dohnanyi and Dietrich Bonhoeffer would ensure. Wishful thinking?

Night had fallen. What could the three of them do? Both ladies were adamant: 'Create understanding and sympathy for our resistance in Britain. Reject the ultra-nationalists, who confused territorial gains with human dignity and pride.' After all, the Dutch had not held on to kindred peoples when they let go of Flanders and of South Africa. 'And New York,' Alexander added laughingly.

In order to harden sympathy into tangible support, a line of communication should be established to ensure that Britain would receive up-to-date and reliable news on resistance progress. If this could be promised, Alexander in turn would promise to discuss the mechanics with someone in Switzerland who had direct access to London. Was this not what Dohnanyi himself had suggested when they met in Berlin? British scepticism could only be eroded gradually. This prompted Emily to ask Alexander to read Dohnanyi's letter to him.

The letter was grammatically flawless, but pedantic, an obvious translation of the German original. It contained a brief statement of principle and a proposal for further action, both uncannily similar to Alexander's suggestions. Only time and patient perseverance could re-establish confidence. It promised to provide relevant documents, accepted that the burden of action rested with the Germans and that arrogance should have no place in their considerations. It was the epitome of dignity, with exactly the reassurance Alexander needed.

Irena next promised to phone the following Wednesday at six to wish aunt and uncle a Happy New Year and confirm her next visit, which they had provisionally set for the weekend of 22 February. The two women radiated relief: some light at the end of the tunnel was visible after all. Clearly Alexander's 'compassion' had succeeded in establishing complete trust. This now had to be turned into practical support and that depended on London and its numerous sceptics. As it would depend on the course of the war.

During the evening meal the aunt now did most of the talking, as if husband and wife had agreed beforehand to take turns. Towards the end she remarked that the three of them had evidently had a satisfactory meeting. Irena confirmed it, then asked whether Alexander could be invited for a meal on New Year's Day when she would phone.

'Alexander is very welcome,' said her aunt, smiling happily.

Her uncle laughed more loudly than was his custom. 'I like this little conspiracy. Our house is at your disposal. We can do with a little excitement. And we won't tell the Gestapo. Ha ha ha!'

Emily, who sat next to Alexander, grasped his hand and pressed her ring into its palm. The old couple went upstairs, shortly followed by the ladies and Alexander. Irena shared most of the night with him. They talked very little.

Alexander reported to Vanden Heuvel, who arranged Alexander's return trip by the same route. Vanden Heuvel suggested that he be introduced to Irena next time she came. He then added ominously that Alexander would in any case be much more valuable at the London end in helping to evaluate the information received from several sources. 'Don't expect too much too soon,' he said. 'In this game one needs infinite patience. The war will grind on and so will Hitler, until something cracks, no one knows where and when.'

On New Year's Day the phonecall duly came and Irena confirmed the arrangements previously sketched out. Alexander started his return journey the next day and arrived in London without a hitch. He spent the next month in a small flat near Whitehall, put at his disposal by Bruce Crane. This time he was allowed to roam freely around the city. He commiserated with van 't Sant about Charles's misadventure, went to tea with Queen Wilhelmina and to dinner with Prince Bernhard. He kept silent about his journey to Switzerland and about the routes by which he had first reached London. All accepted his British connection, none enquired about it. Bruce Crane had clearly taken care of that.

On two occasions Menzies accompanied Bruce Crane to Alexander's flat for a drink before dinner, in both cases excusing himself when they left for a now familiar restaurant. He must have been satisfied because Alexander's mission had provided confirmation of Canaris's bonafides.

Bruce Crane had surprising news. After his next trip to Switzerland Alexander was to use his American passport to try and travel either overtly or covertly to Holland. Which is why Alexander and I came to meet again early April 1941, as I mentioned in the previous chapter.

Chapter Eleven

A DEFECTION AND MY SWISS ADVENTURES

Look at it through German eyes. By mid-1941, almost a year since they had occupied Holland, the groundswell of antipathy amongst the Dutch had caused only minor problems. The strike in Amsterdam had not lasted. Other protests remained muted and scattered. The illegal press was not yet taken seriously. And the civil service on the whole obliged with efficient co-operation, led and directed by the college of permanent secretaries. For the Germans it added up to very little; a carrot here and a stick there would suffice to keep control.

Through Dutch eyes the nazi measures still looked innocuous enough. Most were convinced that the end of the war was in sight, if not that year then surely the next. This was more than wishful thinking, but a persistent myth that determined our attitude. It tricked even the Jews into complacency and, worse, into co-operation, an astonishing and inexplicable episode.

On 10 January 1941 Seyss-Inquart instructed all Jews to register. They did so, with few exceptions. Should Jews be ashamed of their origin? Of course not. Besides they could hardly deny it: the synagogues retained registers and they were known as Jews by friends, neighbours, workmates and business associates. What is more, they were by tradition very orderly, like all Dutchmen.

A month later, on 12 February, in the wake of the Amsterdam riots but before the subsequent strike described earlier, the SS authorities in Amsterdam called in two

138

Ageing: 41 years separate these portraits
Above: Autumn 1983: Prince Bernhard gently pins Cross on my lapel
Below right: Autumn 1942: the vain attempt at changing my face with a moustache
Below left: My home in Holland shows no sign of ageing and stands today as it was when built in 1937

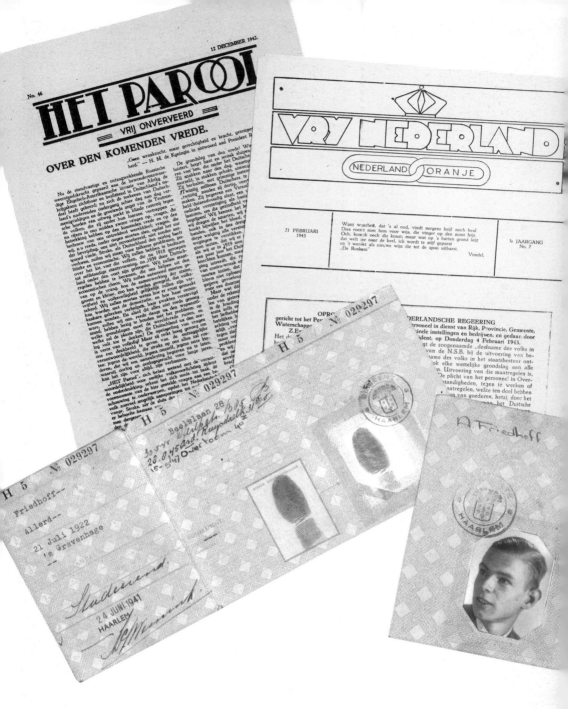

Two of the underground newspapers which shaped public opinion and some of my work, selected for their relevance today: *Het Parool* of 12 December 1942 headlines "The Coming Peace", confidently expected within months rather than 2½ years. I quote from its leading article which defines postwar European integration, one of several foreshadowing the European Community; *Vrij Nederland* carries the "Song of the Eighteen Dead", part of which is also quoted (see page 115) *Right:* The infamous identity card (my brother's, mine did not survive), which explains why today the Dutch sternly refuse its re-introduction, in any form, for any reason

Uncle Stuuf: Dr Herman Bernard Wiardi Beckman (1904 – 1945). Several of us youngsters had their 'uncles', only I had the privilege of one so talented

Above left: Amanda in her early glory
Above right: Theo just before his arrest and execution

Below: Several of the cast of the play *Summer Madness* (winter 1941) were active resisters

Three who kept Holland fighting from exile and its flag at full mast

Above: London 1941, Queen Wilhelmina accepts a cheque from her son-in-law; together they were one of the most fertile teams in wartime

Below: London 1943, Prince Bernhard joins militant Prime Minister Pieter Gerbrandy (with walrus moustache) at a function

Some of those who kept fighting nazism from inside occupied Europe
Above left: Dr Hans von Dohnanyi, political expert at the Abwehr, whom the Gestapo called 'the intellectual head' of the German resistance
Above right: Admiral Wilhelm Canaris, chief of the Abwehr, enigmatic like all spymasters and executed for supporting German resisters and resistance
Below: The College of Confidants, which for the last 18 months of the nazi occupation functioned as an underground government on behalf of the exiled cabinet, shortly after Holland's liberation in May 1945. Wartime Prime Minister Gerbrandy is third from right, Deputy Head of the College and postwar Prime Minister Willem Drees fourth from right

Above: The central exchange of the secret nationwide resistance telephone network, a coup that remained unknown to the Gestapo

Right: Lack of petrol led to ingenious solutions to the transport problem such as this horse-drawn bus

Below: A wedding by bicycle

Above: My mother with my father after her release from prison
Below left: The back of our home and the window from which I escaped the Gestapo
Below right: The view from the window over some of the hedges I had to jump on the way to freedom

prominent Jews and two chief rabbis. They were instructed to set up a Jewish Council. The rabbis excused themselves, the other two – a diamond merchant and a well-known classics professor – obeyed with speed and efficiency, and apparently quite happily. The next day twenty members had been selected and installed, and the Council's first public meeting held. It was to represent all Jews, to register them according to various criteria, to liaise with the nazi authorities on all Jewish affairs and to implement their instructions. This they started to do in the belief that by a co-operative attitude the nazi measures could be slowed down and softened, victims saved or at least helped, and panic averted by the imposition of an orderly system. Order *was* achieved, panic mostly avoided.

It is impossible in a brief paragraph to do justice to the Council's motivations, predilections and actions, or to pronounce judgement. Eventually the Council effectively administered the wholesale deportation of their co-religionists on behalf of the nazis, as similar Councils did in other countries. They tried to save what could be saved until war's end, confidently expected in months rather than years.

No doubt personal arrogance played a part. So did the Council's complete misjudgement of the nazis' ultimate goal. Who did not misjudge it at this point? Some Jews refused a seat on the Council, some refused its authority; the deposed Jewish President of the High Court of Justice counselled caution; the underground press sounded warnings. If the chairman had stood down, others would have done the job, probably more severely. At the time persecution was minimal. Should they have promoted wholesale flight into hiding? In the most densely populated country of the world, highly urbanized, flat, and without the space and the mountainous areas of other countries, Holland could hardly hide 160,000 of its citizens at a stroke, let alone supply them with the false papers essential for survival.

After the war the surviving chairmen were formally accused of collaboration, but it never came to a trial. Had the war ended as presumed they would have been decorated. No guidelines for their conduct came from the exiled government either. For the chairmen it was indubitably an impossible position to be in.

The creation of the Jewish Council had a curious side effect. It started the slide towards unconscious acceptance of the nazi contention that Jews were different in other than religious ways. A split appeared between non-Jews and Jews. As the war ground on, the nazis introduced ghettos. Many Jews lived in Amsterdam, albeit scattered. The Council assisted in moving all Jews into that city and then into designated areas. If the Jews were handling their own affairs, gentiles told each other, then why interfere to help them?

Another side effect was to delay concerted protests against nazi measures until these became palpably worse. The Council of (Christian) Churches did not protest until January 1942, though thereafter it did so repeatedly.

By then resistance on an active level – individually and in small groups – was well established. But the activists needed support from what we came to call 'passivists', for hiding fugitives, money, and the like. That breakthrough can be traced to February 1941. From that early moment dates the birth of the people's resistance. Its motive was to help victims of nazism. At first these were mainly Jews, but when non-Jewish helpers themselves became victims, they too needed help. The circle widened. As victims and helpers both grew in numbers, the need for false papers – identity and ration cards – gave rise to a large sophisticated network of 'falsification centres' for printing and stealing them. Financial relief originally came from private donations, but this activity too grew in scope and led to the creation of the NSF (National Support Fund), backed by bank loans guaranteed by the exiled government.

These events started the process of total resistance – slowly perhaps, but irrevocably and involving even larger numbers. It could not be done by a general uprising, as the Amsterdam strike and two later strikes showed. Nor could people forget that daily life continued, that they had to earn a living, pay for their daily bread, educate and protect their children. They had to weigh the consequences of each and every action carefully.

The nazis, of course, did not confine their restrictive practices to the Jews. On 2 April the boyscout movement was prohibited. On 30 June 500 communists were arrested and 'encamped'. On 12 August so called 'Peace Judges' were installed, political courts outside the jurisdiction of normal courts set up to deal with dirty words shouted at nazis and similar non-criminal cases. Then the executions started, often for ridiculous reasons.

The first, on 3 March, was of a Jewish German refugee. With his customers he defended his ice-cream bar against an attack by Dutch nazi thugs, abetted and encouraged by Germans. No one was killed or seriously wounded, but the owner was still condemned to death. The death penalty for self-defence? Why not? He was a Jew and a renegade German to boot.

The second was neither a Jew nor a German but very much a Dutchman, though a communist. He was arrested on 5 March while distributing leaflets calling for another strike. A record was established: offence, court case, judgement, verdict and execution all within twenty-four hours. Why him and not the hundred-odd others who committed the same offence?

Among the eighteen executed on 13 March, remembered in *The Song of the Eighteen Dead*, three were non-Jewish Dutchmen similarly convicted for incitement to strike. Not incitement to kill, but to protest peacefully against the killing and wanton destruction by the nazi thugs. The remaining fifteen victims belonged to a resistance group which called itself *De Geuzen* or The Beggars, after the sixteenth-century Dutch fighters against Spanish oppression. Several hundred had been arrested the previous November. Only one of them can be said to have acted subversively and also persistently. He was Bernard Ijzerdraad who wrote the first illegal paper as reported earlier, at that time a restorer of ancient tapestries in Haarlem.

Bernard had also started a semi-military group 'to recapture our freedom and prevent Holland from becoming part of Germany'. The group mushroomed. Many were prepared to join, attracted by the promise of action, of weapons, sabotage and cooperation with Britain. They searched for weapons but never found any. Contact with Britain never materialized, if only for lack of a transmitter. No sabotage was committed. In their successful attempts to enlarge and their unsuccessful ones to find the tools for whatever actions, they had to talk to others. Some were so excited that they presented prospects as achievements. Inevitably one sympathizer talked to a sceptic who unwittingly consulted a friend who turned out to be a nazi sympathizer and he reported the existence of a large army and vast armories to the nazi authorities. Searches and arrests followed. Torture did the rest. Confessions procured in this way elicited no more than further names and dreams of sabotage. Their leader never gave anything away and his real role never became known to the nazis. The Court convicted on dreams. Twenty-two were sentenced to harsh terms of imprisonment, eighteen condemned to death, three teenagers having their sentences commuted to life imprisonment. With the three Amsterdam strikers, the total added up to eighteen again. On their way to the place of execution in the dunes they sang, alternating psalms with the national anthem. They were neither Jews nor communists but Calvinists.

News of all these events – though not all the details – were published in the regular press. Their impact both on the active resisters and the passive population was shattering. They stimulated the reconstitution of the Apostles and stirred the groups in which Wiardi Beckman participated. They were fresh in our minds when I met again with Alexander in early April to discuss our approach to Matthew.

Not willing to come to my house, Alexander had suggested we meet at a café nearby. Even his own family were unaware of his presence. The café was an oldfashioned, dilapidated place on the other side of our wood. Faded rugs covered the tables, worn rugs the chairs. When I entered there were few customers. A lone waiter sat smoking in a corner, staring uninterestedly at the persistent rain outside.

When Alexander turned up, he looked different. I stared at him, trying to pinpoint why. He sat down opposite me, laughing. With the fingers of both hands he curled the ends of an enormous newly grown handlebar moustache. Proudly he said: 'Lovely, don't you agree? Changes my appearance. Clearly it works.'

'Rather martial,' I replied. 'And conspicuous.'

He smiled and continued to do so while I recounted my bellicose talk with Laura. 'Matthew must've got under her skin,' he said. 'Apparently he pestered her doggedly and wouldn't take no for an answer. But she misunderstood my advice. I didn't say "shoot him," only "get rid of him". Psychological not physical force. With incontrovertible evidence it would be different of course, but Matthew doesn't qualify as a traitor or you would all be behind bars. A gun was only mentioned as protection if and when the Apostles had matured into a serious unit. Perhaps Laura meant to test you.'

I was only half convinced, until Alexander went on to outline future work for the Apostles. He had found an operator with a transmitter and direct access to London. Luke could still be an asset. Much depended on our joint confrontation with Matthew, to which he looked forward. For our protection Matthew had to be carefully discarded. 'And,' Alexander concluded, 'my identity should not be revealed.'

It was this condition that upset our planning.

The next evening I went to see Uncle Stuuf in his hide-out and there found Alexander again. Uncle Stuuf strongly advised Alexander against the fateful Matthew meeting. His presence in Holland should remain a closely guarded secret to protect his present and future operations. With his dubious connections Matthew presented a potential security risk. The use of a fictitious name would not diminish it. Leyden was a small town, the students formed a coterie, some would see through the disguise, especially in view of Alexander's height and conspicuous appearance. Uncle Stuuf felt I had to tackle Matthew on my own or with Laura and keep it within the Apostle family. I frankly admitted to being apprehensive of my bluntness and lack of diplomatic skills.

In trepidation I consulted Laura, in dread we set out in her car to face Matthew, without prior warning.

Matthew himself opened the door. 'Hello, little one,' he said lightly. 'Come to make amends? Why bring jolly old Herman?' His usual patronizing banter could not conceal his unease. He took us to a fair-sized study on the first floor of his opulent home. On a desk shone a large photograph of a well-rounded and quite beautiful girl with endlessly long blond hair.

Laura sat down in the only comfortable armchair before replying: 'An Apostolic session, Matthew. Nothing else.'

Matthew raised his eyebrows. 'Unannounced, and in my home?'

'I told you we had to be more careful and change the routine.'

'Then why is our precious Luke missing?'

I could not contain myself: 'Luke has already discussed the subject with you.'

Matthew must have understood but he tried to gain time. 'Did he? I haven't seen him since our last meeting.'

I took the plunge. 'He's been talking to you for months about your nazi contacts and he asked you to tell us about it. You haven't. Now you can.' Matthew was the only snooty one amongst us and it had always irritated me.

Matthew stiffened. 'My private affairs are none of your business.'

'I wasn't talking about your affairs,' I shot back, 'but your nazi contacts. That affects us. We're supposed to be fighting them.'

Laura had remained composed. She now said gently: 'Why didn't you tell us, Matthew? Don't you realize you put our lives at risk?'

'That wouldn't be my fault,' he replied, wavering, disarmed by Laura's soft approach.

'You're behaving like a spoilt brat!' I put in angrily.

Laura kicked my shin, then continued as softly as before. 'Matthew, why not come clean? *You* wanted to join the Apostles. *You* agreed there were to be no secrets. You don't now want to betray our mutual trust, do you?'

Matthew did not answer directly. 'Why didn't you ask about it when we met last?'

'Because I didn't know then,' Laura replied. 'You didn't tell me about your girl either. Is that her?' By her tone I realized that their meeting had ended in a lover's tiff.

'It is.' Laura's questions seemed to break the deadlock. 'I need girls, just as you do men. I met Stephanie. She gave me what you refused. I still preferred you. But you refused again. Then I met her father. He helped me to continue my studies, even though the university is closed. I'll be doing my finals next month. He's also offered me a job.'

Laura's voice sank almost to a whisper. 'You could've told me.'

Matthew seemed near tears. He waited, then said: 'Yes. But I wasn't ready. I'm still awfully mixed up. Stephanie's father is quite sensible. So different from the picture you painted of nazis.' He got up, paced the room, somehow contained himself, then went over to Laura, sat down on the arm of her chair, touched her cheek. 'I'm sorry, little one. I'm afraid I've switched sides. I haven't told Luke. Not even my parents. I wasn't sure. My dad will kick me out of the house. But I can't go back now.'

He paused, struggling to find words. Laura did not move. I was too astonished to say anything.

Matthew recovered his poise and went on: 'Stephanie's father has convinced me there's no alternative. Germany will win, no doubt about that. It'll sweep away all the rubbish of our so-called democracy. We need clean, healthy people who're prepared to work, and work hard. There'll be plenty, except for scroungers. Of course, some are better at one thing, others at something else. People who know about running a business should be left to do so – no unions, no commies. People who know about running the country should be able to run it without . . .' He broke off, as if he had said too much. 'Well, you know. Anyway, why be on the losing side with these marvellous opportunities?' Satisfied he sat down heavily in his uncomfortable chair.

I was totally taken aback. Throughout his speech I had veered between wanting to slap his face and to ridicule each flabby assertion. What clean, healthy people? What Holland would there be left to run? But I was too stunned to know where to start and wondered what Laura was going to do.

She looked utterly betrayed. The five Apostles were now down to two. But her voice was still soft. 'We haven't come to argue politics. Not any more. Let's make sure there'll be no killings either way.'

Matthew must have sensed the veiled threat. His eyes widened. 'Little one! What's this about killings? I'll never betray you. Stephanie's father is strongly of the opinion that it doesn't pay to betray friends.' Had he already discussed us? I wondered nervously.

Steel now entered Laura's voice. 'We'll see,' she said coldly. 'I was told you had to be eliminated. There's a war on. One day you might not be my friend.'

I feared we were losing again, but stayed silent, feeling a coward for it. I need not have worried.

'Eliminated?' Matthew's voice rose. 'Why? By whom? Your communist friends?'

'No,' said Laura, icily. 'They don't know. Yet.'

Then Matthew burst into tears. 'Little one, please, please,' he sobbed, 'let's stay friends! I'll never, never betray you, ever!'

Amanda had been right: he was a weak character, pathetic, totally unreliable, whatever his promises.

In the car Laura put a hand on my crotch for a moment. 'You've got balls, Matthew hasn't.' She went on: 'Don't worry. He won't betray us. No guts. I found out when we fucked, some time ago. That's why I refused a repeat. I hadn't expected that this abject stupidity would be the result. Sorry you got involved.'

Now at last I understood her remark when we first met about sex as a sound test of character.

Laura drove straight to her home, forgetting her promise to deliver me to mine first. The reason for this lapse soon became clear. She jumped out of the car, rushed in and up the stairs to her father's study. I followed slowly, slightly puzzled, shut the front door carefully, hung up my coat, walked up the stairs and along the corridor to where a door stood wide open.

Inside stood Alexander. Laura was pressing herself against him, ruffling his hair and touching him everywhere. He remained immobile, bemused. Lady van Alblas laughed at the spectacle they made. Then she went to pour out some wine for us. We drank a lot in the next hour while Laura reported on our experiences.

Later, as he drove me home, Alexander said he would be leaving in a couple of days. He did not divulge his destination, nor did I ask. He suggested I keep an extra eye on his cousin, adding that if she needed physical relief from future stresses it seemed preferable for me to act as her saviour than some unreliable bastard. I laughed, but Alexander was quite serious. 'Amanda won't mind if you tell her why and when. Of course: not too often!' And he too laughed.

When I joined Alexander and Uncle Stuuf the next afternoon, they were deep in discussion, preparing for a meeting planned for that evening. It would be held in a house my father had designed for a prominent alderman. I was to join them to make notes, somehow formalizing my role as Uncle Stuuf's personal assistant. After accepting Laura's assessment of Matthew and warning us to keep away from him, Uncle Stuuf suggested I devote some attention to the question of identity cards.

Designed by a Dutch civil servant before the outbreak of war, the identity card had never been introduced by the democratic government which considered it an infringement of personal liberty. For the same reason the nazis snapped up this golden opportunity to acquire a superb tool to control the masses. The sophisticated design made use of specially prepared paper, various unusual inks and a complicated, almost foolproof, printing technique. Alexander had just obtained his own identity card to take back to England for analysis, though a perfect forgery was never produced. No agent could do without one, nor could anyone in hiding.

Our afternoon meeting fathered another incitement to action. On parting – and outside Alexander's hearing – Uncle Stuuf stressed the need for a line to Switzerland, to help break the communication deadlock with the exiled Dutch government. He had just got hold of an excellent address in Paris to assist me in reaching that haven of neutrality, from where contact with London would be that much easier.

The evening meeting was larger than any other I had attended. We were nine. Notes made at the time were, of course, destroyed, but the spirit of high adventure ensured that I would remember the outcome clearly. Participating were the clergyman-director of the YMCA – Dr Eykman – and Professor Scholten to support Wiardi Beckman in his attempt to forge the planned link between and with the para-military organizations mentioned earlier. These were represented by the effective chief of the OD (Order Service) – Lieutenant-Colonel

Westerveld – and the founder of the rival group LOF (Legion of Frontline Fighters) – Du Tourton Bruyns – each with a colleague. Westerveld, a direct, sensible man, had been a professional gunner but was in business at that time. Du Tourton Bruyns held no military rank because of a foot disability and in order to compensate tended to act like a bully. But thanks to Uncle Stuuf their rivalry turned to friendship and the two agreed to merge their groups as well as form links with civilian groups. Sadly, all four military men were arrested at the end of that month and subsequently shot.

Another attempt to reach Switzerland had to be made. This would mean crossing into Belgium again and then crossing much of France. The omens were not good. Frans van Rijn, my companion of three months before, had gone on to England. I did not know whether the monastery could still help with the border crossing. Spring would soon give way to summer and while that ensured kinder weather, it also made for shorter nights. And my French stemmed from schoolmasters enamoured more of grammar than fluency.

Amanda presented another unknown factor. If I told her about the trip she might insist on joining me. In retrospect that would have been a great help, but I was not to know that at the time.

In June, borrowing a monk's habit and hat from a friend, without informing Amanda, I travelled to Wernhout and thence to the monastery, in broad daylight and warm sunshine. The reception was at first somewhat chilly. The friar who had been our main help last time was unavailable, the prior disapproving of my disguise. His monastery, he said, could not be used as a way-station for stray travellers on illegal journeys. He did not want to involve his flock in undercover activities that would detract from their religious obligations, let alone attract the attention of the Germans. After this dressing-down, he relented and lent me one of his friars to guide me. I was not ready to go any further, but had no option. That afternoon two chattering monks walked into the wood and across the border without any undesirable encounters.

My companion told me that his colleague who had helped

me before had moved to another monastery, south of Eindhoven, equally suitably located for border crossings and whose prior would be more helpful. Much later I heard that a Catholic Dutch policeman had gone the next day to remind the stern prior that straying across borders in wartime should be restricted. As a matter of personal interest he also enquired about the order of the monk with a habit he had not come across before. We had been observed!

Once safely in Hoboken, my friends provided board and lodging again, and promised help, also for future trips into France. That had been the purpose of this brief recce and I could therefore return though not by the same route. Their son-in-law took me to Hasselt, a town due east of Antwerp and due south of Eindhoven, then to a village near the Dutch border. There we contacted the local priest, who volunteered to guide me through the Weebosch, a large wood straddling the border. Again I donned my monk's habit and crossed the border, again without trouble. We were warmly welcomed by a more convivial prior and by the surprised friar, late of Wernhout. All laughed uproariously at my outfit. I stayed the night and laid the foundation for future trips. Three days and two nights after my departure I returned home, rather pleased with these unexpected results.

My real attempt to reach Switzerland started late in July. Amanda had accompanied her father, step-mother and sundry relations on a fortnight's holiday to the Frisian lakes. That saved me from the need to inform her. Using my newly established route, I returned to Hoboken. From there the son-in-law took me to Courtrai near the French border, where he handed me over to a friend in a grimy garage. The friend dumped me in the back of a ramshackle truck, covered me with dusty empty sacks, then drove to Lille, the largest city in northern France. Without stopping once. At the border he waved to the guards – French, Belgian and a lone German. They knew him well because he regularly passed to collect goods in France. My Hoboken friends were well organized.

From Lille another truck took me to Paris. For most of the long ride I was in the seat next to the driver, though I switched to the back again when we neared the city. In Paris I found my way to the address Uncle Stuuf had supplied. An elderly couple, shaking their heads at my audacious intentions, provided generous hospitality. And more practical help. Within forty-eight hours a French identity card turned up in the name of Alexandre Necker, my photograph included. The first name was chosen for its international potential, the second because it sounded German, albeit with a French connection. The Neckers were descendents of a finance minister under Louis XVI, and they still lived in the Alsace. The document gave my birthplace as Colmar, my address in Belfort, near the Swiss border. As a born and bred Alsatian, any accent in my French would thus be explained.

It was an excursion I like to forget, and much of it has been forgotten. Its only success was that I came out alive. Everything else went wrong. I remember the mounting agony of pretending to be Alexandre Necker, even though this allowed me to travel freely in the *zone interdite*, the restricted area near the Swiss border. I picked up a lot of French and improved my pronunciation almost to perfection. An intellectual young man accompanied me. He took me to Delle the first border town, and at night we crept and crawled through gently mountainous country. We were nearly across the frontier to safety when we detected a border patrol. Though it did not spot us, it nevertheless prevented us from reaching our goal, the Swiss village of Porrentruy.

The next night we tried again, further south, via Montbéliard and Hérimoncourt. Again there was a patrol. Much worse, this time it spotted us. We had to run for our lives and became separated. Luck had turned against me. Dejected and despairing I nonetheless found my way back to Belfort in the early hours. The nice young man had not yet returned. I slept a few hours, then learned that he had been caught and arrested. I was advised to return to Paris by the first available train. I did, alone and miserable, only to find that my elderly host had been arrested as well, though not as a result of his assistance to me. With two victims in my wake I decided to give up and go home. As if to prove how finicky memory can be, I do not recall how, only that I must have achieved it within the allotted fortnight, for no one showed any surprise at my presence.

Chapter Twelve

ALEXANDER'S SECOND TRIP TO SWITZERLAND

The meetings with Alexander never really satisfied my understandable curiosity about why he was there, how he got there in the first place, and where he intended to go. I had to wait forty-odd years for the details to emerge.

Alexander had returned to Switzerland by the same complex route as before. On the morning of 22 February he presented himself again at the large villa on the outskirts of Lausanne. The uncle told him that Irena's train had been delayed, and that she would not arrive until lunchtime. That left him two agreeable hours with both uncle and aunt, filled with personal confidences. They proved to be witty, pious and staunchly anti-nazi. They revealed how much they missed their son and how deeply they felt the lack of grandchildren. The Lord had provided for them amply, with a happy marriage and with wealth. But he had failed to provide them with what in old age had become almost an obsession: a replacement for their missing offspring. Hence their attachment to Irena. The uncle even made an oblique plea to Alexander to protect her.

That afternoon Irena handed him a sizeable envelope containing a number of documents. For the first time she showed signs of nervousness. No wonder: the papers contained the names of conspirators and even a brief draft constitution for a post nazi democratic Germany. She had hidden the envelope in her underwear, between several layers, to conceal any rustling. While Alexander tried to absorb the contents of these highly sensitive documents, Irena explained what had caused her delay, even more cogent reasons for apprehension.

During Christmas Emily Smend had suggested that Irena should receive a letter from her aunt with a plea to attend her birthday. The text had been drafted then and there. A month later the aunt had copied it in her own handwriting and posted it – Irena's key to safe travel.

At the German-Swiss border a search had been instigated that turned out to be much more thorough than usual. The train was held up for a long time. Additional Gestapo officials boarded. They started checking the papers of each passenger over and over again and asked penetrating questions. All suitcases were minutely examined and the toilets ransacked. Eventually a male passenger was escorted on to the platform. By then the Gestapo realized that Irena – who had deliberately made no mention of her aunt's letter – carried a special pass from the Abwehr. Whether because of the rivalry between Gestapo and Abwehr or simply because the interrogators felt that a pretty girl with an Abwehr pass could not be as innocent as she looked, two of them returned for further questioning. Formerly polite, the officers gradually became gruff, then even coarse. Irena remained calm, insisting that she was going to Lausanne for purely personal reasons. They stopped short of a body search and thus failed to find the envelope, but inspection of her handbag produced the letter from her aunt. As she had intended, it was this document that became the focus of attention.

'Why didn't you show this letter before?' the two asked almost in unison.

Indignantly Irena replied: 'That's none of your business. It's private. My Abwehr papers are perfectly in order. If you're still worried, why not phone Lausanne? I've nothing to hide.'

This they proceeded to do, thus incidentally warning the uncle of his niece's delay. It had been a close call. On future occasions, she said she would insist on carrying microfilms even though this meant making use of technical facilities which would involve more people.

'Imagine what would have happened if they had found those names?' Irena said, trembling again at the memory.

'Death all round. Torture. The end of all our plans. The end of Germany's future resurrection.'

Alexander restrained the impulse to put his arms round her. 'I'm afraid that's what spying's all about,' he said weakly.

Irena paused. 'It's very frightening, you know,' she said, then for the first time went on to explain how she had become involved.

'I had no idea when the admiral asked me to take Halina Szymanska to Switzerland that it could be anything else than a precaution. After all, what is more natural than accompanying a relative through wartime Germany to safety in a neutral country for the sake of her children? But back in the office he complimented me on a successful mission, stressing that word, a clear hint that there might have been more to it. I started wondering, even more so when they asked me to do other messenger jobs outside my normal work. Asked, mind you, not instructed. In retrospect, those jobs must have been intended as my baptism. Perhaps also to test me. Still, it didn't really become clear until Hans von Dohnanyi prepared me for the first meeting with you. Only then did I understand that something like an active conspiracy actually existed. I felt rather proud that my bosses showed such confidence in me. I felt happy too that the men I respected turned out to be more than silent witnesses, not just anti-nazis but active ones. Their courage inspired me to volunteer for this mission.'

Impressed by this speech with its simple, logical conclusion, Alexander waited a while before reacting. 'You'll get accustomed to such shocks too. Fieldwork is different from deskwork. More strenuous in a sense, which is why couriers and agents get more breaks, let's say holidays. Or should.'

'Do you?'

'I certainly hope so.' Alexander smiled, then waited a while, in some doubt about the next move. But, however difficult, he now had to continue. 'That's why I'm going to introduce you to the man who represents my boss permanently in Switzerland.'

'Oh?!' Irena was clearly surprised and uneasy.

'Your visits can't always be timed to coincide with mine,' Alexander explained. 'Also, I may have to monitor developments in Germany from London. Easy access to Switzerland won't last for ever. But whatever happens, I'll be kept informed. And, you'll be in good hands.'

'But not yours,' she said unhappily.

He laughed. 'Probably more professional.'

'When do I see this man?' She put a brave face on it.

'Tomorrow in Bern.'

'Why can't you stay here? Assist this man?'

Alexander sympathized. It was cruel. After all, Irena expected him to be the sympathetic recipient of her complex confidences, not some 'man' in Bern, and a 'professional' at that. But it had to be done.

'I have to follow instructions, too, Irena. When it comes to evaluating all the information about Germany, London is a better place than Bern. Anyway, why do you really do this work? It can't be because of me.'

'No, mister preacher, it's because Hitler's dictatorship is evil. But it helps to have a sympathetic partner.' She laughed, he smiled, and the tension broke. But he did not want to leave it at that.

'Will you promise me something? Come here to stay with your uncle and aunt when it gets too hot in Berlin.' Thereby Alexander fulfilled her uncle's wish that Irena find protection.

'All right,' she replied.

Then she proceeded to fill him in on the background to the documents. She pointed out that the conspirators worked in a complete vacuum. Although there were quite a few, as the list indicated, and although the brief *curricula vitae* showed them to come from diverse groups and different backgrounds, they acted as individuals without the support of large organizations; without the support of the cowed silent majority or the army; and – more important still – without any idea of what the outside world was thinking.

The silent majority, the general public, was petrified. The Gestapo and its subsidiaries consisted of tens of thousands of able-bodied – though often weak-minded – men, eager to show their importance and prove their power over life and death. Ordinary citizens could be abused, kicked, arrested, even shot for minor offences or presumed ones or none at all. Irena knew of such a case. A family of five had been confronted by SD men looking for a fugitive. Someone with a grudge against the family had suggested he could be hiding in their house. When the search failed to produce anyone or any evidence of his presence, first the husband was shot dead in front of his wife and children, then the three children one by one. Only the mother survived to tell the tale. That was the intention: intimidation by proxy, for she would and did tell of her horrible experience.

At this point Irena halted, swallowed and had to wipe tears away before she could continue.

'In such an atmosphere of fear,' she said when she had regained her composure, 'a revolution of the conventional type becomes impossible.' The only solution was the elimination of Hitler and his immediate entourage. With the support of reliable parts of the army a civilian government would take over. Bereft of their leaders, the henchmen would no longer pose an immediate threat. 'Certainly not once the German people know that the war is going to spread to Russia.'

'Russia?' Astonished, Alexander interrupted quickly. Germany and Russia had been allies since August 1939. They had split Poland between them. They were both dictatorships. They both wanted security on their flanks, the one to the east the other to the west. Had Hitler run out of ideas on how to subdue Britain?

'Yes, Russia! The order to invade had been given. Military preparations have been going on for months, almost since the collapse of France. But the generals opposed it. When England didn't give up, Hitler convinced most of them that there was no alternative.'

'It sounds suicidal.' Alexander still could not believe it.

'It will be, but Hans von Dohnanyi sees it as a blessing in disguise. The people won't accept it. Several top commanders will join the conspiracy because of it. But the real problem is how to eliminate Hitler. He's elusive, almost impossible to approach. He changes his whereabouts and his itinerary constantly.'

To Alexander the information about the planned attack on Russia was far more important than the anti-nazi conspiracy, but he did not say so.

'Do you know the date?'

'Approximately, yes. Early May. To give the army time to finish another *Blitzkrieg* before the autumn.'

'Is there any proof?'

'Isn't my word enough?'

'For me certainly, for others no. What about written orders and plans?'

'They exist, of course. But I don't have anything to show you. It's not my job. Hans told me to concentrate on the resistance. Anyway, military plans come and go. Hitler changes his mind so often.' She saw his sceptical look. 'But he won't change his mind about attacking Russia. Hans says he needs the raw materials because the economy is in bad shape.'

Support for Irena's claim came shortly after. Canaris told Halina Szymanska, who told Vanden Heuvel, who told Menzies, who told Churchill, who passed it on to Stalin. Not that the warning did much good. The invasion of Russia was postponed for six weeks because part of the army was needed in the Balkans and in Africa to bolster Italy. This delay may well have rung the death knell for Hitler's ambitions, for, as feared, foul weather prevented a quick victory. But the delay also increased the doubts in the minds of the Russians about the veracity of the warnings they had received from Britain. Indeed, it contributed to undermining the credibility of information coming out of Germany to the British as well.

Interpreting intelligence can be tricky, sometimes more so than gathering it. Today Alexander recalls that Canaris's over-optimistic forecasts to Hitler in the war against Russia and his over-pessimistic ones for the Western front were subtly devised to harm the Führer's aims. Both suited the Allies admirably. They were further contributions to the honour of his country, in addition to his messages through Mme Szymanska and the support of the active resisters in his Abwehr, including Irena. Canaris was, of course, confronted with the same problem regarding timing which faced resisters all over Europe as well as the Jewish Councils, as reported earlier. When would the war finish or Hitler be eliminated? For someone whose chosen role was duplicity this meant spacing subversive actions carefully. Canaris had a foot in both camps, an improbable balancing act. For the German resisters his value depended on his privileged relationship with Hitler. He would be of little value as a retired and suspect admiral. Canaris knew that his nazi detractors were on to him. He therefore relied heavily on Hitler's fascination with cloak and dagger stuff, and consequently with the foxy spymaster. Time ran out for him in the end. While all this may not add up to the hero some commentators make him out to be, he was certainly not the fake others describe him as.

Irena's list contained the names of a provisional future government, to be headed by Dr Karl Goerdeler, ex-mayor of Leipzig. Only one was a professional soldier – for Defence – all the others being civilians. They represented conservatives, social democrats, members of the centre party and non-aligned experts. Only two were from the aristocracy, neither of them soldiers.

As Irena talked, gaps and weaknesses in the conspiracy showed up. The attitude towards the Allies had not yet been agreed. Some wanted to save the honour of Germany by insisting on the retention of at least some of the conquered territories with a preponderance of German speaking people. Others pointed out that such honour would surely be saved by the revolt itself and that to attach any conditions to ending the war would be insolent and would inevitably distract from the main objective: creating a democratic Germany.

That represented the strongly held view of Hans von Dohnanyi, Rudolf Smend and several other influential conspirators, including Hans's brother-in-law Pastor Dietrich Bonhoeffer. Hans had specifically asked Irena to explain to Alexander their opinion about postwar developments. Europe would be highly interdependent economically. Some institution should be created – even a federation – to secure the necessary co-operation and this would serve as a strong guarantee against a revival of German militarism. Any future German army should also be integrated into a European army. It sounded like an echo of similar ideas surfacing in Holland at the same time and which found expression in the article in *Het Parool* quoted on pages 116–117.

The second document – a draft constitution – was not an

agreed statement either. Dr Goerdeler had requested its inclusion but allowed Rudolf Smend and Joseph Wirmer – the lawyer destined to become Minister of Justice – to add their comments. Loyal Irena was sure this conflict of opinions would be solved in due course by the force of the arguments advanced by Hans et al. The reactionary Goerdeler was known to be practical and on occasion flexible. Alexander felt less sure.

Tea was brought in by the aunt at 4 pm, drinks by the uncle at six. By then both Irena and Alexander were exhausted and, glasses in hand, left the library to join their genial hosts. They retired fairly early, after another elaborate meal. This time Alexander had been allotted a room directly next to Irena's. His bed was not slept in.

The next day in Bern the meeting with Vanden Heuvel went well enough. He came across as a father figure, to establish mutual trust. Like most resisters to nazism, Irena was an amateur and had to be gently coaxed into learning the intricate art of make-believe, its peculiar dangers and how to countenance them. To reassure her, Vanden Heuvel deployed all his charm and succeeded admirably.

Subtly he drew Irena into a discussion of Mme Szymanska. Inevitably this caused surprise and awkward questions from Irena. It also mystified Alexander, who suddenly realized that Irena had not mentioned her distant relative recently, although she too must be in Switzerland.

Irena was quick to react. 'Do you know her?'

'Not really. I just met her at some function.'

'Is she well?'

'She appeared to be then.'

'Where does she live now? I'd like to meet her again one day.'

'I wouldn't if I were you,' said Vanden Heuvel, shaking his head.

'Why not?'

'Well, my dear, obviously the fewer people know about your presence here the better. Security, you know. If the Gestapo came to hear that your visits were not restricted to bringing comfort to an old couple you might be in for more questioning.

They have their informers everywhere, in this country as in yours.'

'Yes, I see. But couldn't I say to her that I've come to see my uncle?'

'Did you discuss her with them?'

'It's funny you should ask that. No, I didn't. I wondered but felt they shouldn't be involved. I didn't even tell them I have a job at the Abwehr.'

'Did they mention her? They must be related as well.'

'No, they didn't. But that's understandable. Their family connection is even more distant than mine.'

Vanden Heuvel nodded, then said: 'For your sake and theirs it'll be better to leave it at that. Don't you agree?'

So this had been his purpose all along, to ensure her discretion. No doubt he had also suggested to Mme Szymanska that she forgo family contacts and had thus succeeded in keeping the two sources apart. Canaris too preferred it that way, as it played up the difference between military and revolutionary activities.

Alexander felt grateful for the rapport that was clearly being established between the two. It might also solve his private predicament, the clash of loyalties to Laura and Irena. He had entered into both relationships lightheartedly, but both had developed into much more serious attachments, with a potential for harmful conflict. Once Vanden Heuvel had gained Irena's confidence, he would be able to stay in London.

Alexander now produced the envelope containing the sensitive documents and explained their value. Vanden Heuvel reacted with genuine surprise. He glanced through them quickly and complimented the conspirators on their thoroughness. The use of that word – if not his voice – should have alerted Alexander, but he was too engrossed in observing Irena whom he might never see again. She smiled with obvious pride at what she took as a compliment. Vanden Heuvel promised to dispatch the papers to London at the earliest safe opportunity. Irena, about to leave for her train in high spirits, did not ask why Alexander himself could not be the bearer. Only when Vanden Heuvel added as an afterthought that the conspirators should perhaps be aware of *too much* thoroughness did Alexander grasp the drift of his thought.

In the days that followed, Vanden Heuvel expressed his worries more openly to Alexander. He admired the pluckiness of the beautiful Irena and the dedication of the undoubtedly important conspirators, and he did not doubt the need for a reasonable plan to back up an attempt on Hitler's life. But he detected a tendency to aim at perfection and as a consequence to postpone the deed until every last nut and bolt fitted. In this revolt of moral dimensions during a war of pure power rivalry – in which the conspirators ran enormous risks – rapid action was essential. Delay might prove more disastrous than failure.

Alexander discovered hitches in the arrangements for his next assignment to Holland, which delayed his departure by several weeks. He was to pose as a State Department official on special assignment to help wind up American consulates in Holland. It was a good cover, for America was not yet at war with Germany. But the American embassy in Bern encountered difficulties in obtaining the visa and travel permits needed for the overt journey through France and Belgium. The German embassy in the Swiss capital took a long time, presumably to check his credentials. The circumspect way the Americans had to be dealt with did not promote speed either. Except for one attaché, none of the embassy staff could be informed of the true nature of his mission, none had ever heard of Jack Taylors (with an s!), Alexander's fifth adopted personality. The ambassador knew that British intelligence had asked for help but did not want to get too deeply involved.

Finally, Alexander left for Vichy – the seat of Pétain's government and the American embassy attached to it – in order to obtain further travel permits. There he was told to proceed to Paris for permission to continue deeper into occupied Europe.

In Paris trouble awaited. Somehow the Americans in Vichy did not know that the building on Avenue Kléber where Alexander had been told to report had meanwhile been requisitioned by the Gestapo. It had been a dependency of the

American embassy dealing with passport control and intelligence, but was not American property and therefore not protected by diplomatic immunity.

When Alexander arrived little security existed yet outside the building. In the dusk no one stopped him from entering. Inside, however, two towering guards confronted him. They were aggressive too. A harrowing experience followed as Alexander found himself in the lion's den. He steeled himself to brazen it out, pretended not to know any German and therefore not to understand what they were saying. He waved his American passport at them and demanded in a loud voice to know where the Yankees had moved to. The guards did not understand him, grasped him by the arm and proceeded to take him further inside.

In the commotion that ensued a Gestapo officer came out, a stocky young man and supremely arrogant. His arrogance saved Alexander who repeated his request, trying hard to imitate a real Yankee drawl and shake off his captors. The result was as unexpected as useful. The officer wanted to show off his knowledge of the world and impress his subordinates by replying in Teutonic English. He took Alexander's passport, noticed the many stamps – including several in German surrounded by swastikas – and ordered the guards to release their captive. Pursuing his newly acquired role as a Yankee, Alexander slapped the officer on the shoulder, snatched the passport and left, shouting 'Thanks, pal,' to the beaming officer.

At a brisk pace he walked down the Avenue Kléber to the river Seine and found himself opposite the Eiffel Tower before remembering that Vanden Heuvel had asked him to pay his respects to some old French acquaintances. This he did and made friends for life with a charming middle-aged couple. The husband was a lawyer with numerous then unexplained contacts. As a result Alexander was advised to travel to Holland at once without bothering to search for an American presence in the French capital. This Alexander also did.

The Flemings showed their happiness with an abundance of pats on the shoulder – from Arthur – and kisses – from Gertrude. It soon became clear that this exuberance had its roots in something more than the pleasure of welcoming a friend. News had just arrived of Charles's death. They were also worried about their son Michael because he had not confided in his parents while clearly involved in resistance activities. Not all was lost, however. Charles's execution meant that he had suffered and died without incriminating anyone. And Alexander could offer reassurance about Michael, on whom he relied to provide the link with Britain until the arrival of new operators.

Alexander met up with Michael at the home of mutual friends in The Hague, where he shared the second floor of the house with his girlfriend Dorothy and his transmitter. Alexander did not like this arrangement but found it difficult to say so. Dorothy was a small busty young lady with very blond hair and very lively. Why involve an innocent girl in such dangerous activities? Was it not a threat to security? When Alexander finally found an opportunity to point this out, Michael laughed. Dorothy came with the flat, the top floor of the house of a respected judge, whose daughter she was. He appreciated Alexander's concern, however, and promised to look for alternative premises for the transmitter, though not for the girl.

Wiardi Beckman was still refusing to leave Holland for London. But recent progress suggested an autumn departure might be convenient.

Alexander also convinced Laura to change from her communist operator to another one with direct access to Britain. He had Michael in mind but also hoped to arrange for another operator to be sent with a transmitter soon after his return to London. She should meanwhile continue to supply the communist with information, but slow it down, thus avoiding suspicion. He further suggested that the Apostles concentrate on general information and forget about the military, for which they were ill-equipped. Laura agreed readily, for she herself had come to appreciate that collecting military details required military expertise which none of the Apostles possessed.

During his fortnight in Holland, Alexander had to visit American consular offices in Amsterdam and Rotterdam in his guise of Jack Taylors, to keep the Gestapo happy. In this he was successful, and he left by train for Paris, where his new found friends told him he could continue by train directly to Spain, an immense relief.

Towards the end of April Alexander reported back to Bruce Crane and Uncle Steve van Alblas.

Chapter Thirteen

THE APOSTLES
RESURRECTED

The Dutch summer of 1941 presented its usual two faces in an extravagant manner: sunshine galore during June and July but an August of rain and cold. The weather reflected the two faces of the nazi authorities. From August onwards decrees restricting freedom multiplied. Slowly it dawned on the Dutch that Seyss-Inquart's aim was to nazify Holland as thoroughly as his master had nazified Germany.

The enemies of this process – whether individuals or groups – had to be intimidated or eliminated. As a warning, individuals could still be dealt with sternly without killing them. Groups were a different matter altogether.

Individuals whom the nazis considered important or opposed to their regime – usually both – began to be taken as hostages, first in tens, then in hundreds. After a failed attempt by saboteurs to blow up a train carrying German troops in Rotterdam, the first five hostages were shot on 15 August 1942. Many such barbarous executions were to follow.

Of the groups, the first targets comprised Jews and communists. On 11 June 1941 a raid in Amsterdam rounded up several hundred male Jews, another on 30 June took in 500 communists. All ended up in camps. None survived.

Next Seyss-Inquart assaulted the professions, replacing existing associations with nazified Chambers into which members were accepted not only for their professional skill but also for their political stance, either embracing nazism or at least acquiescing in its dominance. Among others, Chambers were created for Medicine and Culture, the latter subdivided into Guilds for painting with sculpture, architecture, music, theatre with film and dance, literature with publishing, and journalism. Fortunately it took months to put the decrees into effect, which allowed protest and resistance to build up. Thus doctors could set up their clandestine Medical Contact on 24 August 1941 long before the nazis installed their Medical Chamber on 20 December.

In mid-January 1942 a represenative group of prominent artists addressed a manifesto to Seyss-Inquart. 'The ideas behind the Cultural Chamber and the way it will be organized are incompatible with traditional Dutch artistic calling. It is alien to the spiritual conditions of an artist's life and conflicts with his duty as an artist because it subordinates art to political principles.' Non-membership, of course, implied no public performance, exhibition, publication or building, therefore no income. Adri Roland Holst, the revered poet with whom my father and I had the significant talk during our summer holiday, on receiving a personal request to join, replied that 'the invitation appears not to be a Dutch cultural but a German police measure, which as such I must, of course, respect. However, as the leader of the Cultural Chamber will decide on my being accepted, I equally respectfully express the hope that I will be denied this privilege. Culture cannot be changed into Kultur on police authority.' His letter was widely distributed. The police were at once despatched to his home in the dunes, which he had prudently left to go into hiding, permanently as it turned out.

These decrees affected my family in several ways. One of them was that an element of nazification was aryanization, the exclusion of the Jews. Jewish musicians were barred from orchestras, national, local, or symphonie or brass bands. Nor were they henceforth permitted to perform publicly before non-Jewish audiences. However, the decree forgot to prohibit them from performing privately, at least initially. As a result concerts came to be organized on a non-public basis in schools and homes during the autumn of 1941 and much of 1942. My 'aryan' parents were among those who invited banned musicians – mostly but not exclusively Jews – to perform at

165

our house without fee for friends, many standing or sitting on the floor. Contributions were invited and collected in bags, as in Dutch churches. A fixed entrance charge would have made them public performances and also raised less money.

There were many such events, but one in particular stands out in my memory. During one extraordinary evening my expatriate Spanish cello teacher – Thomas Canivez, non-Jewish – and his expatriate Hungarian accompanist – Geza Frid, a Jewish composer – suddenly stopped playing Brahms' Sonata Opus 38 after the slow second movement. The pianist apologized to the incredulous audience with an astonishing excuse: he wanted to listen to Hitler. He left for the dining room where we kept our radio hidden. No one followed him except me, to explain how it worked. I stayed, watching him as he listened to one of those harangues that maddened most but mesmerized others. Why had he chosen to disrupt a friendly audience and a fellow musician to listen to such rabble-rousing rubbish?

'Hitler is a great artist, a genius in politics.'

'But you're one of his victims!'

'That's different. One can admire one's adversaries.'

'In a civilized society yes, but . . .'

'But this is a civilized society: you and your friends. I'll continue to behave in a civilized manner regardless. If Hitler or his henchmen choose to arrest me, *tant pis*. No one can stop them. But that doesn't give me licence to copy their methods. I hope never to lose my soul that way.'

I had to be content with this. As we re-entered the drawing room the chattering audience fell silent. Frid strode to the grand piano, looked at Canivez, nodded and they resumed with the sonata's gutsy third and last movement, in gay abandon.

At another concert Luke turned up with his parents. I liked him as much as I disliked his friend Matthew. He would be a good doctor, a pillar of society once we returned to normality. He did not say much but on leaving patted my shoulder and whispered: 'Don't worry. Matthew s lost his way, not his soul.'

At a third such session someone asked whether I could help

Jewish friends of his to escape. It came as a shock for I had been careful to hide my resistance activities. As one of the financial supporters of *Het Parool* he may well have made a considered guess at my wider involvement. I pretended innocence. Helping Jews escape to freedom meant not only crossing frontiers, but obtaining false identity cards and Belgian and French currency. All this would surely endanger my other activities, the very mixture Uncle Stuuf had warned against.

After our confrontation with Matthew, Laura and I did not meet for some time, to test whether he had acted as promised. He had: no Gestapo turned up. I was kept very busy with *Het Parool* and Wiardi Beckman's meetings. They included prominent leaders of various parties but also many outside the political mainstream, as well as editors of the increasingly successful newspaper. The basis was laid for the Great Civic Committee mentioned on page 43. In late June Laura and I met again and invited Luke for a reunion. On one of the first days the sun gave warmth, the three of us got together at the beach to make our meeting appear casual. Neither Laura nor Luke knew of my other activities, of course. While cooling our feet in the sea an unexpected turn in the conversation showed that the mutual trust between us had weathered Matthew's defection.

I was unprepared when Laura, usually the leader, invited suggestions for future apostolic activities. I muttered something vague about the need to maintain contact. But Luke opened up. Dejected by Matthew's inexplicable behaviour, he had avoided us for the same reason that Laura and I had not met. But, still determined to be active, he had sought other activists and found them. One was a young lawyer deeply involved with the OD, one an architect and the third a police inspector, all in The Hague. They needed a transmitter for getting important information to England. Did Laura still have access to one?

To his utter surprise – though not to mine – she replied that she did, a different one, directly connected with England. It was, of course, the one operated by Michael Fleming. Later she admitted to me that she needed material to prove her credentials to Michael.

Luke asked: 'Did you drop your communist friend?'

'He isn't my friend,' Laura replied, 'and I haven't dropped him.'

'Then why the change?'

'Let's say that at the moment the Russians are more interested in what happens in their own country than in ours.' And that was the last time her communist connection was mentioned. By then, of course, Russia and Germany were at war.

In early July Laura and I travelled to The Hague where Luke introduced us to his contacts. Carel was the lawyer, Gerard the architect, Bert – nicknamed Brother – the police inspector. It had been difficult to get them all to meet at the same time. They did not constitute a group and had only been brought together by Luke at the prospect of access to a transmitter. They proved to be much more practical, better informed and with a greater range of contacts than the original Apostles.

The meeting took place in Carel's home in the reasonably desirable part of an even more desirable residential district in the northwest of the town, close to the wood with the little royal palace. In a quiet street with a long terrace of medium-sized three-storey houses, his house lay conveniently close to the main exit road to the north, as well as to the main thoroughfare to the beach at Scheveningen, yet not far from the city centre. Carel often received clients at home and our gathering therefore did not attract attention from neighbours or more dangerous individuals. His charming wife supplied endless rounds of tea and biscuits but otherwise left us to ourselves. Laura's appearance clearly made a great impact on the males present, but she was not in a provocative mood, wearing low-heeled sandals, conservative dress and soft make-up. Her matter-of-fact approach clearly impressed them, as did her quick intelligence and qualities of leadership.

Carel, tall, with dark brown hair and a large though well-trimmed moustache, sat on the edge of a deep armchair, slightly bent forward, elbows on knees, hands together, almost motionless when talking, which he did a great deal and incisively too. He explained that the OD had lost several leaders in rapid succession and was in a shambles, aggravated by the clash between different philosophies about the OD's wartime and postwar function. Clearly he was a key man in the OD.

To us Carel was important because he had access to most ministries, could supply interesting information for the government in exile and was anxious they should receive it. He remarked that resistance was coming of age and should not be confined to military espionage or to sabotage by wild-eyed novices without knowledge of the target or experience of the repercussions for the population. It might also be more important to help the civilian population than to support an imaginary invasion force with news about drunken German soldiers. And, with postwar reconstruction in mind, Carel insisted that the queen and her cabinet needed civilian information. An echo of Wiardi Beckman! Gerard and Brother also contributed interesting suggestions.

Thus the Apostles rose from their ashes. The name 'Apostles' inevitably caused hilarity but it stuck nevertheless, although none chose an Apostolic name for cover.

Laura could now provide Michael with more valuable material for transmission than before. She asked the three new recruits for some samples to begin with, and unexpectedly received them: exchanges between German civilian masters and Dutch civil servants, minutes of meetings of the permanent secretaries, an assessment of the Dutch police's attitude towards German demands for assistance, and a report on the feelings amongst doctors and artists about their respective Chambers. Laura suggested the four documents be given a codename and promised to have them transmitted. They clearly required condensing and she took this task upon herself, with my help. To vouch for her credibility she would ask London to broadcast a radio message in a fortnight to confirm receipt. At our next meeting in early August we should consider what methods to use in future and how to guard secrecy, credentials then having been established, or not. Laura stressed that control should remain with her for the moment: the operator had to be shielded from being swamped with trivial material. The documents in their telescoped version did get through and the radio message was broadcast from London. As a result we were to come together frequently at Carel's home, though irregularly to avoid suspicion. Eventually Carel was introduced to Michael, who happened to live only a few blocks away.

On the return journey in Laura's sports car it became clear that her restraint had increased her tensions and that I had been pre-selected as the recipient of her excess energy. One hand repeatedly left the steering wheel to touch and stroke me until she dropped me off at my home with a swift kiss and without leaving her seat. She explained that my role as a lightning conductor had been essential to sustain her determination to succeed at the meeting. I had no choice but to accept this weird argument with pleasure. After all, the Apostles *were* now reconstituted.

Brother preferred to stay outside the Apostles, though promising full support, because of his delicate position as a member of the police force. Towards the end of that year I learned that his role also hid his many other resistance activities. After one meeting I confessed to Carel my relationship with Wiardi Beckman, a gaffe which I regretted the moment his name was uttered. I need not have worried, for although politically more conservative, Carel shared Uncle Stuuf's religious approach with the passion of a committed Calvinist and admired Uncle Stuuf's practical solutions, proof, if that were needed, of Uncle Stuuf's ability to bridge the political chasm. On the question of whether the military should be subservient to the politicians or vice versa, Carel stood firmly on the side of the politicians. As an equally dedicted reserve officer he would make an ideal addition to the top levels of the OD.

When I duly reported the resurrection to Amanda, little problems emerged to cloud the clear sky of our remarkably lasting relationship. For one thing, I was so involved in resistance activities that she felt somewhat neglected. For another, I tactlessly mentioned Laura's remark about my usefulness as a lightning conductor in conjunction with

Alexander's earlier request of a similar nature. Amanda frowned coolly. Realizing the unintended impact of my innocent gaffe, I protested my eternal love and devotion to her. Typically, Amanda then took another line. To my amazement she suggested I try Laura out and report back with full details. She was probably intrigued to find out what made Laura tick erotically. A clever ploy, for it avoided the absurd incentive to promiscuity that obstinacy supplies. It made her an ally too, which assured her of my ultimate loyalty.

Her advice was soon put to the test. When I arrived at Laura's palatial home for our exercise in reducing twenty pages of bureaucratic jargon to two pages of transmittable gibberish, she had abandoned the subdued attire worn in The Hague, for a sophisticated dress, high-heeled shoes and pronounced make-up. When I remarked that I did not deserve such attention, Laura explained: 'I do it because I'm starved.'

'I don't believe it.'

'You should. It's about time you realised that I'm in love with Alexander and much more loyal to him than you seem to think. There haven't been any others.'

'Then why all the war paint?'

'Because Alexander has chosen you as his stand-in. And like all males you like female war paint, as you so charmingly call it.'

I should have protested about such successive unflattering statements: first I was a lightning conductor, now a stand-in. But I had already lost.

'Amanda doesn't wear any war paint.'

'She's got her super figure. I have to make do with war paint. It's very good for my self confidence. A woman should be proud of herself and show it. Besides, it's a compliment to her companion.'

She smiled, and then became serious.

'Let's get to work. We've got to complete our Apostles job first. You'll have to be patient until it's finished. After that, no holds barred. You can stay the night. Don't worry about Amanda. I've no intention of taking you away from her. She's much better for you than I am.' All my defences had come unstuck and now Laura wanted to work. Patience is not one of my virtues. All I managed was: 'How can I work in this atmosphere?' I protested, my emotions in turmoil. 'I haven't brought a toothbrush either. After all, why me?'

'Because your legs are like war paint to me.'

Torn between desire, loyalty and work, I nevertheless followed Laura's professionalism. We did concentrate on the texts for almost three hours without any amorous diversions and succeeded in construing a credible abridgement. Somehow I then survived a night of passion.

Upon leaving the next morning Laura even suggested that Amanda be informed about the particulars, as she herself would in due course inform Alexander. When I reported to Amanda, she calmly concluded that I must have been a weak surrogate. Having thus deflated my male pride, Amanda restored my self-respect by pointing out that Laura's was, of course, pure animal greed and lacked the tenderness of our love.

Thus did resistance evolve, a random, chaotic, emotional progress. Certain in our determination to do something, we felt uncertain as to what form it should take. The nazis were just starting to demolish that uncertainty by insensitive measures which gave us both direction and method. At that time we were still relatively unhampered by the V-men, whose infiltration was to cause such havoc later on. Arrests were made and executions occurred but on a scale that caused only ripples outside those immediately concerned Initially the Germans were cautious with executions. Thus most of the OD members arrested in the spring of 1941 – including Westerveld and du Tourton Bruyns – were imprisoned and only executed a year later: 72 of them in all.

Slowly, steadily the nazi triumvirate of SD/Gestapo/Grüne Polizei grew in numbers and effectiveness. The two methods used were well-established police procedures: applying pressure on those arrested to obtain information and infiltrating informers into subversive groups. But the nazis came to apply them with a vigour that added a whole new dimension. Pressure turned into torture and spies in the guise of V-men or confidential agents proliferated.

We were totally unprepared and not brought up on a regular diet of *Darkness at Noon, The Gulag Archipelago* or any of the numerous atrocity stories in today's press. We knew nothing about Stalin's excesses and were hardly aware of nazi atrocities. We even felt that betrayal of fellow resisters following arrest showed weakness of character. This is one of the youthful errors of judgement I feel most ashamed of in old age. But we learned fast and realised we had to be careful. Anyone connected with someone arrested – provided one knew about the arrest – had to scramble for safety and go into hiding. For one arrest often led to several others. If arrested we were taught to hold out for a couple of days to allow for that scramble, then feign a breakdown and confess to what was already known. Still, the crude practice differed from the comfortable theory. Nothing much could be done once informers infiltrated.

Most V-men were Dutch, occasionally even arrested resisters threatened with reprisals against members of their family. The nazis had luck on their side when they found several devious Dutchmen prepared to act as resisters, for substantial monetary rewards and very capably too. They infiltrated some groups and in a few instances tricked very security conscious leaders.

This was made easier by a great tragedy, one of the greatest in the history of Dutch resistance.

In March 1942 a Dutch SOE agent was arrested with his transmitter and offered his life if he turned operator for the Germans. He agreed but when contacting Britain omitted his security check. Although the British clerk made a note of its absence on the decoded message – and did so on subsequent occasions – the possibility of arrest was discounted and the agent's lapse put down to working under stress. The British supervisors thus ignored a safety device they had themselves introduced, with tragic consequences. It enabled the nazis to play a wireless game with SOE for eighteen months which cost the lives of some 60 agents, who were all arrested on arrival. But the fall-out for the resistance was infinitely worse. By using an eventual eighteen transmitters, the SD and the Abwehr gained entry into numerous resistance groups. The bonafides of their V-men could now be established by asking the BBC to broadcast a message agreed with the resister or the resisters. That undermined almost any code or other precaution we could take. Hundreds died as a result.

As a victim-manqué I may be forgiven a footnote here. Much has been written about the military aspect of what has come to be known as the England Spiel – in Britain as in Holland – but less about its effect on the resistance. The military failure was a battle lost, with the sad loss of 60 lives but little impact on the war. For at the time Holland lay outside the battle areas and some lines of communication were kept open in other ways. But the impact on our resistance was devastating and continuous, with at least ten if not twenty times the loss of life as well as a poisoning of the atmosphere. Thus the most notorious V-man could continue to substantiate his credibility with messages from the BBC and infiltrate the painstakingly built up master-organization of the resistance, the Great Civic Committee. In addition it offered the nazis the opportunity to enlarge their small band of V-men. As will be seen, one of them came to cause me infinite trouble, while Alexander became involved in clearing up the ashes and recreating a viable espionage operation.

For this abject SOE failure I have no new evidence to offer. There have been many investigations over the past 45 years and none support any other conclusion than human fallibility. Yet some commentators continue to dabble in conspiracy theories, either nazi traitors or communist moles in Britain. I do not believe any of them, nor does Alexander. They all depend too much on human perfection and ignore human imperfection.

The England Spiel originated in Holland – not Britain – on 31 August 1941, seven months before the wireless game could start. On that day one of the operators whom Charles had set up was caught with all his messages in clear and in code. He refused to talk but German experts gradually unravelled the code. Later a V-man infiltrated another espionage group and supplied it with information concocted by the Germans to trap its operator, the first one sent by SOE. When he was finally tracked down and arrested he carried the coded message with this information. During his interrogation he appreciated the

Germans' inside knowledge, which even included the existence of security checks. But he spotted the gap in their knowledge: they did not know which check. Therefore he decided to co-operate in order to warn SOE in Britain. And caught them off guard. New agents were sent to dropping zones where the nazis awaited them.

A series of coincidences had combined to enable the Germans to play a wireless game, which they proceeded to do with great care and ingenuity. So did the British, when MI5 successfully used captured German agents to play a similar game with the Germans (the XX or Double Cross System). Conspiracy afficionados will point out that some such co-incidences could have provided the traitor-mole in Britain with his opportunity. It could not, for this assumes the presence in Britain of the masterminds and the massive resources of a well-organized machine which the Germans used. No one of the conspiracy theorists has ever suggested that such a nest of traitors or moles existed in hostile Britain.

The shrewd way the Germans used the Spiel for their V-men caught the resistance at a vulnerable stage. We did not take rumours about infiltrators very seriously, as the story of Matthew illustrates. We knew everyone else in our groups. We had yet to acquire the professionalism which ultimately defeated this German ploy. The revived Apostles were still friends and functioned well for quite some time.

Chapter Fourteen

ALEXANDER LANGUISHES IN LONDON WHILE DISASTER STRIKES

Alexander's debriefing straddled a quiet weekend and lasted more than forty exhausting hours on either side, spread over four days. Much of it was taken up by gazing into the crystal ball to see Germany's future. It was early May 1941. Germany's future looked bright. Hitler firmly controlled a large part of the continent. Surprisingly no one queried Alexander's revelation of the imminent attack on Russia, all seemed to accept it as a fact. If that venture were handled in the same effective military way, Hitler would soon be in charge of all continental Europe. To discuss his demise and what was to happen after sounded rather unreal in a prostrate Britain. But his interrogators doggedly pursued their questioning. After all, Britain had stood up alone for almost a year. Somehow it would muddle through.

Alexander faced seven people in all, six men and one woman, in succession not at once. The woman was an attractive blonde of around thirty, who probed Alexander on his relationship with Irena and started flirting with him, presumably to test his reaction to the opposite sex and disclose a vulnerable side. As they were leaving after the last meeting she suggested dinner, out of everyone's hearing and for the following Saturday. He accepted with alacrity: a free meal in the presence of a beautiful lady should not be refused. They went to a quiet place. He thoroughly enjoyed the evening.

Conversation was highly intelligent without touching unduly on Intelligence. She referred to Irena only once, briefly and innocently. Then, near the end of the meal, she subtly but unmistakably invited him to bed. Sorely tempted, Alexander nevertheless gently declined. Back in his flat alone, he suddenly realised that at no time during those elaborate interviews had he mentioned the frolics with Irena. A surprise, because he could not find a good reason for an omission which the shrewd intelligence officers must have considered. They were much too polite to say so openly and might therefore have interpreted his silence in a sinister way. As it did not materially affect any of the issues, he decided that continued silence would be the best course. When at their next meeting he enquired of Bruce Crane about the lady's motives, it produced one of the dour man's rare outbursts of laughter. The poor girl had fallen for Alexander and had faithfully reported her regret that the affair had not been consummated.

The discussions on the implications of Hitler's demise and its possible repercussions led nowhere. His questioners agreed only that little else could be done than monitor developments. At the last session Crane confirmed that this would become Alexander's job. However, they disagreed on almost everything else, particularly about the weight to attach to German resistance. Alexander detected distrust of Germans, all Germans, and a coolness towards his contacts.

One opinion made him cringe: by all means let the Krauts do their own dirty washing and if they needed soap it could be provided, but were not all Germans sullied, pro- and anti-nazis alike? This attitude was to bedevil his work for the next eighteen months.

One man from the Foreign Office kept referring to Europe as a separate entity from the British Isles, which provoked Alexander. 'You're only twenty miles from France!' he said sharply. 'Japan is 120 miles from its continent, yet it's part of Asia. The British Isles have been populated by successive waves of Belgae, Romans, Saxons, Angles, Normans, Huguenots and sundry other tribes. They shoved the Celts aside and the Celts too originated in Central Europe. Britain belongs as much to Europe as Crete and Sardinia. What else could it belong to?'

To Alexander's sense of fun his adversary retorted: 'To the world. History can be used to prove anything, like the Bible. We live in the present, not in the past. No invader has succeeded since William the Conquerer. Those twenty miles of sea are quite enough to keep unwanted foreigners at bay. And all those tribal invaders amalgamated with the local population. They adopted local customs, in some cases initiated changes. As a result a coherent nation was forged.'

'*Touché*!' It did not, of course, resolve the issue. 'Still, Britain did involve itself voluntarily in the continental war. You started it. Surely you want to help shape its destiny?'

'Unfortunately yes, to some extent. That depends on the outcome of the war.'

'But also on the people who will lead the nations after its end. Therefore also on the men of the German resistance. You'll have to take an interest in them.'

'We do, we do. Would your German chaps listen to what we might have to say? And not try to hold on to the Sudetenland, slices of Poland and Austria and whatever else they happen to have seized?'

That was indeed a problem. In need of a receptive audience, Alexander asked Crane for another meeting with his boss. The request was granted at once. They were four in Alexander's flat for drinks: Crane, Menzies, van Alblas and Alexander. Alexander voiced his unhappiness: 'I'm afraid, Sir, German resistance doesn't seem to be taken seriously. The anti-nazis deserve a more receptive audience.'

Menzies puffed at his pipe, a glass of whisky in the other hand untouched. He appeared to be deep in thought and took a sip before speaking. He did not mince his words, yet contrived to make them sound kind.

'The evaluation of German resistance is a political matter,' he said. 'Decisions rest with Mr Churchill, not with civil servants. We only collect information and summarize it as impartially as possible. There are more sources of information than yours. The Prime Minister has to decide on facts not foibles. We wouldn't have offered you this rather delicate job if we doubted the quality of your German friends or distrusted your approach.'

Alexander could do no more. Yet he wondered. A chasm had opened up between two apparently conflicting loyalties. It seemed quixotic to fight a moral battle for one set of Germans in the midst of a military battle against another. Distrust of all Germans had infected Britain as much as the countries on the continent. The moral imperative for the crusade against nazism was swamped by the military imperative to wipe out its physical presence. All Alexander could do now was to make the best of a job so generously offered: monitor events conscientiously and try to foster the spirit of the moral crusade as and when an opportunity arose.

Alexander was allotted an office in Broadway, Westminster, and had to find a flat of his own, which he did, in Earls Court. He became a fairly independent part of a group of five. Soon enough he discovered there were many sources, including intercepted German wireless traffic. It taught him how to unravel fact from fiction and put the pieces together. And to look at messages from agents with a more critical eye than, as an agent himself, he would have liked. Masses of documents passed through his hands. They took much time to read, digest and file properly. Dangerously, they also tended to induce a false feeling of achievement which diverted attention from the real issues. Still, he appreciated why he was being employed in London and not in Switzerland, and said so in the few guarded letters he was able to send to Irena, in which he assured her and her co-conspirators that their material was receiving due attention. But his moral crusade, however dispassionately presented, failed to penetrate the screen of anti-German feeling which he suspected stemmed ultimately from the Foreign Secretary Anthony Eden himself. And Churchill is alleged to have remarked that he had little time for chivalrous windbags.

Postwar research has confirmed this impression, though the problem was a lot more complex than need be explained here. The resistance in Germany was suspect and opportunities were lost. One of Alexander's interrogators, Maurice Oldfield, who went on to occupy in the 1970's the same position that Menzies had in the 1940's, admitted after his retirement in the 1980's that chances were missed to finish the war earlier by

179

neglecting the German resistance and mistreating Canaris, who had been a vital factor in the Allies' favour. There were a few in the British establishment who discredited both Canaris and the resistance. One man had a particular interest in doing so: Kim Philby, uncovered twenty years later as a Russian mole. It was not in the Russians' interest to promote a democratic Germany.

All this sapped Alexander's energy. His disappointment made him gradually focus more on events in Holland and ultimately led to his decision to quit. Crane had demanded that Alexander should not be tempted away by any Dutch authority for at least a year. His job was important and should not be compromised by other involvements. But he was nonetheless allowed some contact with a chosen few.

Wiardi Beckman had given Alexander three documents to take to London. One was a very long 'Memorandum concerning the position of Holland during the German occupation'. It had mainly been written by the chairman of his party and edited by Beckman. It described in passionate terms the potential conflict between politicians and militarists and requested support for an underground provisional government to avoid a military take-over. It assumed the end of the war to be imminent and gave a detailed situation report. The second paper was a one-page summary of the tasks for a transitional government, the third an equally succinct statement of intent for postwar reconstruction, both by Uncle Stuuf.

One day Alexander and his uncle, Baron van Alblas, were taken to the queen by her charming ADC, the son of the vice-president of the Council of State, whom they found present as well. The venue was a large villa called Stubbings inside a well-walled garden just outside Maidenhead, an unpretentious and unimaginative home for the queen, comfortable and bourgeois. After living for sixty years in the grandeur of palaces she disdained ostentation, one way of showing sympathy with her beleaguered subjects. It did not, however, lessen her regality or her insistence on formality. Indeed, she chided those – like some of her ministers – whom she accused of petty-bourgeois attitudes. But within those sometimes awkward constrictions she was generous and considerate. Tea with biscuits became her hallmark for no other reason than that it was a Dutch custom, like wearing a hat when outside on all occasions, rain or shine. In her spare time she fiercely knitted socks and woollies for her deprived subjects once they were liberated. Still, she could be devastatingly sharp, unaware that the recipient of her scathing remarks might be hurt and was prevented by protocol from responding in kind. Her obstinacy may well have derived from a strain in the Oranges but it was fostered by the conflicting pressures of old-fashioned values and the demands of a modern world. Her upbringing had been restricted, one-sided and unfinished, her marriage a sad failure. Her simple religious ideas bordered on the puritanical. Yet this turbulent mixture produced the powerful personality needed in the circumstances. Churchill called her the only man amongst exiled statesmen.

The four of them sat in comfortable easy chairs, the queen on a higher straight-backed armchair which held her ample body and offset her diminutive stature. Abundant grey hair topped a slightly pudgy face and bluish eyes that often looked blank and undistinguished but could dispense bolts of lightning at times. She looked like a mother hen and was very much in charge of the proceedings.

'I'm most impressed by the clarity of thought in Dr Wiardi Beckman's brief papers,' the queen began. 'Of course I also appreciate the long paper, but it strikes me as rather verbose and imbalanced.'

Alexander winced, hesitated, then replied: 'Perhaps, Ma'am. May I point out that the author is a very volatile man and lives under great stress. He sincerely feels that a confrontation with some of the new OD leaders is inevitable. That would be disastrous for democracy and hamper the effective coordination of the resistance. Dr Wiardi Beckman simply waited and then summarized. I can assure Your Majesty that they have no quarrel with each other.'

The queen smiled. 'But perhaps there's a difference in emphasis.'

'Indeed, Ma'am,' Alexander agreed. 'Or rather a difference in approach. Dr Beckman agrees that a potential danger exists. Which is why he got military and civilians together. He relies more on the common sense of the OD leaders and is convinced that common interest will prevail.'

Again the queen smiled: 'That was a most loyal defence, Mr Paul. Still, the long paper concentrates a lot on the excellence of pre-war institutions, whereas the brief ones breathe an awareness of their weaknesses and a readiness to consider changes.'

Alexander nodded. 'Dr Beckman looks for strong personalities with an open mind. These would be more dispassionate when considering existing institutions, including political parties and their dogmas.'

'Talking about dogmas!' said the queen, laughing, 'One of Dr Beckman's papers reads like the Ten Commandments. Except there are only five.'

Alexander smiled happily: 'That was the point, Ma'am. As an exercise he reduced political dogmas to three principles and added two more to appease others. Party programmes so often tend to present each wish as a dogma. With fewer "commandments" action can be more relevant and visible.'

The vice-president broke in: 'Do I understand, Mr Paul, that Dr Wiardi Beckman tries to build bridges?'

'Yes, Sir,' Alexander replied. 'One has already been built. Leaders of the parties and other people from different walks of life are on it. Quite an achievement in our fractionalized country. And more important than blueprints. But the bridge is still rather rickety. That's why some sanction from Her Majesty would help.'

'Are you suggesting a rival government, Mr Paul?' asked the queen teasingly.

There was restrained laughter, then silence, as all eyes turned to Alexander, who found himself at a loss. The vice-president came to the rescue. 'May I suggest that Your Majesty might like the bridge to be kept intact? The legitimate ministers could eventually join their illegitimate colleagues in reconstructing our nation.'

The queen said quickly: 'I'm not eager to argue about illegitimacy. But I do like the idea of coordinating the resistance and having a bulwark against my legally constituted fuddy-duddies.'

She promised to reflect on the issues raised. They proved to be pointers to the future. After the defeat of nazism the weary population would rejoice to find a widely representative team ready to revise the state's institutions. As reported, such co-operation did come about in Holland, boosted by the support of queen and Cabinet. And good intentions for postwar renewal proliferated. Unfortunately, the war went on for nearly four more years, the weariness turned into exhaustion, the good intentions failed to pave any way. The College of Confidants, when it finally emerged as the 'rival' underground government, could only mop up, not map out. One of the reasons for this book's title.

Much philosophizing went on in this and similar meetings. Also in Holland. Uncle Stuuf, however, realised that lofty ideals might all too soon evaporate once the pressures of war had been lifted. Hence his stress on bridge-building rather than blueprinting. We underestimated the danger inherent in this emphasis on people. It proved a mortal danger, for once those people disappeared behind bars and into graves the bridge would be left unmanned. And too many did do disappear.

The queen avoided taking sides but made it abundantly clear that she was as addicted to renewal as she was to consensus. Her razor-sharp mind cut out woolly thoughts ruthlessly, impatiently and occasionally unkindly.

Sometime later Uncle Steve took Alexander to see their prime minister. He expressed admiration for the documents and informed them that arrangements were being made to extract Dr Wiardi Beckman from Holland to join the cabinet as deputy prime minister. He did not say when or how. This worried Alexander. To extract someone from Holland in late 1941 presented a problem that could not be solved as easily as Alexander's when he had slipped in and out of his native country disguised as an American consular official. Escape routes were strewn with failed attempts and some corpses. But Alexander had a reliable address in Paris, as they must have known, and he felt sure that his French hosts would be able to organize a safe route into Spain. Remembering my Belgian friends, he also envisaged sending a message to me with the request to accompany Uncle Stuuf on what would in any case be a perilous journey.

Discreet enquiries revealed that the head of MI6 Dutch section was in charge of the plans together with van 't Sant. A few young Dutchmen had recently arrived after a daring escape from Holland, two of them, like Alexander, alumni of Leyden University. They were intelligent, knowledgeable and keen. They would be tutored by Crane's MI6 colleague as well as van 't Sant. SIS resourses were at their disposal. It sounded a competent team and Alexander felt satisfied with these gallant musketeers.

It remains on his conscience to this day that he failed to persist in questioning the plan in detail. Had he done so, Alexander's ideas about a land journey could have been pitted against the sea route that was chosen. The various dangers could have been more carefully considered.

On our side, in Holland, we aired our reservations the moment Uncle Stuuf received the news, a message from the queen in her own handwriting. It was then already late in November. I offered at once to take him to my friends in Antwerp and make a recce to Paris. Uncle Stuuf even remembered the address in Paris that Alexander had discovered. He nevertheless refused to consider my proposal for one decisive reason: Her Majesty had sent a messenger – a reliable one too – and she would have made sure the escape route was the best available in the circumstances. He remained unshaken in his trust even when several attempts had failed and winter set in with a vengeance.

The original plan to land agents and transmitters on the Dutch coast was not designed to collect prospective prime ministers. One-way traffic had been envisaged, not two-way. That would add another dimension and demand exquisite timing.

An MGB with a speed of 50 knots would set out, taking less than five hours to cross the North Sea. Such speed would enable it to skim over sea mines. Near the Dutch coast two of its engines would be cut, the noiseless third driving it along at 8 knots to within half a mile of the coast. There the agents would transfer to a dinghy which would take them through the breakers and drop them into the sea to wade the last few yards to the shore. Agents would be dressed in a dinner jacket, protected by a bulky waterproof overall, which a companion was to retrieve and take back to the dinghy. To avoid being spotted, the crossing had to take place during darkness, with a little light from a tiny moon. In addition, the sea had to be reasonably calm near the coast, the breakers of the surf small, which meant an easterly wind. All these conditions prevailed for only a few days each month. Moreover, a curfew was in operation between midnight and 4 am. Landing and collecting therefore had to be carried out just before or just after.

The landing site chosen was even more audacious: the beach in front of the Palace Hotel on the seafront boulevard at Scheveningen. It housed the headquarters of German coastal defence for the entire sector from Denmark to Spain. There were several reasons for this unusual choice. The musketeers were familiar with Scheveningen and could recognize its skyline in the dark. There were many houses, and trams ran frequently to the main railway station in nearby The Hague. Most of the Dutch shore had been booby-trapped, but because of the German passion for swimming the officers' beach in front of their headquarters remained clear. Nightlife in the town just behind was lively and not yet restricted to Germans. Drunks of both nationalities frequented the boulevards. Hence the agents' evening dress which would be liberally sprinkled with brandy.

However, the sea crossing might last a little longer, the breakers turn out to be a little higher, the MGB slightly off course. Landing an agent by sea was not much different from parachuting one in: the hours mattered, the minutes did not. Collecting someone demanded much more precise timing and siting. The person to be collected could not stay too long on a forbidden beach without being detected. Collector and collected might miss each other in the dark. It also required a properly functioning wireless communication. Although their plan – called Contact Holland – did envisage such collections eventually, the musketeers wanted to practise first on a few operations to test its feasibility. And, of course, for strictly military, not political purposes. Unaware that Wiardi Beckman was intended to become deputy prime minister, they called him a 'bloody politician'.

The musketeers set out to sea six times between mid-October and late November 1941 and had to return six times without achieving anything, though for different reasons. The engines broke down several times, the windscreen shattered once, they went off course twice. At the seventh attempt, on the night of 22–23 November, the messenger with the queen's request was finally put ashore. A wireless operator, parachuted a week earlier, had not been heard of. The messenger would therefore have to find out what had happened to him as well as approach and convince Wiardi Beckman. They were to be collected three days later – a tight schedule.

Uncle Stuuf and the messenger duly arrived at the beach in evening dress as arranged, but there was no one to pick them up. The MGB had left a little late, found itself fifteen miles south and had to return without making contact. Thanks to Brother, our Apostolic Michael Fleming used his transmitter to relay messages to London. As a result four more attempts followed, all of which failed, three times due to the weather unexpectedly turning bad, the fourth time because the correct signal was omitted. The boating party landed, but did not find anyone. Each time Uncle Stuuf and the messenger went to a safe-house near the beach, donned evening dress, sprinkled themselves with brandy and walked out into the freezing cold, only to have to return again. Somehow they never despaired.

For the next six weeks Uncle Stuuf kept away from all but the most urgent contacts, hiding with a relative in The Hague. He neglected his wife and two young daughters. They had already suffered from his failure to pay them the attention they deserved during the preceding eighteen months, as he came to be more and more engrossed in resistance activities. I met him twice during those agonizing weeks when he was preparing himself mentally for an utterly different task in utterly different circumstances. He had come to relish the idea of working with Queen Wilhelmina. She might be stubborn, but so was he, and he sensed a great empathy. He did not doubt that the same approach which had proved so successful in the resistance would succeed in England as well: bridge-building by patiently trying to find common ground on the basis of deeply held convictions. After all, the Great Circle Committee – as it soon came to be called – existed in embryo and would shortly start functioning as an umbrella organization covering the broad church of resisters. He told me that I should maintain contact with one of its designated secretaries, Freek van Hattum, an Amsterdam lawyer with five initials (F.W.D.C.A.), and watch developments in the OD. Sadly the OD was once again leaderless and in turmoil after another round of arrests. Uncle Stuuf hoped Charles would rise to its top because though young he sounded sensible.

Once, in broad daylight, we ventured out and strolled along the boulevard, and he pointed out the stretch of beach where he would be picked up. I shuddered as he recounted earlier failures and pleaded with him to let me take him to Paris and the address he told me Alexander had given him. But he retained his confidence in the sea route and I too became impressed by the boldness of the plan. It remains on my conscience that like Alexander I was too easily swayed by its sheer audacity and failed to push any more. After all, my cross-border ventures had not been foolproof either.

Uncle Stuuf's absence came to be noticed and created rumours as the weeks went by. The explanation for his virtual disappearance – illness – did not satisfy everyone. As a result of pressure from various groups two more people were to use this unique opportunity to reach England. They joined the escape party at another attempt on the night of 17–18 January: Frans Goedhart, founding editor of *Het Parool* and, to Uncle Stuuf's delight, a young representative of the OD. His presence would avoid conflict in future because the OD would be represented and potential conflicts could be discussed before they might be able to do any damage.

Another result was more serious: the Abwehr too came to know about this attempt, a week before the due date. In retrospect it is surprising that none of the German intelligence units had been aware of the previous goings on. There had been talk of course. Yet it was not garrulousness that upset the carefully sheltered plans but the breakthrough achieved by the V-men. The most notorious of them – van der Waals – had established a relationship of trust with a senior member of the OD who was involved in the choice of its young representative for the sea trip. Van der Waals reported to the Abwehr boss, Hermann Giskes. It formed part of the preliminaries that led to the England Spiel, in which both were to play decisive roles.

Giskes heard only that three people were to be collected from the beach between 11 pm and 1 am on the night when Radio Orange opened its broadcast with the national anthem spoken instead of played. When this happened Giskes distributed guards along the beach, some with a machine gun. That was abandoned at 1 am when no one had turned up. The senior OD man had not known the departure was timed for 4.30 am. As a precaution, Giskes nevertheless kept several guards on duty. A large group of Dutchmen went to the beach shortly after 4 am in 20° C of frost. Three of them hid in a disused bunker to shelter from the numbing cold, two went to the water's edge, then into the sea for fear their dark shapes might be spotted against the white, iced beach. As indeed they were. The guards then searched the beach and found Uncle Stuuf, Frans Goedhart and a temporary assistant in their hideout. Their capture satisfied the guards — who therefore failed to spot the two others — because three had been the number mentioned. They marched off to the hotel and did not bother about the two in the sea. These came out, covered in ice and marched in the opposite direction without being accosted.

Thus, after a seven-week delay, the operation came to a disastrous end. This time too the MGB failed to arrive. It had left East Anglia late, turned up fifteen miles north and eventually returned to England. It tried again the next night, safely landing two agents. The two Dutchmen who had so miraculously escaped the previous night's arrests, having heard the national anthem spoken again, went to the designated spot, again in evening dress, but were halted on the boulevard by a German patrol, thus failing once again to reach the rendezvous. Fortune smiled on them again, however, for Brother had been following them, saw their arrest and used his badge as a police inspector to bully the Germans into releasing their captives into his care. The two reached London the following April via the land route. The musketeers had no idea about these events and returned to the safety of East Anglia.

Michael sent wireless messages to London with the news of the disaster. This did not stop the activities of the musketeers. Several more agents and transmitters were successfully beached, though at other places along the Dutch coast. But no more attempts were made to collect anyone. Contact Holland was wound up early that summer, a victim of rivalries between various Dutch authorities.

Despite the numerous mishaps, no one in authority in Britain called off what had clearly become a foolhardy operation. Ineptitude bordering on incompetence allowed a brave appetite for action to eclipse vigilance, and pride to take precedence over wisdom. Not unlike the England Spiel that had just started. But, unlike the England Spiel, no one has ever suggested treason as the cause of this disaster.

The British naval officer, who had rowed the dinghy and waited for many hours near the surf, received the MWO, the Dutch equivalent of the VC. So did the musketeers for their perseverance and physical courage, from a queen who bypassed convention and the military committee that awards this highest decoration for valour.

Uncle Stuuf's perseverance was rewarded by imprisonment. Holland had lost a prime minister designate, the resistance an indispensable leader, and I an irreplaceable mentor.

Chapter Fifteen
MY JEWISH QUESTION

Occasional intense actions, like that just described, should not hide the fact that inactivity was our constant companion. Take the naval officer in the dingy, bobbing up and down for most of a freezing night, waiting for passengers who might not turn up. Or the men on the shore, waiting for a radio signal that might never come. Or Wiardi Beckman during those seven weeks of enforced idleness, with action only on five out of fifty days. For me too the autumn of 1941 and the winter of 1942 harboured too many hours and days devoid of meaning. Some were filled with private tutorials, some with gathering material and distributing underground papers, a lot with reading, others with theatrical rehearsals.

That severe winter the amateur dramatic society mentioned on page 7 rehearsed a play incongrously entitled *Summer Madness*. Its cast included Alexander's brother Peter, my erstwhile school classmate. Somehow we had never made use of him in our resistance work. The reason for this neglect seemed simple then, though less convincing in retrospect: strict rules of silence. Peter is also reticent by nature; he never imposes himself on anyone nor seeks action for its own sake. Moreover, he then studied at Delft University, where he got involved in subversive activities as unsatisfactory as those of the Apostles mark I. To his utter surprise, he was arrested. Fortunately he had to face a judge who was a professional German navy officer, not a professional nazi. The officer in turn was surprised, at the lack of evidence, and quickly acquitted Peter. Still, the seven days he spent in jail caused him a severe shock. They also gave Peter time to reflect on the poor prospects for effective resistance. So, one day in March 1942, he left Holland and ended up in Switzerland. There Peter found a more congenial and – as it turned out – immensely important job with Willem Visser 't Hooft, the Dutch Secretary-General of the World Council of Churches in Geneva. Dr Visser 't Hooft had been empowered by the Dutch cabinet-in-exile to establish regular contact with occupied Holland. At his request, Peter went back to Holland to set up staging posts between the two countries for smuggling documents of military and civilian value in microfilm, which would be passed on to the Dutch government in London. On his return to Geneva at the end of 1942 Peter had opened up the very route which Alexander and I had vainly tried to establish earlier. A regular fortnightly courier service ensued which also delivered copies of most underground newspapers.

He did not know about us, nor did we about him, evidence that not all resisters talked too much. To talk or not to talk, that was indeed one of the basic questions. Without talk no worthwhile contacts could be made, no agent dropped from England could find a foothold, no persecuted people find a home to hide. The evolution from Political Convention through the Great Civic Committee and ultimately to the College of Confidants would have been impossible without talk, nor would the underground press have achieved its professional quality and vast readership. Without such risks being taken by wave upon wave of resisters – where women came to outnumber men – no resistance would have been possible and without resistance in both its active and its passive form nazism would have triumphed by default.

Our despair over Uncle Stuuf's arrest was relieved by the news that the only charge against him was attempting to reach England. No details of his resistance roles became known. He carried no documents, nor did he need any. The Gestapo was puzzled, but the German civilian authorities came to realise the importance of their catch. Seyss-Inquart clearly appreciated that one day Dr H. B. Wiardi Beckman might be used when a compromise peace had to be negotiated. Attempts were even made for his exchange via Sweden for nazis in Allied hands although nothing came of them. He was kept in various prisons for a long time and allowed to read books of his choice, amongst them the complete Homer in Greek, to exercise the mind and remind him of Odysseus's ups and downs. This benevolent treatment failed to save him. Nazi bureaucrats at a low level mixed him up with a group of 'real' resisters and when the tide of war turned and the nazis intensified retribution, he was transferred with that group to a *Nacht und Nebel* camp.

He might still have survived the night of terror and the fog of anonymity – as some did who went on to tell the tale – if he had not volunteered for service in a typhus-infected barrack, against the advice and entreaties of his fellow inmates who wanted to save him for our country. He caught the disease and died on 15 March 1945 in Dachau, only a few weeks before the camp was liberated. His new friends held widely different political and religious views, but, as one of them reported later: 'Stuuf was a friend to all of us not because of his political beliefs, or because of the conviction with which they were held, but because of his strength of character and obvious sincerity, which commanded respect, and because of his great talent and wide learning, which enriched us.'

Emotionally Uncle Stuuf's arrest had a tremendous impact on me. Amanda renewed her plea to leave the country. But in practical terms his disappearance did not affect the Apostles. They continued to meet, as did Laura and I. There was little to link me with him. Only Brother knew of my involvement, for we had met at Uncle Stuuf's hide-out in The Hague. Luke guessed something but sensitively asked no questions. Hardly anyone knew anything for certain. There was little chance that the arrest and torture of others might incriminate Uncle Stuuf.

So the Apostles continued to gather information, Laura and I to condense it, Michael to be supplied. He had encountered two problems. First, the messages from the Apostles took up a lot of time, both in coding and in transmitting, notwithstanding our strenuous efforts at reducing them to a fraction of their original length. To alleviate the burden I offered to try and find a land route. They were, of course, unaware of my earlier attempts.

Secondly, having found a safe place to transmit from, he discovered that reception both ways was unsatisfactory. It gradually became so bad that he had to abandon it. He therefore temporarily moved his unwieldy transmitter back to the flat he still shared with his girlfriend Dorothy. It was, of course, too comfortable an arrangement, and he waited too long before moving to another site. The result was disastrous.

I never found out why the SD arrived that night at Dorothy's home. Michael was just signing off when he heard a commotion upstairs, climbed out of one dormer window, along the roof and into another one – luckily unlatched – a few houses further on, then escaped into the black night. The incriminating transmitter had had to be left behind, but he took the messages and his code. Dorothy was at home with her father, a well-known judge, in the drawing room two floor below. Both were arrested, both denied any knowledge of what went on in the attic. Both were nevertheless charged with harbouring and abetting a spy, a criminal offence liable to the death penalty. The news was published in the regular newspapers and by radio. As intended, it made a great impact on The Hague society. Clearly, the nazis expected the prey that had escaped them to feel enormous pressure and give himself up to save judge and daughter.

Michael did not run to his parents, where the SD could be expected to look for him first. Nor did he want them implicated in any way. He went to a friend who phoned another friend who phoned Doctor Fleming. He immediately removed all traces of evidence that might point to activities unusual for a doctor. There was not much: a few papers and Alexander's belongings. When the SD arrived, the Flemings were all innocence, with apparently no idea of what had happened or any knowledge of what Michael had been up to. The SD accepted their protestations, especially when Gertrude started crying inconsolably. As she told Alexander more than a year later, weeping came as a relief. At first tears filled her eyes unwittingly, but she noticed their impact on the nazis. Her sense of drama then took over. The real shock came later when they read the announcement in the press.

Advice came from Carel, whom Michael had met twice and come to trust. He stayed with Carel for three days and nights before moving to Amsterdam, an address unknown to either Dorothy or his parents. Carel argued against Michael giving himself up. The nazis would not have created such a furore about the judge if they really wanted to harm someone who seemed genuinely innocent. Best to wait and see.

When after a month the warning was repeated, Michael could not face the responsibility for their possible deaths. Without telling anyone he went to the main Dutch police station in The Hague and requested the promised exchange. He was lucky. Brother happened to be around and phoned the SD with a demand for the immediate release of the judge and his daughter, promising to deliver Michael as soon as this was confirmed. He did not tell them Michael was sitting right next to him. The judge was duly freed, his daughter remained in custody. Accompanied by Dutch policemen, Michael walked to the SD office. Assuming daughter and father both to be free, he shook his friendly escorts off and ran away again. Dorothy was sent to a concentration camp and never returned. Shortly after his release the judge suffered a heart attack and died.

The following year was agony for Michael. Although bravely going through the motions of yet more resistance activities, he could not forget Dorothy and her father. His capture came quite by accident, when he fell victim to a random raid by Grüne Polizei. At their station one of the Gestapo officials checked the papers of those rounded up against a list of wanted fugitives. Michael's papers survived the scrutiny, but his face did not. He was executed soon afterwards.

All these happenings confused the Apostles. They upset me even more. The Apostles had lost their contact with England, but I had lost my mentor and employer as well.

The nazi measures took a turn for the worse during those months. On 5 January 1942 the Council of Churches had protested to Seyss-Inquart about what they called the 'complete lawlessness' of the treatment of the Jews. If it made an impression on the Dutch, it made no impact on the nazis. Five days later 1,402 what were termed 'unemployed Jews' were rounded up and 'put to work' in a 'camp', euphemisms all. At that time no one outside a small inner circle at the top of nazi Germany knew that the fatal decision of the *Endlösung* had just been taken. In Holland despatch to labour camps was not then suspected to be any more than the term implies, serious enough but not a death sentence.

More restrictive measures followed relentlessly. On 17 January the first Jews living outside Amsterdam – in Zaandam – were ordered to move to the capital city; during the course of the year Jews from all over Holland followed. Amsterdam became a ghetto. It was also turned into a transit city. On 6 August one of the regular raids yielded a contingent of Jews who were despatched directly to Auschwitz. Another protest from the Council of Churches just before had failed to stop the evolution of evil.

In these winter months resistance came of age. It changed irreversibly, both in general and for me in particular. During the previous period small groups of, mainly young, enthusiasts had groped for a useful way to act, to continue the war by some other means, not in the first place to resist. There was little to resist. Separately – but at the same time – other small groups of more mature and politically conscious people tried to co-ordinate and co-operate. Their aims ranged widely: to assess nazi measures and the response to them, to give guidance where needed – from permanent secretaries to activists – to create goodwill across political and religious divisions, ultimately with a view to adapting national parties and institutions as well as international ones. Initially some even argued the need for a master organization to include underground newspapers, espionage and sabotage as well, but this was soon discarded as too ambitious, dangerous and unnecessary. Many, including Uncle Stuuf, feared that wild acts of sabotage would rebound on the population and should be discouraged. The change came with the escalation of nazi measures and the formation of the Great Civic Committee (GCC) with narrower aims but more impact. It was for this reason too that Uncle Stuuf felt he could leave occupied Holland and be useful in England.

His arrest represented the nadir in my life. I confided in Carel and consulted Freek. Both urged me to re-activate the land route to either Switzerland or Spain, but neither could help. Carel was too immersed in the tribulations of the OD, Freek with the embyro GCC. I knew that Laura would not be able to help either.

All this happened at the same time that the request to assist Jews was repeated and stories of woe were multiplying, unconnected events that combined to make me take the plunge. And thus my activities came to be directed at relief for victims, as others had done before and more came to do after. It reflected the sea change in the movement, from the minute resistance of the few to what would become the massive resistance of the many, ultimately involving some one million people, activists and passivists alike.

For me the turning-point came when Brother introduced me to Theo, a specialist in the falsification of identity cards. I did not know him, he did not know me. We set up elaborate precautions to convince each other that we were not V-men. Brother phoned Theo and so did I. My password was 'Apostles', his 'Peter'. In addition I was to carry a copy of *Het Parool* under my coat and he was to show me a copy of *Vrij Nederland*. Brother described each of us to the other.

So, without telling Amanda, I took a train to Amsterdam and a tram to the vast square where Theo lived. At its centre was a sizeable sports field, on three sides tall housing blocks, the fourth side covered by an architectural monument designed by my father. I rang the bell two floors up in one of those six-floor buildings that contain two-floor flats and was welcomed by Theo himself.

Theo, a student of economics at Amsterdam University, had developed an ingenious system for changing one identity card into another. In early 1942 falsification of essential papers was still in its infancy and, with a colleague Theo was a pioneer in this intricate service industry which came to be essential for survival. Theo also supplied ration cards: the person with a new identity still needed to be fed. Having ventured into unchartered territory beyond the range of the Apostles, Theo quickly established himself as a trusted ally and friend.

His character was a peculiar mixture: self-assured yet self-effacing, a natural organizer yet casual in details, great potential frittered away in the manifold activities of the resistance instead of being applied to a brilliant career. Of medium height and sturdily built, he was always well dressed, had a sharp mind usually several steps ahead of most others', and was adored by his parents as well as his fiancée. His steel-rimmed glasses hid restless eyes which in his case truly reflected a restless soul. What brought us close in the span of only six months was our combined effort to slip Jews – and some gentiles – out of Holland and into a neutral country. Once his initial reservations had succumbed to his craving for planning, he assisted untiringly with the necessary papers and with his apparently limitless resourcefulness.

A few days later I looked up a charming middle-aged Jewish couple in Amsterdam. They were friends of the man who had pleaded with me at the house-concert and who supported *Het Parool*. I think they were called Jacobs, the name of many Dutch Jewish families and one which is vaguely familiar. And it must have been early spring 1942, for the sun shone benignly after the tough winter when I arrived at their home. The desperate desire of Jews to escape from the encroaching nazi tentacles thus merged with the urgent need for an Apostolic line of communication with the free world.

Mr and Mrs Jacobs received me with restrained cordiality which soon turned into warmth. Well educated, cultured and civilized, they were obviously bewildered. They could not understand what was going on, nor accept the inevitability of the process that would eventually rob them first of their harmless pursuits, then of their possessions, finally of their lives. They were resigned to whatever fate held in store, but deeply concerned about the younger of their two sons. In his early twenties, he was just married – far too young as they said, restless, impulsive, a do-er, in complete contrast to his more contemplative brother. They were afraid he might act irresponsibly, perhaps attack nazis and be killed in the process. They did not want to know anything about me or my job, not even my name. Although not wealthy, money would be no object. When I waved this aside they insisted that their son's expenses be amply refunded. Would I please go and see him, only a few blocks away?

Holland's cities abound with such blocks, which have a peculiarity: an open staircase that leads to the upper flats on either side without a communal entrance door. The system, now discontinued, provides some protection against the weather and more privacy. But it also fails to give warning of unwanted callers.

I walked the quarter of a mile in good sunshine and good heart, found the street, the number and the staircase, which led me to a door two floors up. Slightly breathless, I rang the bell. The front door opened an inch or so enough to tauten the latch chain and provide a peep at the intruder. I mentioned the name Jacobs to the girl behind the door and asked to see the son, whereupon the door was slammed in my face with a cry of 'don't know any Jacobs'. Puzzled, I retraced my steps, down the concrete stairs, along the sunny street and up another concrete staircase to the parents' home. The Jacobs were equally baffled, tried to phone, failed to get through, then accompanied me on a second attempt to enter their son's home. This time we were received with great relief.

The girl who opened the door was the same one who had refused me entrance earlier and turned out to be the sister of the younger Jacobs' wife. In between bursts of tears it transpired that all the family had been glued to the window after Jacobs senior had phoned to announce my arrival. They had noticed a green German prison van further along the street. Consequently, when I rang they took me for the Gestapo. They had panicked. Junior had rushed up the inside stairs to the top floor – followed by his frightened wife – opened a window, grabbed the gutter, and moved along it to the neighbouring house, perilously suspended six floors up. He had kicked desperately at a closed window, in vain. His wife lacked the height and perhaps the courage to follow him and was left behind, crying wildly. Had the Gestapo come she would have given the whole game away. Now Junior was stuck to the gutter, frozen by fright, eyes tight shut.

I raced upstairs with the girl at my heels, passed some crying people, poked my head out of the window and saw a body dangling rigidly a few feet beyond my reach. Meanwhile Senior had caught up with me, with a walking stick. Touching Junior might have sent him headlong to his death sixty feet below, but the risk had to be taken. The closed window belonged to a top house on another staircase. To go there meant running down all these flights and up again, and then either answering awkward questions or finding no one in. So I tapped on his bottom with the stick.

The head slowly turned in my direction. The eyes opened and took in the three faces, two of them familiar. Miraculously the hands moved, the still stiff body came within reach and I grabbed it round the waist. Though terrified of heights, when stretching myself perilously outside that window sixty feet up I felt no fear. With the father's help I somehow managed to hold on and gently let the body subside on to the floor inside. For a few seconds he remained motionless, as if dead. We held our breath until a loud cry rended the silence. It came from his wife who proceeded to kiss him and shake him into consciousness. Junior slowly came alive, staring round at his family, shaking all over. Soon he calmed down and got up without any assistance. He looked at me and uttered his first word: 'Sorry'.

The experience so unnerved me that I told Amanda, despite my resolution to leave her out of this new venture. But she reacted sweetly, almost maternally. Some time later I discovered the reason for her sweetness. She guessed that her wish to escape had come nearer fulfilment. During the following months, determined to strengthen the bond between us, she took over much of the work of distributing *Het Parool* and *Vrij Nederland*.

Jacobs junior and his wife became friends while waiting for the completion of the preparations for their flight. He was intelligent and lively, albeit still impulsive, she was pretty, slight, with sparkling eyes. Theo had prepared identity cards with the Jacobs' photographs but in the name and with the fingerprints of others. We were to travel by train and bus to the Belgian border and he would accompany us because the cards had to be retrieved to serve on another occasion. I would continue across the border and escort them to my Belgian friends in Antwerp, then as far as arrangements would allow me to go, if possible well into France. Young Jacobs and his wife would cross into Switzerland on their own and deliver Apostolic documents to the Dutch military attaché. Junior would then return to the last staging post on the French side of the Swiss border to report their safe arrival. That message would be passed back along the line to me. Junior could either stay in the safety of Switzerland or act as courier across that border. The temporary lack of identity papers in Belgium did not worry us unduly because like France it only had a military nazi authority and at that time checks were rare.

I looked forward to another meeting with the friars at the monastery near the border after a gap of eight months. We presented a mixed bag to the Catholic community – two Jews and two Protestants – but to the friars we were just fellow human beings in need of their practical help.

They carried their religion lightly, all the more impressive for its innocent simplicity. We set out from the monastery early that afternoon in cool but lovely sunshine through the woods to and beyond the border. There was no need for any monks to accompany us for I knew the way. We walked in silence for about a mile, treading softly to avoid accentuating the gentle rustle of leaves from an unusually subdued wind, and carefully weaved our way through the trees. A couple of hundred yards from the invisible border I stopped, for Theo to collect the Jacobs's identity cards. They changed hands. Then Theo's curiosity got the better of his prudence. He hid the cards in some undergrowth and continued with us.

A few seconds later, suddenly, from behind a dense cluster of shrubs, someone shouted 'Halt', in an unmistakably German accent. A soldier, quite an old one, appeared pointing a rifle at us.

For the first time the reality of arrest stared me in the face. I had a feeling of utter disbelief followed by shock. Memory of rehearsals of just such an event fell away. I simply stood, staring at this unexpected representative of the nazi war machine. I was paralysed. All possible avenues of escape were closed.

In retrospect, I suppose we could have made a run for it or even overpowered our poor old captor. We had assumed border guards were highly trained young men from the Grüne Polizei armed with high velocity revolvers. But our soldier had only one bullet which might well have missed any of his four targets. Even if it did not, three would have escaped. But then the crack of the shot might have alerted his colleagues. And where would we go? Fortunately none of us made an attempt.

Theo kept his cool, so did Jacobs junior and his wife. In good German, Theo said: 'Hello, nice weather'. The soldier, surprised at such equanimity, dropped his rifle. That woke me into devizing a strategy for survival. But at once the soldier remembered his duty and politely asked for our identity cards. Undaunted Theo searched his pockets and handed his over. Jacobs, his wife and I did nothing. The soldier looked at the card as if he had never seen one before, looked at Theo and was about to return it when, recalling his training, he changed his mind and pocketed the card.

Next he looked at me and asked for mine, rather apologetically. Having regained my faculties I too searched a while before handing mine over. He accepted it with a friendly nod, studied it with interest rather than suspicion, took Theo's out of his pocket, compared the two, looked at me and at Theo, nodded appreciatively and was again about to return the documents to their owners. Again he had second thoughts, slipped the cards in his pocket and looked enquiringly at Jacobs. Junior appeared completely at ease, searched his various pockets, patted them, then smiled. He spoke in Dutch, his eyes moving from the soldier to Theo.

Theo translated: 'They haven't got one.' No greater contrast can be imagined than between the lifeless body hanging from the gutter and the self-assured Jacobs facing another crisis.

The soldier said: 'Sorry, I've been instructed that all Dutchmen should carry identity cards at all times.'

'Didn't know that,' Jacobs replied lightly. 'Why should I? This is Dutch territory.'

The soldier now leered slyly and we realised the danger had not yet passed, had perhaps even increased. For we stood face to face with an enemy with limited intelligence, not the typical German who was reputed to follow instructions automatically, but a human being debating with himself whether to believe a fellow human being and relent. There seemed no reason why he should not implement his instructions. I thought one of us might retrieve the buried cards but realised that this would only rekindle his suspicion.

Our two cards went back into his pocket and he invited us to accompany him to the command post. The situation was beyond his competence, he said, and the sergeant would sort it out.

'Nonsense,' said Theo. 'We're on our own territory in our own country. Why should a foreigner interfere with a nice afternoon walk?'

'But you're on the frontier, maybe already across it.'

We all showed excessive surprise, and initiated another round of discussion. We explained, we cajoled, we argued, the cards popping out of his pocket when he seemed satisfied and back into it when he remembered his duty and the possible repercussions of ignoring it.

Slowly he revealed details of his life. He explained that he was on recuperation leave from the Russian front. He added that Russia was awful, cold, dreary, endless, hopeless. He did not want to return there, ever. He admitted to disappointment which had gradually turned into resentment. He had been shifted straight from the Russian steppes to the West and Holland without any permission to see his wife and four children on the way. He had not seen them for a year and was clearly demoralized.

After some three hours of this it seemed we were on the verge of a breakthrough. But when Theo touched the cards in the soldier's hand, he held on to them. 'Nein, Sie gehen mit,' he insisted, determined not to upset any chance of seeing his family.

At this point Mrs Jacobs junior played her part. She had remained quiet throughout, silent but alert, her pretty face and pretty figure not unnoticed by the soldier. She started crying inconsolably and so convincingly that I went over to her and nearly snapped 'Shut up!'. The reaction of the soldier was immediate. He softened and asked her to sit down and not be distressed. She continued to shake with sobs, large tears welling up into her eyes. The soldier put a hand under her armpit, helped lift her up and asked for a kiss. She put her arms round him and kissed him fervently on the cheeks, even once on the lips. He told her gently to make sure that the burgomaster of her town give her an identity card and not to be so near the frontier. She gave him another cheeky kiss and said she was sure he would soon see his wife and kids. Then we returned to the monastery. Theo even retrieved the Jacobs's identity cards.

The incident made a deep impression on me, and a lasting one, for a simple reason. We claimed we were resisting nazism on behalf of human values. Anti-nazis, however, easily spilled over into anti-Germanism. Yet here was a human being whose humanity shone through his German uniform. The incident has remained an object lesson in avoiding blanket prejudice.

We tried again the next day. This time all went according to plan. Theo reclaimed the Jacobs's cards immediately after leaving the monastery and went home without bothering to investigate the invisible frontier. We three wound our way through the wood, apprehensively and silently, and safely reached my Antwerp friends.

The next night saw me in the splendour of a four-poster in the prime guestroom of an imposing late-eighteenth-century house, owned by the main Belgian steel company Cockerill, but occupied by its Dutch director. His son Eddy, an old friend, had suggested I visit him if and when in Hoboken. This turned out to be a stroke of good luck. The father advised me to travel to Namur, the seat of a Cockerill steel plant, which I did, with the Jacobs couple.

They had meanwhile been provided with Belgian and French papers by my Belgian friends. One of the managers of the Namur plant was a tough anti-nazi Belgian engineer who had used his contacts in France to help messengers cross into Switzerland. He assured me that the Jacobses would arrive there in two or three days, but begged me not to proceed any further in order to protect this escape line. I therefore returned to my Antwerp four-poster to await the news of their safe passage. This included, of course, the Apostolic documents Jacobs now carried. That news duly arrived in the form of a coded message arranged between Junior and myself only. I thereupon returned home, relieved and pleased with my achievements.

During the next few months several more Jews – and two gentiles – went the same way, including the elder Jacobs son, whose parents refused to budge. Our travel agency appeared to function smoothly.

One incident in particular sticks in my mind. It concerns a Jewish couple in their early forties. I will call them Cohen. The husband was a distinguished teacher of piano and harmonics at the most prestigious academy of music, the Amsterdam Conservatorium, where the wife taught the violin. They had a gentle, studious son of 11 and a lovely, lively daughter of 13 who, although like all the Cohens very musical, showed a preference for discovering and enjoying life's many other pleasures. I had met them twice before to discuss the practicalities of escape and its complications. Each time the children were present and treated as adults. Should they give up a life dedicated to music and civilization or stick it out and let the devil take the hindmost?

The third time they invited me for lunch at their opulent flat it was to make the final decision. Theo had already changed their identity cards, which I brought with me. The Cohens had just been told by the Jewish Council to leave for a smaller, indeed tiny, apartment elsewhere in Amsterdam. This meant leaving behind the grand piano, most of their valuable antique furniture, paintings, books and other cherished possessions; no doubt to enrich some uncivilized German. Would this be the beginning of the end? Or just another temporary cross to bear until sanity returned, as the Jewish Council had put it?

Parting with their worldly goods they accepted as a small price to pay for the privilege of continued dedication to music. They agreed with me that the chances of the war finishing in 1942 looked dismal. However, would they be permitted to stay with their small upright piano in the new apartment until liberation in 1943 (which all of us were convinced would happen)? The Cohens trusted the Jewish Council but distrusted the nazis. They had taken precautions and found a friendly buyer for their furniture and library. Should they go or stay? With the successes of the past escapes in mind I said unhesitatingly: 'Go'. All four of them nodded their approval.

Cohen then offered me the grand piano and a substantial sum of money for my practical assistance 'and moral support'. A piano for four lives? I never considered it a temptation. I could not even guarantee success.

The meal disposed of, we sat in the comfort of the drawing room drinking coffee with a glass of brandy. At a gesture of his father the son produced a pill. Unwittingly I put out my hand, unaware of the grave look on the boy's face. He held on to the pill, however.

'No, Sir. I'm not to give it to anyone, ever. It's my safeguard.'

I looked puzzled, and felt a rising sense of foreboding.

The girl explained cheerily: 'It's our way to heaven if we can't reach Switzerland.' They were cyanide pills provided by a medical friend.

I felt too deeply moved for words. This lovely, talented girl, her face as pure as Leonardo's 'Madonna with St Anne', accepted with utter calm the possibility of suicide.

'Well,' the girl added unemotionally, for she must have seen my expression, 'it's better than torture and death at the hands of these savages, isn't it?'

That, ultimately, must have been the decision that ended her short life, for as far as I know the Cohens never arrived in Switzerland.

Forty-five years on, the face of the girl still haunts me.

Chapter Sixteen

THE GESTAPO ON MY TAIL

Since Michael Fleming's disappearance. the Apostles had once again found themselves without a transmitter. Still, we were more fortunate than similar groups; whereas they lacked all contact with England, we at least knew that two more consignments of documents had reached Switzerland, and presumably therefore London. Also, Dorothy had clearly not divulged any information or names, for none of the Apostles were arrested or even shadowed. Many groups had been less lucky. When one member fell into the clutches of the Gestapo most others followed swiftly. We were given a new lease of life and I was determined to improve the service provided by the travel agency.

How did we know the documents had arrived? Because the Jewish escapees had sent coded messages through the various stages back to me. These were inevitably brief, but in words that could not possibly have been invented by anyone else. Still, the useful line of one-way communication had not developed into the expected two-way system. No one seemed to have recrossed the Swiss border back into France. Although not unduly worried I nevertheless decided to investigate. This time I would insist that my Cockerell friend in Namur let me go all the way to Switzerland. Again I intended to take advantage of the holidays and planned my departure for 8 August.

Contact with England was as much an obsession on our side of the North Sea as it proved to be on the other, though for different reasons. We felt – rather pedantically – that our exiled government required reliable information about nazi measures. How else could they give reasonable guidelines for our conduct? On the other side military information was sought and sabotage contemplated, although gradually the value of political news came to be appreciated as well. We entered the long night of the England Spiel. Dawn did not arrive until spring 1943 when the newly founded Dutch Bureau of Intelligence – BI – forged an alliance with MI6 instead of with the tarnished SOE as its predecessor had done.

That period was not only bleak for active resisters but also for the population as a whole. In addition to the anti-Jewish measures already mentioned, a wide range of orders attempted to coerce what the Germans proclaimed to be their 'brother' people. Some brother! In February 1942 all actors were required to join their guild of the Cultural Chamber on penalty of a prohibition to act. Many joined, for what is an actor without a stage, an audience and an income? Others refused, only to be accused of breaking ranks by those who joined. The controversy was echoed among musicians, painters, sculptors and architects when they in turn came to face the same dilemma, followed by doctors, teachers and workers. The ensuing discord left a scar that survived the defeat of Hitler.

Some restrictive measures could be classified as 'military necessity'. On 1 May 1942 all beaches were proclaimed prohibited territory and part of the coastal population was forced to evacuate their seaside homes. While resented, the move increased hopes of an early Allied invasion. On 15 May all professional officers of the disbanded Dutch army were instructed to report at various barracks. Though puzzled, most did so to honour their oath, only to find themselves locked in, then transported as prisoners-of-war to camps in Germany, more than 2,000 of them. Many interpreted this as another sign of an imminent Allied landing.

Individual anger became national when on 19 July the nazis requisitioned bicycles in all sizeable towns. They were needed to ensure greater mobility for the German army, presumably inspired by fear of the expected Allied landing. Soon 50,000 had been collected. As *Het Parool* commented: 'Hardly any move by the occupying forces caused such wild anger, such deep bitterness as this bicycle theft.' Lack of petrol had halted private cars and many communal buses, scarcity of coal and electricity restricted the frequency of trams and trains. To take their main means of transport from the Dutch constituted the ultimate crime. It initiated a new and separate branch of the resistance: protection and servicing of bicycles. My family saved ours.

Resistance now also involved raids on distribution centres to obtain identity and ration cards for persecuted compatriots. The first took place in a remote village in the remote lake-province of Friesland, the most daring and spectacular in Amsterdam. On 27 March 1943 the huge population registry was set ablaze, destroying thousands of personal cards and also yielding hundreds of blank identity cards to be used for fugitives, Jews and non-Jews alike. None of these activities was organized, directed or even inspired by the exiled government or the Allied agencies. Nor were they of much help to the Allied war effort: their intention was to support the Dutch people and sabotage the nazi occupiers.

The nazis also turned on the universities at about the same time. The Gestapo detected that many of those arrested for subversive activities were undergraduates. This is not surprising as the universities had been prone to erratic closures and its members could more easily spare the time than those with jobs. The nazis demanded that 6,000 undergraduates – out of a total of 14,600 – register for labour in Germany 'to support the war effort against communism'. The governing bodies of the universities unanimously refused co-operation, which would have included providing names and other details of all members. A universal strike resulted and the demand was rescinded. Next they employed cruder methods: random arrests. But they followed this up by a more subtle demand for a 'declaration of loyalty', which would earn each student a stamp in his university card without which entrance to university buildings and participation in lectures would be prohibited. On the requisite date – 13 April – only 14% complied. My brother was among the 36% who refused to sign and who then received a demand to report at various centres on penalty of dire consequences for their relatives. Most did not; those who did were transferred to holding camps, then to labour camps, some even to concentration camps. Again the nazis achieved little else but the alienation of ever larger sections of the Dutch.

The nazis lost their touch altogether when on 29 April 1943 they announced that the entire conscript army – disbanded in June 1940 – was to be recalled. All ranks had to report to barracks even before call-up papers had been served. There were 300,000 of them, almost the entire able-bodied male population between ages 19 and 35, an administrative night-mare of gigantic proportions. Again there was the threat to 'all persons supporting those concerned in their attempts to withdraw from this duty'. The order was sent by telex to all newspaper offices on the morning of 29 April. The printer of one newspaper at once stuck the text in a large typeface to his windows in the centre of the main textile city in the east of Holland. During their lunchbreak workers read the amazing news and that afternoon eastern Holland was on strike. By Friday morning factories all over Holland stood idle. The strike had become general. No one had organized it. There were no demonstrations or pickets, nor was there any thought of what to do next. People had simply had enough and downed tools; management and workforce alike went home. Even in one electronics factory controlled by the Germans work stopped, and, as no one could leave, people sat down.

It could not last without outside support, nor did it. No Allied landings occurred. The nazis resorted to summary justice. On the Saturday a farm labourer was executed for refusing to deliver milk to the factory. Eighty more executions followed that weekend. Moreover, the railways refused to join the strike. Throughout the war management and unions co-operated to ensure that railway management remained in Dutch hands and that existing unions were absolved from joining the nazi union. This guaranteed the smooth running of the railway system, which benefited Germans and Dutch alike. The nazis used it for transporting Jews into exile, the Dutch for food, coal and – covertly – underground newspapers. The long-term aim had been from the start to use the strike weapon only as a last resort: to assist Allied armies. In April 1943 none stood on the continent. Nor were there any instructions from the exiled government. Consequently the railways continued to function normally.

The strike swiftly petered out. It nevertheless served its main purpose: the Germans called their reprisals off as well as their demand for the return of the Dutch army. It taught the Dutch the lesson that a general strike would only succeed if its aims remained restricted to protest. Any wider purpose – such as the overthrow of the nazi clique – must await the arrival of the Allied armies.

In mid-summer 1942 my own contribution to the resistance came to an abrupt halt. On 7 August at 7.30 pm – just twelve hours before my planned departure – the Gestapo arrived in force at my home. It was a warm Friday evening. My brother and sister were on holiday. My father had left that morning for a meeting in The Hague where my mother would join him the next day for a wedding, the first night since the start of the war that the two had been separated. My mother had stayed behind in view of my departure the next morning, disguised as a holiday with friends.

Amanda and I were chatting in my room upstairs when my mother called me to the telephone downstairs. Just as I arrived in the hall, the doorbell rang. My mother and I opened the front door together, leaving the receiver off the hook. Outside were two men in civilian clothes. One of them asked for me. It was not unusual for strangers to do so and it had happened before. In due course some code would be used to establish their bonafides. We Apostles had devised a clever system of codes, so intricate that I have forgotten it. Completely relaxed I began to ask questions intended to elicit that code, without divulging my identity. I had no reason to expect them to be anything but bonafide. My mother, however, suspected them at once and – as she told me later – thought I had as well since I failed to reveal my identity. She interrupted my questions with an outright lie.

'Herman's on holiday,' she said without blinking and, turning to me: 'Allerd, you go and take your phone call.'

The enormity of witnessing my mother blatantly lying registered only slowly because this first lie came to her as such a matter of course. She seemed to function on two different levels, as I started doing while walking to the telephone, which stood within sight – but not hearing – of the front door.

My mother continued chatting to the strangers. The shock of her unexpected denial of my identity – which led to my recognizing the strangers as enemies – would have paralyzed me if it had not been for the experience with the German soldier at the Belgian frontier, still fresh in my mind. It now galvanized me. I put aside the myriad questions the revelation raised and picked up the receiver. It was Luke, who said rather nervously:

'The Gestapo are on the way. I've just heard: Carel and Theo were arrested.'

Softly and unemotionally I replied: 'You're right. They're here. I'll try to scram. Ring you later.' Then added loudly: 'Herman's on holiday. See you soon.'

All the time I was eyeing my mother, who blithely continued her conversation with the strangers. Cunning seemed to be called for, since making a run for it at that moment might invite bullets. I decided to brave it out and play it my mother's way, hoping that an opportunity for a less dangerous escape would present itself.

Replacing the receiver and returning to the door, I heard the first stranger ask: 'Who's he?'

My mother replied without a blush: 'He's Allerd, my second son.'

This clever and entirely convincing switch of her sons' identities prompted the second stranger to talk in German to the first, who then asked me: 'May I see your identity card?' That confirmed who they were.

'Of course,' I said. 'It's in my room. I'll go and fetch it.'

My mother kept up her barrage of words, and made some remark about the nice weather. 'His brother will surely enjoy it, don't you think?'

Now came the opportunity we had both been waiting for. Calmly I strode to the stairs and up the first steps. The staircase then turned out of sight of the hall and I raced to Amanda who stood at the top with a small box in her hand. The box contained my only secrets and evidence: various identity cards – my own, a false one in the name of Alexander

Optenoord, and the Belgian and French cards in the name of Alexandre Necker – as well as some money in the three currencies.

Amanda had listened to the talk downstairs, grasped the implications as quickly as my mother had done, grabbed the box of whose existence only she knew and opened a window at the top of the stairs. This gave onto the roof of the garage which protruded beyond the house into the back garden.

She did not say a word, nor did she have to. I climbed through the window, jumped onto the roof, ran across it, jumped down at the end, scaled an eight-foot fence into a neighbour's garden, then carefully walked past his house into an adjoining street – only to spot men in uniform at both ends. Retracing my steps I climbed over several more fences, blessedly lower, before looking out into another adjoining street, the third of a triangle that enclosed some sixty houses. Uniformed men were everywhere. It was the only time I nearly panicked. I slowed down to regain my breath and my wits.

Amanda, meanwhile, closed the window, then walked imperturbably down the stairs into the hall, past the surprised strangers, out of the front door to her bicycle on which she rode away. This galvanized the strangers into action: they raced up the stairs, searched everywhere and, defeated, rushed down again to confront my mother, who still stood equally calmly in the hall. She understood what had happened.

The German shouted at her: 'Das war Ihr Sohn!' She nodded.

'You've lied!' shouted the Dutch speaker.

To which my mother retorted blithely: 'What would you have done?'

They took her to the drawing room then, and started to question her about my activities, first gently but soon with increasing roughness. She, of course, knew next to nothing about what I had been doing. Then: where was I likely to go?

Indignantly she replied: 'He wouldn't be a such a fool as to go to any address that I know.'

By then I had my panic under control. I ran through several more gardens, hurdled dividing fences, and arrived almost full circle at our next door neighbours' house, which I entered by the back door. They were great friends of ours and therefore trustworthy. Luckily the door was not locked. Luckily too the husband and wife were at home. They took me to their attic where I hid in utter darkness.

Two hours later the husband bravely went to our house to investigate, carrying a book as an excuse for his visit. The front door stood wide open. In the drawing room he found my mother surrounded by four men, two of them in uniform pacing up and down. The Dutch-speaking Gestapo man asked him aggressively what he had come for. Our neighbour put the book on a table: 'To return this book,' he said. 'Sorry to disturb you.' He winked at my mother and hurried away.

The four men did not follow him, too deeply involved in the battle of wills with my mother. Only when he had gone did one of them ask whether it was normal for people to call after 10 pm.

'With friends it is. After all, lights are blazing everywhere.'

Another hour passed before my hosts, watching from their darkened front room, witnessed my mother being escorted to a waiting car and driven off. Two more cars followed.

The motorcade went to Amanda's home, about a mile away. My mother had provided the address, confident that Amanda would not be there. I phoned Luke, who asked me to come to him. I borrowed a rather tight dark mackintosh and a hat several sizes too large, then walked the half mile to Luke's home through the quiet moonless night.

At Amanda's house her father had been furious. When the Gestapo arrived, she had not left and bravely opened the door herself, having pushed her father away for fear that in his anger he might let weakness prevail over wisdom. Coolly she faced the same two nazis and denied any knowledge of my activities other than as a 'nice kisser'. Alternating between injured innocence and female charm, she clearly rendered her prospective captors speechless for they departed dejected. They had left my mother between two guards in one of the cars and presumably felt that one chatty lady was enough.

Amanda's father was less easily appeased. After the Gestapo had left, he called me a scoundrel who had bewitched his poor daughter, a 'nice kisser' too! Whereupon he lapsed into self-pity. Amanda's self-assurance started to weaken. The decision to stay at home rather than flee had been cool calculation, but doubts now surfaced. The Gestapo might have second thoughts. She phoned Luke, who told her of my presence. So she rapidly filled a suitcase and told her father firmly that she intended to share exile and hiding with me. Perhaps she hoped we would at last escape nazi Holland and start on our way to freedom in England. Her father had become soft. We were not even engaged, let alone married.

Ignoring his laments and planting a kiss on his balding dome, Amanda cycled into the night; to Luke, where astonishingly we were re-united. Months later, when we furtively met, her father was his jovial self again. And he begged me to protect his 'darling little kid', generously adding that I had already proved to be a gentleman. I never told him that she had protected me rather than the other way round.

Meanwhile Luke had warned Laura and kept her informed of developments during the evening. They decided we could risk staying that night at his home, arguing that if he were on their list the Gestapo would already have arrived. Fortunately the guess proved right. All four of us congregated the next day at the home of another friend. Laura and Luke had also decided to go into hiding, at least for a few days, or until we discovered what had put the Gestapo on to Theo, Carel and me. There was no clear indication. I hinted at Matthew as a candidate for the role of informer, Amanda supporting me. Laura kept an awkward silence, torn between the conflicting demands of mind and heart. Luke was sure, however, that Matthew was innocent.

'It doesn't make sense. Why betray you and not Laura or me?'

'Because Matthew promised never to betray Laura and you are his best friend,' I replied. 'But I was the harsh one at the showdown last year.'

Laura interrupted: 'It still doesn't make sense. How could he betray Carel and Theo when he doesn't even know them? And why wait so long?'

'He could've had me followed,' I persisted. 'By selecting me he had his revenge, kept his word to you and enhanced his standing with his father-in-law.'

Laura shook her head. 'Very clever, but much too contrived. It doesn't sound like Matthew at all.'

I was undeterred. 'But you didn't expect him to turn nazi either.'

Luke put up his hand. 'Hang on. Matthew's not a really fanatical nazi. He's still my friend, in a way. I see him occasionally. I've also met his father-in-law. Neither seem treacherous people.'

I had nothing to add, for I was slowly coming to the same conclusion. The scenario was too complicated, although the facts, when they surfaced, turned out to be equally bizarre. The discussion continued for a while, with Amanda disparaging Matthew's weakness and Luke talking about his blinkered idealism. But I had lost interest. The mystery surrounding the arrests remained.

Thus started nine months of life as a fugitive, with my mother and my mentor both in prison. We went our diverse ways, promising to keep in touch. Amanda and I left for Amsterdam by train, a safe enough journey as all trains were crowded. At our first hiding place another vital meeting took place the next morning, which determined my future course of action.

The only other person who had to be warned was Freek van Hattum, the lawyer involved with the embryonic Great Civic Committee, and as such Uncle Stuuf's successor. When I phoned him, he rushed from his office in the centre of the city to our suburban safe-house. There, politely but firmly, he pushed our kind hosts and Amanda out of the drawing room to confront me alone. Up till then discussions and actions had been rational, practical, geared to the immediate future, with longer-term considerations pushed to the back of our minds. Freek changed all that.

He was slight, with hornrimmed glasses and unusually large – though beautifully slim – hands, which he used a lot while talking. He meant to be kind and supportive but at that moment, forcing me to confront the real issue, his incisive mind and fierce determination made him acerbic.

215

'Will you give yourself up to release your mother?'

It was perhaps an obvious question, but I had never considered it. Having successfully escaped the Gestapo's clutches, I was appalled at the prospect. Still, I nodded, though without giving any thought to the implications.

'Do you realize that that would endanger Stuuf's life?'

I had not, and shook my head in bewilderment.

Freek persisted: 'You're one of the few who know most about Stuuf's work. The Gestapo are unaware of his many activities and therefore won't harm him. They might even release him shortly. But they will torture you. And you won't be able to cope with their brutality. That will inevitably lead them to us.'

The ramifications of the situation now struck me in their full horror. 'What about my mother?'

'They won't harm her. She's only a pawn, to get you.'

I got angry at this lack of logic. 'If they're that brutal they'll torture her!'

Freek remained calm. 'Does she know anything?'

'She doesn't,' I shot back, but then remembered: 'Of course she knows my connection with Uncle Stuuf and some of my involvement with *Het Parool*. But nothing else.'

'We'll just have to rely on her common sense in not telling them. They have no clue and won't ask. She'll probably deny any knowledge of your activities.'

I was less sure. I realized at last that I was expected to make a choice between my mother's life and that of my mentor. Curiously, I was not concerned about my own death. I realized for the first time that I had come to take that for granted. So many admired people had died already that my own death seemed trifling. Where the sense of calm came from I was not sure. The *Song of the Eighteen Dead* came to mind and the image of Jesus that so profoundly influenced me as a teenager. Realizing that I had accepted my own death, I regained my composure. It is a strange fact that ever after death never worried me, and from then on I was able to contemplate ways to avoid it without panicking. But I was very frightened of torture.

'There's only one way out,' I said coolly. 'Give me your gun.'

Better to kill myself right now, I thought. That would save the Gestapo the need to keep my mother as a hostage and avoid giving away secrets under torture.

Freek remained completely calm. 'I haven't got one,' he said. Though some months later he let slip that he always carried a loaded one.

I must have burst into tears then, for Freek got up and put his arm round my shoulder. 'Buck up, Herman. You've done the right thing so far. Don't spoil it. Brave it out. Stay in Holland, continue to work for us, for you've still got knowledge that few have. You can always leave later. I'll help. I'm sure Amanda will help too.'

I felt deflated, but I had no option. Amanda, who had occasionally poked her head through the door, did help, loyally supporting me with the considerable sympathy and common sense she was blessed with. She had guessed the problem, and the solution. When Freek left no more was said about it. That came later. We stayed at numerous homes of invariably kind people, most of them unknown to my parents, many also to us, sometimes together, mostly apart.

On the Saturday my father, still in The Hague, worried when my mother failed to turn up at the wedding. He phoned our home. Failing to get a reply, he rang our neighbours and heard what had happened. He rushed back home, where he found two men from the Gestapo rummaging through piles of papers. They told him to find me as soon as possible and threatened to send his wife to a concentration camp if he failed. They firmly refused his offer to replace her as a hostage, correctly assuming that her incarceration rather than his would give them a stronger hand. Shocked, he promised to do his utmost, which in theory gave the Gestapo a second trump card. They reckoned without the strength of their hostage, without the rationality of her husband, and without the bureaucracy that finally defeated them in their efforts to rattle or remove our family.

My father, of course, tried to locate me but lacked any clue to my whereabouts. It was Amanda who approached him three weeks later through our faithful neighbours. They met in a wooded park on the outskirts of our city. Amanda could move about reasonably safely because girls were not then prone to the irregular security checks that bedevilled men, especially young ones like me. She continued to meet him there regularly.

At their first meeting my father reported that the Dutch police had issued a warrant for my arrest on behalf of the Gestapo, that my picture had been distributed to all police stations, that a reward of two thousand guilders was promised to anyone who led them to me, and that he would broadcast an appeal to me to save my mother. He considered the amount of the reward high and a clear sign of the importance the Gestapo accorded me. He was wrong on both counts: I was only one of many and the amount far less than for more adult resisters.

My father added that as he was unaware of my activities, he could not judge the penalty if I did give myself up. Nor was he sure that his wife would then be released. Therefore he bravely left the decision to me. I use that adjective because to Amanda it seemed that he found it difficult to contain himself, to keep back the tears. Undoubtedly he felt that he had lost his wife and consequently his life's main support.

Amanda listened attentively, secure in the knowledge of my father's fondness for her. She told him that I had been advised by Freek not to give myself up. My father knew Freek was a sensitive man as well as an excellent lawyer and accepted the simple though crude reasoning behind the advice.

My mother – whose behaviour my father rather unfairly described as 'cocky' – called her period of captivity a 'most interesting experience'. She shared a single cell with three other women, one a communist, the other two prostitutes. Class distinction and other differences were quickly forgotten. There was one bunk, which the women shared in rotation, the other three sleeping on the concrete floor. They also shared the talk. Today, my mother at 94 still proudly proclaims she discovered what made people turn communist and women become prostitutes.

What annoyed her were the 'interruptions', twice weekly for five weeks. Each time she was taken to a large bare room for endless interrogations. There the Gestapo repeated the same questions over and over again, only to receive the same replies: 'don't know' or 'don't be silly' or variations on these phrases. The only information she could have provided – but never did – was my connection with Uncle Stuuf and our involvement with *Het Parool*. Uncle Stuuf's resistance work had been constantly on her mind, even though she lacked details. 'But the fools never asked me about him.' She had never realized how easy it was to lie, something she had been brought up to despise. After ten such sessions the Gestapo gave up and passed the responsibility on to the prison authorities, forgetting to keep track of her or ask the Dutch to do so. She became a burden to the prison management, who needed the space, and they released her at the end of October.

The question of how and why the Gestapo decided to arrest me remained. Enlightenment came after my mother's release. We had learned soon enough that Carel had been arrested the day before me, whereas Theo had landed in jail about a week earlier. Neither Laura nor Luke nor Brother attracted the Gestapo's attention. They were therefore not after the Apostles. In early November I met Theo's fiancée who provided the pieces that completed the puzzle.

In tears she handed me a letter which Theo had somehow smuggled out of prison. He had been caught *in flagrante delicto* at the place where he manipulated identity cards, on 1 August. A V-man had managed to ingratiate himself with one of his associates with the help of a radio message from the BBC through one of the wireless lines of the England Spiel. Eventually Theo had put the Gestapo on to me. I have never blamed him. As I read about the atrocities he had suffered – the first time I heard the details – I too wept. The abundance of horror stories today threatens to blunt our perception, but it was then news to me. He lasted forty hours, without sleep, food or drink, mostly standing up with his hands manacled behind his back; he was kicked, slapped, spat upon and ridiculed, until exhaustion took its toll and he mentioned my name and that of Carel. He did not mention any others, specifically avoiding Brother whose position as a Dutch police captain was more delicate than any other. Our names were thus deliberate choices. Theo correctly assumed that two names would satisfy his torturers, but guessed wrongly that we would be aware of his arrest and that we would therefore have scrambled to safety.

Carel is reported to have admitted at once to being anti-nazi. He proudly claimed that his Calvinism determined his opposition to irreligious racialist nazism and that the legal irregularities of the occupying forces put him into active opposition. He therefore had to fight nazism and this he repeated ad nauseam, like a record stuck in a groove, without once lapsing into details. He took the initiative and attacked the enemy, a policy he had recommended to me. He realized that such blatant confession might itself incur a severe penalty but it circumvented the need to mention names and incriminate others. As the Gestapo could not link him with Theo's activities, and did not know of any of his own, they left it at that without physical abuse. But he did not escape the death sentence, handed down on manifestly spurious grounds. The nazis were never ones for legal niceties, as Carel, the trial lawyer, pointed out with great eloquence at his trial. He was executed with Theo and others near Schiphol Airport on 20 February 1943.

During the long months of hiding I fell victim to bouts of depression and a feeling of guilt which even today occasionally crops up. Totally unprepared for inactivity, I felt humiliated. I was unprepared too for coping with the captivity of my innocent mother and the not-so-innocent Uncle Stuuf. My feelings for him came to border on hero worship. I worried too about Carel, Theo, Michael, Dorothy and the Apostles. And, yes, about the future of our ideals. I believed in them fervently – still do – and was distraught at the prospect of their loss. Dissatisfied with my lot instead of grateful for my luck, I came to despise myself. My mood must have affected Amanda, but she took care I did not notice. Although she could move about fairly freely, even returning to her college of crafts, she continued to share my life as a fugitive, loyally and lovingly.

Mine was a twilight existence, immobile, fearful, frustrating. I had to remain comprehensively hidden, sometimes in opulent rooms, sometimes in bare attics, never able to go for a walk without suspecting every passer-by of being a spy ready to pounce on me. I relied totally upon contributions from what I have called 'passive resisters'. Some thirty gave us shelter, others provided ration cards. Many were active in small ways in offices, factories, shops. For every active resister there must have been at least ten passive ones. All risked discovery and retribution in one form or another, including death. I have calculated elsewhere (see the Epilogue) that they add up to one fifth of the adult population. In my dictionary they are defined as 'the Resistance', the people's contribution to the defeat of nazism. Of course, many did not want to know or be bothered. Inevitably the latter ones attracted the spotlight of publicity after the war. However, in a democracy like Holland's with twenty-odd parties, any one of them receiving 20% of the vote is quite happy and likely to be a partner in our coalition governments.

I started resistance work again, this time for Freek. He belonged to the group based around Professor Scholten and acted as secretary to the Great Civic Committee. Although much of it was desk work, it gave me back some of my self esteem. Freek's office was on the ground floor of a seventeenth-century patrician house on one of the canals for which Amsterdam is renowned. In this grand room I reflected that with the GCC well established, one of Uncle Stuuf's ideals – the bridge – had been achieved.

The creative episode did not last long, but work cured my depression to a large extent. It also restored enough of my confidence to believe that our ideals might yet be realized. And that with care I might avoid the Gestapo.

I soon saw these were vain hopes. Thus, in March 1943, just before the mass arrests, my brother, on his way to his university laboratory, jumped from a moving tramcar in Amsterdam, a youthful exuberance prohibited by Dutch law. Unfortunately a Dutch policeman stood nearby, stopped him and requested to see his identity card. A quick glance brought an unexpected question: was my brother me? When my brother correctly denied it, there came the surprising advice: 'Whoever you are, with a name like that you'd better scram.' He was what we called a 'good' policeman, a patriot. But it struck my brother – and me when I heard the story – as ominous that even a simple constable remembered my name so long after the event. The incident also influenced my brother's decision to report to the nazi authorities on 13 May as demanded of undergraduates, for any other course would have doubled the danger for our mother.

The next disaster came in the last days of March and on the first of April: 150 people involved with the GCC and including its members were arrested. Freek miraculously escaped arrest because he did not appear on the Gestapo's wanted list. Not yet. I did, of course. News of the massive arrests spread rapidly and astonished everyone by the sheer numbers. I was stunned into near-panic, like many, for we felt sure that the havoc was caused by a traitor and we lacked any indication of his identity. He must have infiltrated much earlier and laid his trap carefully. We were right. The culprit, unmasked only after the war, was the notorious van der Waals. He had made use of the SOE wireless services during the England Spiel to establish, confirm and re-confirm the bonafides he never possessed. In 1946, during a brief spell in which Holland introduced capital punishment for war crimes, van der Waals became one of the few condemned to death and executed.

Freek strongly advised me to leave. Not much urging was needed, for I was sick of my shadowy existence. Freek pointed out that my already reduced usefulness had now slumped to zero. Amanda had, of course, wanted to leave for years and eagerly backed his advice. Freek, almost a generation older, decided to stay and attempt to recover some of the ground lost, in which he succeeded admirably. The College of Confidants owes its existence in part to his persistence and shrewdness. That argument did not apply to me. I was a hunted man even after eight months had elapsed since my flight from the Gestapo.

Before my family leave this book their vicissitudes deserve a postscript. Shortly after Amanda and I left Holland, my brother received the expected demand to report in Amsterdam. He was 20 and felt it his filial duty to avoid endangering our mother a second time. He went to the assembly point, a madhouse of disorganization, and ended up in a camp near Jena, now in

East Germany. He owes his survival to another bureaucratic fluke. His university card contained the subject he was reading: medicine. Someone found this too complicated and on the list accompanying the transport my brother was promoted to 'doctor'. And in that capacity they used him. On his return after the war he completed his studies in a proper manner.

A few days before we left, I also met my mother, surreptitiously and for the first time since her ordeal. Her last words echoed the thoughts of Amanda's father, though she expressed them in a different way. The previous year Rawi, the son of her best friend, had been granted permission to marry his pregnant girlfriend in prison before being executed. On parting my mother referred to this dramatic event when she said quietly: 'Remember Rawi.' The nature of my relationship with Amanda had never been discussed between us, but she knew anyway. However, it was not impropriety that bothered her but the idea that Amanda might become pregnant. She was greatly relieved when I told her that Amanda had been to see a doctor when we went into hiding together. The medical examination revealed a twisted womb, sad yet fortunate in the circumstances.

Four weeks after our departure and two after my brother's, my mother was asked to adopt a nine-month-old Jewish baby. The exodus of Jews had started in earnest. They were instructed to report at a disused theatre, henceforth dubbed the 'Jewish Theatre'. Although closely guarded by nazis, it did not prevent members of the Jewish Council in attendance from smuggling out babies and toddlers. Thus the resistance gained another job. Several thousand were saved. They were passed on to non-Jews who found them suitable homes. Too young for identity cards they still needed ration cards. My mother never hesitated, my father supported her and in this way they acquired another son. It caused some hilarity amongst friends, for he had arrived out of the blue and was also rather large for a new-born child. My parents were, of course, well aware that discovery of this humane crime carried the penalty of being put on a par with Jews and all that this entailed. But the risk paid off: now in his forties, my foster brother lives near New York with his own family, all Jewish, all happy.

One week I hid at Laura's home. Only once was I required to

223

stand in for Alexander. With less sensual success than on previous occasions but, as she sweetly remarked, more sensitive satisfaction. My heart had gone out of it. Laura had lost two more Apostles. Undeterred she searched for new recruits. She also tried to identify and eliminate the V-man who had caused Theo's arrest and for that purpose had even acquired guns for herself and Luke. Her efforts were doomed, and the V-man proved elusive. Then, in that same spring of 1943 Brother and Gerard were also arrested and shortly afterwards executed. With Luke, though without an operator or any other means of communicating with England, she carried on gathering information. Ironically, collecting it proved easier than passing it on. Civil servants were now quite ready to co-operate.

It was not until Alexander arrived a few months later that she came into her own again.

Chapter Seventeen

ALEXANDER RETURNS TO HOLLAND

In London, after a full year at his monitoring job, Alexander's life changed again. His frustration was sapping his stamina. On 5 April 1943 Hans von Dohnanyi was arrested in Berlin together with Dietrich Bonhoeffer and a few others. Irena took Alexander's advice and left the next day for a permanent stay with her uncle and aunt in Lausanne. Alexander had now lost his only personal contact with the German resistance. He asked Bruce Crane to relieve him of his duties and Uncle Steve to accept him as an assistant.

The latter had other plans, however. Now a Commodore, van Alblas had come to know and appreciate an army major called Somer, in charge of the new Dutch intelligence unit BI. He introduced Somer to Alexander. The two rapidly established a rapport and this developed into admiration. As a result Alexander accepted Somer's invitation to be dropped into Holland again, this time as the special envoy of the exiled government with the revitalized OD. In May he started on a much improved training course near London. All contact with the German resistance and with Irena was lost and a chapter of his life ended. Or so he felt.

When he parachuted down in the early hours of 22 June, eastern Holland presented its peaceful self, the countryside exactly as remembered. He came to realize the deceptiveness of this first impression soon enough. The human situation bore little resemblance to the one he had left behind two years previously. The resistance was no longer confined to the handful of surreptitious amateurs among the mass of a dour, dispirited population. It had spread everywhere, as had its support from the now grimly determined people. A sense of professionalism prevailed.

To Alexander this came as a revelation. He felt elated in one sense, though deflated in another. To him the war had primarily been a fight against the evil in nazism. Hence his empathy with the German resistance. After Wiardi Beckman's capture, Dutch resistance had been relegated to second place. His elation stemmed from discovering the maturity of the Dutch resistance, his deflation from the fact that the German resistance lacked the widespread support now prevalent in Holland. To him the arrest of Dohnanyi, Bonhoeffer and others signalled its ultimate failure. In this he was wrong, as he now admits, for others – in particular Claus von Stauffenberg – took over and nearly succeeded with the bomb plot of 20 July 1944. Without massive support from inside, the resisters needed outside support. They never got it.

One of the reasons – revealed only recently – was Kim Philby, then head of the Iberian desk of MI6. Part of his role as a Soviet agent was to use his official position to block approaches from the German resistance, among them Otto John. New German emissaries had contacted MI6 agents in Spain and Portugal; their reports did not get beyond Philby. As Philby himself explained after his defection to Moscow: 'It would have been dangerous for the Russians to think we were dickering with Germans.' Consequently, neither Menzies nor Churchill nor Eden were fully aware of the continuing struggle of the anti-nazi resisters in Germany. Alexander still wonders what would have happened if a more constructive approach had been adopted by Britain.

Alexander's instructions for his work in Holland seemed straightforward enough, if rather ambitious. The exiled government believed that the OD had collapsed, yet someone unidentified was apparently still acting as its chief. He was to find out who, and liaise. Secondly, the GCC had been arrested in its entirety. He was to find out who was responsible for the disaster and what chances there were of a re-grouping. Thirdly, the underground press had become a national force. He was to contact the editors of the main papers. Fourthly, the England Spiel had virtually wiped out military intelligence gathering. He was to find, introduce and instruct a string of local agents — operators with transmitters would be sent — to improve communication with England. Finally, he was to provide contacts for resistance groups and their communication with London. In all a formidable and daunting task.

Alexander was not expected single-handedly to change the course of Dutch wartime history at a stroke. Two BI agents had already been dropped in March and a third one early in June, ten days before Alexander. More were to follow. All did excellent work. However, during the summer and autumn of 1943 Alexander was undoubtedly the motive force behind the establishment of an efficient communications network with England and the creation of a broad base on which others could build.

He did not immediately contact either the Flemings or Laura or anyone else who had been involved previously. He did not know who was still free let alone free from nazi surveillance. But he did not want to delay the search for the unidentified OD chief. He therefore took the plunge and went to see the local GP of a town in the extreme north-east, an important member of the OD. The town boasted a port from where coasters still scuttled to Sweden. One of the coaster captains carried messages to and from the Dutch consulate in Stockholm. In this way the GP had been informed of Alexander's arrival and the GP gave him the swift introduction to the OD chief expected.

In the months that followed, Alexander established a perfect rapport with the OD chief, a scion of an old aristocratic family, single and, however security conscious, rather reckless as he went around on an unusual racing bike. The OD turned out to be well organized and a much more potent force than it had ever been before with a fairly substantial intelligence gathering unit. Alexander was now able to carry out most of his instructions.

SOE played no part in Holland. Although it successfully dropped twenty-five two-men sabotage crews, they landed in the wrong place at the wrong time. It was therefore all the more important that Alexander and his colleagues from BI should succeed in establishing a satisfactory spy network. Inevitably he encountered practical problems. His identity card contained six errors of which he was quickly made aware by his new friends. A perfect one was promised though never received. It had been made but fell into the hands of the Gestapo. This would not have mattered but for two details. The name and most particulars were, of course, pure invention, but it carried his photograph with the impressive handlebar moustache, and it mentioned his exceptional height.

More and more identification papers were required as the war went on. For to wage what already looked like a lost war, Hitler needed not only raw materials but also raw recruits to replace his own nationals conscripted into his armed forces. An identity card – flawless or flawed – would not on its own prevent arrest. Exemptions too were needed, a pass which proved the bearer's value for the Dutch economy. These existed in great variety and the falsification groups had their work cut out. They produced German stamps, German letter-headings, German signatures, even German typefaces, almost on demand. Alexander's pass made him an official of the Central Crisis Control Service (CCCD) which regulated rationing of food and clothes, a very important person indeed.

Another problem was finding a home where he could hide. It solved itself more easily than anticipated when he carefully went to the Flemings to retrieve his belongings. They welcomed him like a lost son, for in some way he did replace Michael, whose traumatic experiences were recounted with resignation and pride. Through them he also contacted Laura, where eventually he enjoyed hospitality of a different and more complex kind.

Yet another obstacle complicated his work: transport. Like most people Alexander was thrown back on the trusted bicycle. He took to the splendid machine the OD provided with relish. But it gradually lost its attraction. A bicycle is a sound and secure means of transport but frustratingly slow. It also demands a lot of energy, especially for long distances, as Alexander found out when he had to receive some new operators, parachuted with their transmitters in a triangle of farming country where public transport did not exist any more. He had to cycle for days, always, it seemed to him, in rain, always against a head-wind. He still calls Holland 'Windland'.

While he noticed the improvement in the resistance, he also witnessed – and came to be embroiled in – its squabbles. These revolved around the vexed question of the transitional period between the defeat of the nazis and the return of the legitimate government. Who would be responsible for law and order then? A clash materialized between those who produced the main underground papers and those who led the para-military OD. The publishers claimed to be best suited to take ultimate control, the OD maintained that it was better equipped for what looked like a police operation. The old antagonism between smart politicians and simple soldiers reared its head, aggravated by a clash of personalities. Ironically, the publishers were not professional politicians, nor were the para-military groups led by professional soldiers. Both sides reverted to dubious methods to support their case with the exiled government, both requested authority for that purpose.

There were, of course, potential dangers from both left and right. The communists might proclaim a revolution and make use of the expected chaos to impose one as some of them wanted. Few of us trusted them anyway. The communist leaders were openly confronted with this possibility, denied it and remained loyal to legality, crown and cabinet included. The communists also lost more lives than any other group, but always maintained contact with the main underground press and with the politicians at the highest level.

Danger also threatened from the other extreme. Para-military groups might impose rule by royal decree without parliament. However, they lacked the means and support of the queen, even her silent acquiescence. And Alexander soon found out that the OD chief, while strongly in favour of a dominant role for the OD during the transitional period, harboured no dictatorial ambitions. Still, there were many areas of agreement. Thus the danger that everyone wished to avoid was Hatchet Day, the day of reckoning when the population would revenge itself indiscriminately on the nazis and their Dutch collaborators, a free-for-all that would betray the very values we had been fighting for. Agreement on this potential danger made disagreement on its prevention all the more serious. Alexander should have intervened and arbitrated. He failed to do so in the short time available, thwarted by the complexities of the resistance. Resistance had become warfare, but underground, in great secrecy. Postwar commentators should take this into account before passing judgement on perceived lapses.

Disagreements could not be openly aired as in peacetime. The protagonists were in deep hiding, forever changing locations and cover-names. Meetings of more than three people were deemed too dangerous. Transport had become arduous. All this complicated communication. Although Alexander sensed the core of the conflict soon enough, he gave priority to the twin tasks of setting up a spy network and liaising with the OD, both of immediate military importance. The squabbles appeared irrelevant. Meanwhile the antagonists started to woo the exiled government vigorously through their two separate courier services to Switzerland. This led to a 'spy scandal' that still reverberates today.

The OD found a way to see what its newspaper 'rivals' sent there. The photographer who microfilmed documents for both was persuaded to let the OD have copies. Alexander saw little harm in what purported to be an exercise in gaining more information. But the OD used it to tarnish its 'rivals' in a report to London. Poaching had become spying on fellow resisters with a view to undermining their influence with the exiled government, a despicable act. The rival route was also accused of bias in the selection of and the comments on the material sent to London. Dr Visser 't Hooft wrote the comments, Peter helped with the selection, scrupulously impartial. It did not remain secret for long: the report found its way to the newspaper 'rivals' even before it reached London. The row that ensued was finally settled by a member of the College of Confidants. Peter has never forgiven his brother Alexander for sanctioning the initial poaching, though he had no hand in the infamous report. Otherwise they remain the most amicable of brothers.

Three months after his arrival Alexander finally met Laura. The delay was caused by the determination to get his operation going before getting entangled in affairs of the heart. And entangled he became.

By stealth he had come to know a little about her vicissitudes, her return to apostolic activities with Luke, as well as my flight. He heard too that she was well, living at home as before, and that his brother Peter had left for an unknown destination.

Alexander met Laura on the neutral ground of a café in Amsterdam. It did not stay neutral for long. The other customers first threw furtive glances in their direction but soon stared at the unusual couple. Alexander and Laura hurriedly departed after paying for their ersatz coffee, walked to the nearby station and took the train to her home.

He was happy to find that their amorous ardour had not cooled after two years' separation. The night passed in sleepless surrender to Eros. However, the passion elicited a chilling note. There was never any doubt about Laura's dedication to Alexander, nor about her absolute loyalty. She reported on the few frolics with me, which he himself had suggested and therefore taken for granted. But he had not bargained for one other dalliance, which had ominous implications.

The approaching dawn threw faint light into the room, where they drowsed between bouts of lovemaking. Laura was fondling him with her slim fingers and long nails, and complimented him on his stamina. Perhaps understandably she compared it to mine, which she described as reasonable. She then followed this harmless confidence with another about Matthew, whose performance she called totally unsatisfactory.

'Well, perhaps his prowess has been improved by his marriage,' said Alexander playfully.

'No, it hasn't.'

'How would you know?' Alexander asked, unsuspectingly.

'Because I had him last month,' she replied casually.

His voice did not betray his sudden anxiety: 'Why?'

Laura, still unaware of the significance of her confession, pointed out that she had not 'had' Alexander for two years, nor me for six months, that Luke was untouchable, and that Matthew had been desperate.

231

'But why a traitor?'

'He's not a traitor in the sense that you and I attach to it.'

'How do you know?'

'Feminine intuition, if you like. Too wet anyhow.'

'Still, fairly risky.'

Laura chuckled: 'Not really. A harmless and adoring man seemed preferable. He's quite attractive too. He didn't ask any questions and never stopped talking about his frightfully domineering wife. Apparently *she* finds solace outside the marital home in abundance.'

Laura had met Matthew a few times at the increasingly rare social occasions which she continued to attend to keep up appearances. Matthew had seemed happy enough at his job, admired his father-in-law, but was dissatisfied with the daughter. Alexander decided not to pursue the subject nor to show his growing concern. He could no more leave Laura out of his life, even in wartime, than Laura him out of hers. Also, the depleted Apostles supplied valuable information, and he resolved to introduce one of the new agents to Laura and Luke as soon as feasible.

But for safety's sake, Alexander determined to make enquiries about Matthew, to restrict the time he spent at Laura's home, to avoid giving her any of his hiding addresses and in future to meet her on neutral ground. His enquiries – of necessity limited – basically confirmed what Laura had told him. After all, Matthew had not betrayed Laura or Luke, nor anyone else during the past fifteen months, although in a position to do so.

Some four months later – at the end of January 1944 – it ceased to matter. Alexander suspected that something was wrong when Laura did not turn up at a rendezvous. He tried to phone her home but did not get a reply and went to investigate. Surreptitiously making his way to the house, he found it teeming with uniformed nazis. Puzzled as well as desperate, he pedalled swiftly on past the grounds, unable to understand how the subtle but successful lines of communication could have failed to disclose such a major event.

His borrowed bike took him the twenty miles to the

Flemings. They were the only ones with secure access to his aunt. Doctor Fleming could phone his colleague whose patients included members of the van Alblas family. It worked. The doctor's news, however, was shattering. Something terrible had happened, involving Laura.

Desperate for details, Alexander made arrangements to meet his aunt in the same park where Amanda had had her regular meetings with my father. It was a very courageous decision of Lady van Alblas', as she was obviously in great distress. It was also rather risky for Alexander, for she might be shadowed.

She was not and, however painful, she clearly wanted to share the memory of what she had seen. The van Alblas house, she explained, had been requisitioned for a German general. Most large houses in the area had suffered that fate much earlier. German occupation of the property was only postponed because of the status of its owners, of which Lady van Alblas had arrogantly reminded German military personnel on a previous occasion. A lieutenant had demanded to inspect the house on behalf of his general. 'My husband is an admiral. No one of lower rank will be admitted.' A month later the nazis returned, in force.

Laura and Luke had just finished a meeting and Laura accompanied Luke to his bicycle near the entrance gate. Lady van Alblas had gone upstairs and was standing at a window watching the two walk down the long driveway with a clear view of the scene.

Suddenly two armed uniformed nazis came through the gate. She felt no real concern, just slightly surprised. Nazis abounded. She saw Laura halt, then Luke. To her horror one of the nazis pointed a gun at them. The other followed suit. That did not fit the scenario. It was now that Lady van Alblas felt a twinge of fear.

Laura must have panicked, for she drew her revolver. Lady van Alblas next heard several shots without seeing who fired first, and then saw one of the nazis fall. Appalled, she tried to wrestle the window open, and failed. Helplessly she spotted Luke drawing his revolver. The other nazi, in equal panic, started shooting, but apparently missed. Laura aimed coolly, carefully fired again and he too fell.

Now all hell broke loose. More nazis rushed through the gate, machine guns blazing.

With a crash Lady van Alblas at last threw the window open. Silence reigned. It was all over.

Both Laura and Luke lay riddled with bullets on the grass beside the drive.

Lady van Alblas could not believe it, made it to her bedroom and collapsed. 'The first time in my life,' she said to Alexander. 'And the last, I assure you.' She was sedated by the family doctor who had somehow been alerted and rushed to the scene.

The next morning Lady van Alblas awoke in hospital, from where her sister took her home. She had regained her composure when she met with Alexander in the park. She could not be sure about some details but about the shooting itself she was in no doubt. During the telling she occasionally stopped to swallow, not to cry. 'Laura went down fighting. A true daughter of a sailor.'

Alexander was shattered but restrained himself to avoid another breakdown of his brave aunt. The full impact came later, when it made him determined to find out about the missing details. For instance, why had the nazis come with guns in the first place? If they wanted to requisition the house it seemed rather excessive. Lady van Alblas did not understand, and just kept muttering through clenched teeth: 'Traitor!'

Two days after the meeting with his aunt, Alexander was riding his bicycle in Amsterdam when a German staff car passed, paused and stopped, releasing four nazis who jumped out and arrested him jubilantly. The senior SD officer had recognized the tall figure with the handlebar moustache from the photograph on the identity card. A month earlier the arrest of several of Alexander's collaborators had raised the suspicion that the tall man with the moustache was an important agent.

There followed more than one hundred hours of uninterrupted interrogation, like Theo's, but even longer: five days and five nights. More than forty years later Alexander and I debated whether the fact that the SD *Sachbearbeiter* – the official in charge of his case, the same man who had arrested him – was a professional policeman and not a sadist contributed to his ultimate survival. Professionals do respect professionalism in others, even adversaries. Alexander even complimented his adversary on his skill during the more relaxed periods of the *Dauervernehmung*. The *Sachbearbeiter* was justifiably proud, and returned the compliment.

Alexander was condemned to death, as were his collaborators. The latter were executed almost immediately. Surprisingly, Alexander and one of his main assistants were transported to Germany. Alexander believes that the nazis wanted to extract more information, for they must have sensed that he had not divulged much. In different surroundings with nothing to lose, with perhaps further reprieves or even commutation of the death to a life sentence, Alexander might co-operate.

He, of course, looked for every opportunity to abscond. His chance came in November 1944 when he and his comrade jumped out of a moving train in Germany. That was Alexander's second train jump to safety, though less fortunate, for he broke ribs, gashed his head and was concussed for some time. His comrade sustained no injuries, and tended to him until he awoke in a deep ditch. After strong pleas from Alexander he then found his way back to Holland, leaving Alexander to make his way back on his own when he could, and to solve the mystery of his aunt's last words about Laura's death: 'Traitor! Traitor!'

Chapter Eighteen

MY ESCAPE TO ENGLAND

The dramatic events of the past few weeks had made me tense, Amanda strangely excited. On 30 April 1943 most of Holland was in the grip of a strike, with the fortunate exception of the railways. We had been sheltering with the wife of Ad Viruly, a KLM pilot then in England, famous for captaining a daring flight of a rickety Dakota to Australia in 1934 and for his popular books on flying. But we spent our last night on Dutch soil in the centre of Amsterdam within walking distance of the station. It should have been a memorable occasion. Our hosts were great friends of my parents. The house was a seventeenth-century gem with antique furniture dominating a scene reminiscent of an interior by Pieter de Hooch. Slim though surprisingly spacious, the house nestled on a small canal which connected two wider canals where grander patrician houses vied with each other. Our room at the top contained an old but extremely comfortable four-poster. The hospitality was warm and supportive. Yet the joy of this ambiance and the prospect of our dash to freedom from persecution did little to raise my depressed spirits. I felt I had failed my country in its hour of need by being of no use to the resistance. Even Amanda's ardour took time to dissipate my tenseness. It did, of course. Content, we fell asleep.

Only to be shaken out of it by an awesome bang.

The noise was followed by the cracking of flames, the sirens of fire engines and a sky brightly lit up.

Sleep did not return, we dozed fitfully. If another attack by a resistance group were taking place, it would surely be followed by stringent restrictions on movement as well as tighter security checks. The railways too might join the strike and we were depending on the train to take us south to the border. Not only was I hunted, I now also *felt* hunted, and useless. Amanda was hardly affected by any of these considerations, still excited at the prospect of an adventurous trip to London. She lacked experience and relied confidently on mine.

After venturing out early that morning we learned the cause of the night's explosion: an American bomber had crashed on the Carlton Hotel, half a mile from our abode. The nazis were too busy dealing with the strike to bother about us. Indeed, the very anarchy prevailing as a result of these disparate events may well have helped us as we made our way to the station.

Once in the crowded carriage I continued to fret, however, and took every passenger for a nazi on my trail. It was my sister's birthday too, which I would fail to attend for the first time in her fourteen years. She might resent my absence more than enjoy the special present my mother would give her on my behalf. Amanda, though, was magnificent. She kept telling me that I had no choice. 'Grit your teeth and smile,' she said. Slowly her equanimity cleared my mind of its conflicting feelings of fear and excitement. We were on our way.

I was bolstered too by the friars at the frontier. They showed surprise only at my long absence and at the fact that there were just the two of us. Rather shamefacedly they confessed that their bishop had forbidden any more help with border crossings. However, they added shrewdly that I knew my way across anyhow and that sheltering old friends fell outside the ban. They showered hospitality on us that night and, stimulated by their cheerfulness and obvious rapport with Amanda, I fully recovered my sanity and stamina.

Much relieved, we arrived in Antwerp, and went on to Hoboken by tram, where we found 'For Sale' signs on both the house with the green door and the house with the yellow door, which I had come to know so well ten months earlier. We next tried the grand home of the Dutch engineer in charge of Cockerill shipbuilding. His wife, charming but clearly nervous, gave us lunch. The manager in Namur, our lifeline to Switzerland, had been arrested and her husband had become much more careful. However, she gave us an address in Brussels whose occupants could help us along better than her husband. Anxious to move and mindful of her embarrassment, we politely declined her offer of hospitality and the four-poster.

Towards dinnertime, travelling again by tram, we found the address in Brussels, a huge multi-storey block of flats with a concierge. He looked us over, then whispered 'scram!'. The Gestapo, he explained, had that very morning arrested the people we had innocently asked for. We quickly followed his advice, turned into a park and sat down on a bench, totally at a loss.

After all these setbacks in one day I felt dejection returning, but Amanda refused to be downcast. She suddenly remembered the name of a widowed aunt. A café telephone directory provided the address. With the help of passers-by we finally arrived at an opulent block of flats only three storeys high, landscaped, with a drive and a uniformed porter instead of an ordinary concierge.

Aunt Agnes van Doetighem had vaguely heard about us through a letter from Amanda's father, couched in puzzling terms, and was happy to harbour obvious fugitives. Saved by the bell. 'Only one spare bedroom I'm afraid, but twin beds,' she said with a twinkle. Not to worry and no more worries at least for a few days. Sleep, just sleep.

We were very obviously at a dead end. Aunt Agnes, in her early sixties and an incurable busybody, showed her joy at helping people in need by a shower of hospitality. Her husband had died a few years before, leaving her well-off, but with little else to occupy her stupendous energy than bridge and gossip. She was also very practical, hid us from her nosy bridge cronies, seemed content to keep us forever and discussed various courses of study we might follow.

One day she disappeared, left us to our own devices and returned three days later from a mystery trip, carefully timed between bridge sessions. She had gone to Holland, talked herself past the border guards, and seen Amanda's father for the first time in years. She had also been introduced to my parents. The trip served two purposes: it reassured the parents and confirmed our story. She even managed to lay hands on the police demand for my arrest.

Why had she done this? One of her rich bridge cronies harboured communist sympathies, which the ultra conservative Aunt Agnes accepted as the harmless quirk of a much maligned millionairess. The lady's unhandsome but intelligent daughter had a relationship with a supposed communist, a miserable hairdresser with a pencil moustache and plastered-down hair, who was said to be suffering from an unfortunate wife and awful children. This seamy appearance hid an Englishman working for MI9, the escape organization of the British secret services, and probably also for MI6. Not even his mistress's mother recognized his true identity. His communism – and his 'family' – formed part of his cover. In reality a bachelor, he was truly in love with the wealthy lady's daughter. Aunt Agnes had guessed he truth and now, armed with the documents she had collected on her trip to Holland, she asked him for help. London agreed in part: I, and I alone, could take the established route to Spain. Amanda was judged to be in no danger and of no value in England, and therefore had to remain behind, a silly decision which the hairdresser was at a loss to explain. There was nothing we could do about it.

Depressed, I left for France without Amanda. She would attend an art course in Brussels and act as companion to Aunt Agnes, a wonderful woman who, while clearly delighted with this unexpected arrangement, nevertheless sincerely shared in our distress. I began the journey by crossing the French border on foot, not too many miles, and ended up in Wattrelos, the grimy suburb of Roubaix, twin town of Lille. I was billeted with a local policeman and his wife: Paul and Angèle, who were extremely helpful within extremely limited resources. Paul drank a litre of wine each day in the company of his colleagues after duty hours, a rather risky ritual as several of them were either nazi sympathizers or strictly dutiful. Often Paul came home the worse for drink, but he never disclosed his undercover activities. Although forever complaining about this stupid habit, Angèle tended to his need with loving kindness. Perhaps she suspected, as I did, that the unfortunate indulgence constituted part of his cover-up. They formed an ideal couple.

The money they were paid for their pains in harbouring fugitives barely covered the cost of the food that Angèle expertly cooked for the many unknown victims of nazism. That was their contribution to the defeat of the *'sales boches'*, who had killed both their fathers in World War I. They had also lost their only child recently, a fifteen-year-old daughter. This contributed to their wish to atone. Not everyone acted so selflessly.

Paul's resistance chief was also British and from MI9, again perfectly camouflaged, this time as a Frenchman. When Paul and Angèle heard the dismal story of my separation from Amanda they pleaded with him for justice and the reinstatement of the *status quo ante*.

A fortnight after my lonely departure from Brussels, Amanda duly arrived, unannounced, unexpected and in a happy mood. MI9 had relented and Aunt Agnes had let her go. MI9 had given her a password for Spain – 'Shakespeare' – and added a condition: we should tell everyone we were married until our arrival in Britain. The ban on women had been provoked by the habit of some Belgians and Frenchmen of escaping with their mistresses, not from the Gestapo but from their wives. We happily told the British agent that we intended to get married.

One night an unusual sound woke us up. Surprised, we could hear loud singing outside. Frightened, we rushed downstairs where we found Paul and Angèle glued to the window. Paul turned round, a finger on his lips, and pointed to a small group of drunks in the street, weaving their way past. In the silence of the night their songs could be clearly distinguished as English. By the light of a half-moon and the stars, we recognized them as British pilots, like us in hiding to await the day of departure, unlike us oblivious of the danger their behaviour presented to all those involved in helping them to safety. We were desperately frightened as we watched helplessly. Luckily the folly went unobserved by the nazis and their collaborators.

A few days later we left for Paris. We were six: three of the British pilots we had seen had joined us together with a Belgian, with a Frenchman as our guide. We travelled in pairs to reduce the risk of arrest, for if one pair got caught the others could escape. Although our papers were supposed to be perfect, this could not be said of everyone's French, a distinct disadvantage when awkward questions came to be asked. Our French guide shuttled between the pairs but showed an unfair preference for the two of us, not because of my then fluent French but because of Amanda's appearance. He was clearly a lady's man, small but handsome and very self-confident. He claimed to be the lucky husband of a lovely wife in Lille and the proud father of a boy and a girl, aged eight and six, and he had photographs to prove it. Amanda liked him, but I distrusted his preening over-confidence.

Luckily only one cursory check occurred during the train journey to Paris when our papers proved their reliability and our speech was never tested. We transferred from the Gare du Nord across the city on foot – strung out like ducks behind our guide – to the Gare Montparnasse for the fast train to Bordeaux. There we had to switch to a very slow train because the *zone interdite* started not far beyond at Dax. Stringent checks would follow.

That brought increased tension. Since each carriage was composed of a number of separate compartments with their own exit doors on both sides, we could be closeted with nazis scrutinizing our papers and asking awkward questions for the full five to ten minutes between stops. Suspects were put in the rear carriage for further scrutiny at Hendaye on the Spanish border. At Saubusse the British pilots suffered that fate, as did the Belgian. We saw them being led along the platform. Our guide then advised us to get out at the next stop and walk to a café in St-Jean-de-Luz. Too late: no sooner had he slipped away than two nazis climbed in.

At this point in our saga Amanda became more than a lovely companion and occasional morale booster: she saved our lives, the first of three such occasions and the most inspired one.

The only other passenger in our compartment was a young man attired in a black, tight-fitting coat and an equally fashionable hat. Why had someone so clearly from Paris taken the slow train instead of the fast train unless his papers were less than foolproof? A question Amanda and I had whispered to each other. He looked a good deal more suspicious than we did in our shabby raincoats, Amanda with a dirty scarf, I with a Basque beret.

The door closed, the train started and the two severe-looking nazis viewed their charges, wondering with whom to begin. At this point Amanda cuddled up to me and gave me a kiss, then another one. Perhaps it might be thought there was nothing unusual in this show of affection between young adults whose papers moreover proclaimed them to be married, certainly not in France. But after our recent harrowing experiences and in that tense situation, petting was far from my mind.

The nazis fell for it. They went for the Parisian. He produced his papers in a self-righteous and arrogant way that invited animosity. Then the questions started. Each brief answer was followed by more long questions in elaborate French. The clicking rails and my racing pulse ticked the seconds away. Seconds seemed minutes and minutes hours. At last the train slowed down, and stopped at St-Vincent-de-Tyrosse. The nazis took their prey on to the platform and out of sight, slamming the door shut.

Amanda and I waited until the engine gave a whistle and the train started to move. We then jumped out only to see the exit crowded with uniformed men, checking passengers. We rushed in the opposite direction, down on to the track, then through a gap in the fence and, still undetected, on to a road, walking swiftly, controlling an impulse to run. I glanced back: no one was following us.

A sign, pointing to Bayonne and St-Jean-de-Luz itself, thirty miles on, told us we were on the N 10. It was almost empty of traffic. We walked for many hours, delighting in our good luck. Then with less than ten miles to go, we rested by the side of the road, basking in glorious afternoon sunshine.

Another mile on, around a bend in the road which was protected by fir trees, we were shaken out of our complacency by the roar of aeroplane engines. Puzzled, we glanced round. Then we saw the planes, only a few hundred yards to our left. And soldiers too. To our horror two were moving in our direction, gesticulating. Only then did we see we were on the perimeter of an airfield, the southernmost Luftwaffe base. Something had gone badly wrong, for them as well as for us.

The soldiers must have been sentries. 'Slow down,' I muttered and put my arm round Amanda. We walked on, arms intertwined and heads touching, the occasional kiss. It worked a second time. The soldiers, now close, stopped, waved, then clapped before making ruder gestures. Amanda waved back cheerily. We carried on until trees hid us from view.

I went down on my knees, stretched my joined hands upwards and whispered 'Thank you'. Amanda, unsurprised but surprisingly, joined in the exercise, but got to her feet quicker, remarking rather coyly that she was of some use after all.

At dusk in St-Jean-de-Luz, we found the café and waited for Pierre to turn up. Impatient, we asked the owner who directed us to the guide's house. Pierre himself opened it. To our surprise a stunning young woman stood by his side and a toddler boy peeped through their legs. He welcomed us with kisses, going on tip-toe to reach our cheeks, and introduced the beautiful lady as his wife, with a finger on his lips. As he explained later, when the lovely lady had disappeared with the boy to prepare a meal, the dutiful husband of Lille turned out to be also the dutiful husband in St-Jean-de-Luz, 640 miles separating the towns and the wives. It was not the distance that protected his bigamy but the barrier created by the *zone interdite*, which neither wife could cross. Well-known in the town, he was desperate to keep the bigamy a secret from the inhabitants as well as from us and the ladies involved.

Once a pilot in the French airforce, he had been disappointed with his commanders and equally disgusted with the generals. He used his wits to trade on the war situation and thus get his own back on these pompous characters. He was friendly with Germans, French, British and sundry nationals and had some legitimate business interests that enabled him to become one of the few to enter and leave the prohibited zone at will. He was thus able to collect large sums for acting as a guide. All six of us had paid in advance, without a guarantee, but only two had got through so far. He was clearly a smart operator: treble the amount per 'head'.

The resistance did throw up flotsam and jetsam, scavengers as well as caring people. Even the one redeeming feature in this unscrupulous behaviour – the readiness to help escapees – evaporated when he innocently admitted that the money was essential for his bigamous set-up. He justified his attitude by pointing out the enormous dangers, which were in fact fairly limited, as he implied by promising that the next stage across the Pyrenees would be simple.

The next day we left St-Jean-de-Luz at 6 pm on foot, with a new guide, a Basque 'passeur', to whom I also had to hand a substantial sum in advance. He did not speak French or even understand the few words of Spanish I had learned.

The small country road was flat for a few miles, then started to climb. At dark we left the road for a path that wound its way up the mountains. On the map they may not seem high – between 1,500 and 3,000 feet – but their base was at sea level and they looked forbidding to us. The hours went by as we struggled up ever higher ridges and slid down ever steeper paths. At each ridge we asked the same question: 'España?' and got the same reply, a negative shake of the head. At one stage the passeur suddenly grabbed our arms and pushed us into a cave. He had sensed something, but it took some time before we could dimly discern two Germans passing by, talking and playing with a ferocious dog. The talk kept the fierce animal distracted and saved us from detection. After that I did not begrudge the Basque his fee.

We waited a half hour before proceeding. He then pushed us out and on our way again, up another mountain. This one levelled off to a plateau. The sky was clear, a sliver of moon and masses of stars lighting up our rocky terrain. On we walked until a hint of dawn dimmed the stars.

My watch showed 6 am when a small farmhouse loomed up. The Basque took us inside for some food, a drink and a rest. The occupants' only language was again Basque. The passeur stretched out in the one easy chair, leaving us a bench. After no more than twenty minutes he got up, beckoned us outside into the dawn, and pointed with an outstretched arm to some small hills. 'San Sebastian!' he said, and returned to the house, leaving Amanda and I looking at each other in utter surprise. He clearly did not intend to guide us any further. We were completely dependent on him, did not carry anything – not even a toothbrush – let alone any food. I went back inside the dark house and started arguing, as best I could, with hands and fingers rather than words. I even offered more money, to no avail. He waved me on and repeated 'San Sebastian'.

We were on our own again, more than 3,000 feet up, with unknown miles of mountainous wilderness to navigate, without a map or a clear direction. But at least the going would mainly be downhill and the sun had kindly started to warm our cold bodies. And we were in Spain. We shrugged at each other, held hands and walked on in our torn espadrilles – the local footwear acquired in St-Jean-de-Luz – joyful, disregarding our tiredness and distress at the passeur's behaviour.

At noon we hit a road, winding but paved, which eventually joined a wild stream. A bus rattled past, displaying the name of Oyarzun, a village which Pierre had told us was some six miles from San Sebastian. In mid-afternoon, just after we had passed through a hamlet called Ergoyen, we were suddenly confronted by two members of the Guardia Civil, Franco's dreaded national guard, in their resplendent uniforms and hats. While in France, rumours had circulated that the Guardia Civil sent fugitives back across the French border to the Gestapo. So far we had been lucky not to have met any. As seasoned experts, the trick of the cuddle and kisses now came automatically. It succeeded a third time. It even inspired our potential captors to whistle and blow kisses.

We entered Oyarzun at close to 7 pm and found a tram-stop with people waiting. The tram duly arrived and took us to San Sebastian. We were exhausted and looked like tramps. No one seemed to notice until one of the passengers, a woman on her way out, leaned over to me and asked in uncannily good English where we were going. 'British Consulate,' I said, surprised. She took a piece of paper and wrote down the address, told us to get out at the third next stop, wished us good luck and hurriedly left. Only then did I realize it must have been obvious where we came from. We got off, hailed a taxi, showed the driver the piece of paper, and after a few minutes arrived at a big office block. I stared at the plaque in relief: 'Consulado Inglaterra'.

It was just after 8 pm, but the door was still open. Ahead

loomed a staircase. To me this looked like another mountain. Although we had only one floor to go up, those twenty-six steps demanded more effort than the previous twenty-six hours. Having got to the top we found the door to the consulate closed but our luck still held: it was unlocked, and a tall, middle-aged lady was packing a briefcase ready to depart. Amanda fell into a vast easy chair, I stood there with just enough strength to make a joke of the codeword that MI9 had supplied: 'My name,' I said shakily, 'is Shakespeare.'

The lady took one look at us and burst out laughing. Having already lost my stamina, that made me lose my sense of humour as well. 'It's not my real name, of course,' I explained heavily. 'It's our password.' The lady nodded, still smiling, then explained that the consul was away for a fortnight and she uninformed about such secrets. But she relented, took pity on us and deposited us at a comfortable pensione, where we got a room with a view of the Atlantic Ocean.

It was June, hot and beautiful, and we swiftly regained our stamina, and got restless. Luckily, after a few days, Amanda conjured up another relative, this time a distant uncle, based in Madrid. He turned out to be the Dutch minister to Spain. With the help of the kind lady at the consulate we secured the necessary papers that enabled us to take a train to Madrid. And thus we avoided the sad plight of most escapees who were confined to prisons.

The uncle proved to be very gentle, but he was also a worried man. On his advice the pretence of our marital status was carefully preserved. Not only because of our instructions but because Madrid in June 1943 was a hive of spies and unsavoury characters, among them unfortunately the Dutch consul-general. The uncle's wife kept dubious company too, he explained sadly. He compensated for the complexity of this situation by introducing us to nice people and volatile *corridas*. He could not help us when in September Amanda and I moved to Portugal. There we came face to face with another bureaucratic hiccup that threatened our being together, more serious and an ominous portent of the future.

We stayed at a holiday resort near Sintra on the Atlantic coast, some twenty miles due west of Lisbon, with several tens of compatriots, all waiting to be flown to England. A week or so later the first counter-intelligence officer arrived at the Dutch legation from London to test our reliability, a sensible screen to alleviate the burden on British security. He was a happy choice, for he had himself escaped earlier, had been active in the Dutch resistance and was therefore knowledgeable as well as appreciative of what we had been through.

The interview turned out to be more like a friendly talk than an interrogation, but it led to an extraordinary incident, which now seems farcical, but at the time was very serious. Protocol required a senior member of the legation to be present. He happened to be a middle-aged consul with a high sense of propriety and a peculiar name that proved to be rather fitting: Drogeboom or 'Dry-tree'. My interrogator was aware of some of my activities as well as of Amanda's involvement and was eager for me to fill in the gaps. Towards the end he congratulated me on extricating Amanda as well and, as a matter of personal interest, asked when we got married. I felt relaxed, and released from the promise made earlier, so I told him the true situation. He laughed uproariously.

Not so the consul. He had been abroad much of his diplomatic life. As befitted someone unfamiliar with conditions in Holland, he had been silent up till then. He now interrupted sternly: 'That means you've lied.'

Our renewed laughter did not impress him. 'Lying,' he said pompously, 'is not a laughing matter.'

'No?' I retorted glibly: 'In the resistance it can be a matter of life and death.'

'But you're not in the resistance now.'

I started feeling slightly uneasy. 'And I didn't lie now, did I? And, incidentally, the instruction to say we're married came from the British agent.'

So far this unreal exchange had remained fairly good-natured. But I could not resist concluding with a tendentious dig. 'There's a war on, you know.'

It was intended as nothing more than a flippant remark, but the consul took it seriously. 'Oh, so you're happy to use the war to cover up indecent behaviour?'

'Indecent behaviour?' I reacted angrily. 'You call that indecency? Well, if that's indecent, you can marry us right now. We're ready, you know.'

The consul remained icily stubborn. 'That's beside the point. First you lied, second you're co-habiting illegally.'

At this I completely lost my temper. 'You've no idea what nazism is like to live under, have you? Perhaps you think our escape was indecent too? The nazis certainly think so. Why don't you do the decent thing and go to Holland to find out for yourself?'

My anger at such bureaucratic nicety only served to harden the consul's attitude. 'Whatever your excuses for past co-habitation, there are none now,' he said stuffily. 'I'll have to treat it as an illegal act.'

'You haven't got any jurisdiction over us!' I shouted back.

The consul sensed victory. 'Oh yes I have! First, you're a Dutch national and I represent the Dutch government here. Second, you're dependent on our generosity. I can stop your allowance and refuse to pay your hotel bill.'

'That'll suit me fine! Put us on a plane and let London deal with us!'

'I haven't any say about planes,' he said. 'I now instruct you to leave the room of your mistress at once, and find another hotel.' I could not believe it. Even then, when the moral climate was very different, the whole thing seemed ridiculous. However, the consul too was now losing his composure. 'Find another hotel!' he shouted. 'Otherwise I'll stop your passage to England on the grounds of unreliability and unlawful behaviour!'

The security officer had followed this verbal battle in silent surprise, uncertain of his status, though increasingly certain about the absurdity of it all. The consul's words now drove him to intervene, calmly and firmly. 'With respect, Sir, the decision about reliability and entry into England is mine, not yours.'

The consul had one more card to play and did. 'True, but only for men of military value, not for mistresses.'

At this I stormed out of the room and out of the legation, found my way back to the hotel and reported to Amanda. She could not believe it at first, then chuckled and said we would obviously ignore the instruction and had better forget the whole episode. We did at first and remained in the same room in the same hotel. But we were not given a chance to forget.

The next day the consul, in his determined pursuit of decency, committed another mistake when he told one of our fellow escapees about us. Who was unreliable now? That evening the entire Dutch community knew of our 'indecent co-habitation'. It caused great mirth and gained us much-appreciated moral support. It did not alter our new official position, however. Some ten days later I left, alone and depressed, on a ship to Gibraltar, where I had to wait for more than a fortnight before a second ship took me to England.

I arrived in Plymouth on 6 November, and was in London the next day, some five months after our arrival in Spain and seven after the start of our journey. The free world proved to be rather slower and hemmed in by ifs and buts than the free enterprise adopted in the tightly controlled occupied territories. But the warmth of the reception made up for many of the setbacks suffered in the past.

Baron van Alblas told me about Alexander's return to Holland. This prompted me to volunteer as an agent too, but he gently pointed out that as a wanted man I would not be of much use. Like all escapees, I was introduced to Queen Wilhelmina. This led to two lunches with Her Majesty alone, followed by a meeting in the presence also of the vice-president of the Counci of State, his son – her ADC – as well as van 't Sant.

They wanted to know all about Wiardi Beckman. The queen's interest focussed on the person as well as on what he stood for: the religious motivation and the radical political conclusions he drew from it. The Orange queen a radical? That much abused term can certainly be used for her ancestor William the Silent in the sixteenth century. And, like him, she was ready to reform what rationally needed reform. Thus she instigated a review of the relationship between Holland and its colony the Dutch East Indies, now Indonesia, and openly advocated dominion status in the middle of the war.

As a result of these interviews, I joined the staff of the Ministry of Foreign Affairs, then in Stratton House, Stratton Street, Mayfair. This enabled me to participate in discussions about Holland's future. I vividly remember one meeting – on 18 January 1944 – that saw escapees of various ages and persuasions gathered around the queen and Prince Bernhard. She explained her attendance as that of an observer and – amazingly – stuck to this self-imposed constraint and kept mostly silent. For several hours no one minced words and everyone disregarded the royal presence. The occasionally emotional clashes did not prevent a consensus on many issues. The queen clearly loved every bit of it: democracy in action, witnessed not from a pedestal but in its midst. We felt her to be truly the Mother of the Fatherland. making for a unique parental couple, with William the Silent as the Father. One minister commented: 'In the absence of parliament, Queen Wilhelmina represented the Dutch people. It may have been unconstitutional, but in those circumstances was not unreasonable.' She herself once pointed out: 'Those who accuse me of unconstitutional behaviour have not understood my policy at all. I am not anti-constitutional. On the contrary, the changes which I desire must come into being along constitutional lines.'

It was a hectic life, fascinating and rewarding. Sadly it lasted only a few months, but while it did boosted my morale, sorely needed. The bizarre experiences in Spain and Portugal, culminating in the separation from Amanda, had depressed me. The escape itself came to prey on my conscience as too much of a negative act, an escape in the true sense of the word, and consequently an abdication of responsibility. Yet it had initially been motivated by a positive urge to pass on the ideas for renewal generated by Uncle Stuuf and his allies. These much admired men had become prisoners of the nazis and might even be dead, whereas I was alive and free. The torch they had lit should be carried to other great men, in England. Such dedication to ephemeral concepts beyond my grasp vastly overrated my youthful abilities of persuasion, of course. And the intensity of my zeal inevitably caused agonizing frustration during the interminable months of waiting. It made me blinkered as well as single-minded. This surprised Amanda and affected her. But now, in London, my escape was clearly vindicated. Hence the euphoria.

The rewards proved ample. Many people were kind and seemed genuinely interested. Among them was Dr Jan Willem Beyen, the father of a friend in Holland. As a director of the Bank for International Settlements he had found himself trapped at its headquarters in Basel, Switzerland, when the nazi war machine engulfed Holland, whereupon he made his way to London. Beyen was clearly delighted with news of his family, trapped in Holland, however stale. He allowed me to use one of his two superb cellos occasionally. He also involved me in discussions about postwar European development. I had mentioned the article in *Het Parool* quoted on page 116 and tried to explain to him the thoughts prevalent in the resistance.

Beyen turned out to be fully engaged in preparations for European co-operation and a staunch advocate of the functional approach. In contrast, I championed federation, even though Uncle Stuuf did not share my enthusiasm. Indeed he had smiled at the simplicity of the solution for complex problems: set up a supra-national authority, give it the tools and there will be no wars. Uncle Stuuf had painted a vivid picture of devotees producing grandiose schemes for federal structures in endless detail without any regard to reality. As indeed did happen. But Uncle Stuuf had disappeared before the subject was adequately aired and some of his allies preferred the clear federal route to integration, until they too disappeared.

Beyen now greatly convinced me that federation for Europe was a utopian dream. Existing federations had been created for different reasons in a distant past in circumstances that did not exist in the twentieth century.

'International institutions have to grow organically,' he argued, 'and they must be adaptable to changing circumstances. Today a European federation is too tight and inflexible, nor will it be accepted by proud states. Political co-operation will inevitably follow once a web of international activities and agencies has spread. That splendid spirit of co-operation between nations you described will still be needed, for the states must enact the necessary legislation. But in this way the community itself will be a living body, not through a written act of faith – however important too – but through tangible and active organic development.'

This is, of course, what happened. As Holland's foreign minister after the war Beyen contributed largely to the shape of European integration. His pragmatic idealism was at the core of the EEC. In London he purposely remained outside our government. His affable lifestyle and his international outlook did not go well with the stuffy, parochial attitude of most of the exiled cabinet members. The few exceptions were happy to listen to him. My enthusiasm about this subject did not meet with much response from Dutch civil servants either. What preposterous pretension from a half-educated escapee!

Yet I thrived on these and other activities, and this compensated largely for Amanda's absence. I did not forget her, of course, and talked to whoever wanted to listen, as well as to some who did not.

At the foreign ministry I discovered that the consul in Lisbon had written to the head of the consular service about Amanda and me in disparaging terms. He had not consulted the Dutch minister – his superior at the legation in Lisbon – nor the security officer. That proved his undoing. He was suspended and then retired for breaking the rule of diplomacy, not for his unfair treatment of us. It did nothing to stop ugly rumours about us from filtering through to London. With the sympathetic help of the permanent secretary – my boss – the ban that had prevented Amanda from finishing her journey was once again reversed. But it took a lot of time.

This provided the opportunity to make preparations for our wedding. The Dutch community in London looked forward to so unusual and exciting an event as a marriage between two escapees. They did not have much fun, had not had much for years and even looked askance at escapees. Why? First, because some were indeed rather wild youngsters and most of us had an exaggerated opinion of our own importance and a scarcely concealed contempt for the staid settled Dutch residents. Secondly, because the queen pampered us, their queen whom *they* rarely met except at formal functions and at a distance. Escapees were few and far between: over the five years only some 1,600 reached the British Isles. Still, a wedding was not to be despised. To show my awareness of the divided loyalties I asked the minister of the Dutch Reformed Church to officiate instead of the vicar at my own Church of England. It proved to be of no avail. For when Amanda at last arrived in late January, the wedding, arranged in some splendour for a week hence, had to be postponed, indefinitely as it turned out.

Actually, Amanda sneaked into freedom before I could welcome her. British security dispensed with her in four days, one day less than me and a lot less than most. I spent many frantic hours chasing around London before I finally caught up with her and overpowered her with the elaborate plans for our wedding. Instead of the expected praise Amanda stalled, then said gently but firmly: 'Please wait.'

This did not make sense to me. Clearly a gap had opened up. As I found out in the next few hours, Amanda had tasted freedom from tensions during the four months she had spent in Portugal after my departure. She had shed the encumbrances of the straightened circumstances under nazism and found peacetime life most enjoyable. To her the war was finished, bar a few battles which others would fight. It had given her the time to reflect that I lacked. She had accepted my single-mindedness initially with approval, but gradually came to find that it clashed with her more fanshaped approach. She also realized that for me the war was not over, nor the fight for a better society that formed an indelible part of my resistance. Her involvement with the resistance had been practical, whereas mine was emotional and idealistic as well. Confronted with the momentous decision of marriage with a splash, Amanda repeated that she needed time.

I was shocked to the core. I pointed out that the meetings and discussions represented the prolongation of resistance by other means. It failed to impress Amanda. I did not know how to react and got angry, tried to convince her of the un-reasonableness of her stance, implored her to change her mind, even argued that postponement would be unfair to those who had helped her reach London. I may well have said: 'Wedding first, reflection later.' Or words to that effect. I then set her an ultimatum: forty-eight hours to make up her mind, when I would come to collect the answer in person. It cannot have been a pretty scene.

Those two days and nights were the worst I had ever

experienced. When I came to collect the answer, the flat where she stayed with a girlfriend was empty. An envelope with my name on it was pinned to the door. The note inside apologized but pointed out that forty-eight hours was peanuts in terms of a lifetime, repeated a plea for patience and promised contact 'in due course'. I did not see it for the reasonable request that it sounds in retrospect. I felt totally let down. I turned my back on the wonderful past and scribbled on the reverse of the note: 'Finito'. Like a spoilt child.

It is, of course, useless to speculate about what would have happened if we had gone through with the ceremonies or if I had shown the patience which maturity gave me many years later. The irreversable does not allow for reversing and the result probably served us both best. I can only record that the shock of the abrupt cancellation of the wedding sent my credibility with the Dutch community plummeting.

There is a happy sequel to this sad episode. Eventually Amanda met and married a man who contrived to re-arrange the twisted womb the doctor had diagnosed in 1942, which enabled her to have the children she craved. And I had the immediate and inestimable support of friends, who shook me out of my lethargy and misery and set me back on the road to normality.

Some months later this led to a brief, uncomplicated yet bitter-sweet affair with Sylvia, the daughter of a shipping magnate. Like most young women in Britain of all ranks and stations she was on active military service. Some historians attribute Hitler's ultimate failure to his reluctance to involve women in the war effort other than as breeders of perfect Aryans. Sylvia belonged to the ATS as a dispatch rider. A liberated woman with an infectious zest for life, not unlike Amanda's, she was otherwise totally different: blonde, blue-eyed, well-rounded rather than slim, with an innocent face rather than a shrewd one. Sylvia's fiancé had recently been killed in action somewhere in Africa, my fiancée had been lost to the whirl of a new life. Both of us wanted to forget the past, both of us needed sympathy.

Apart from attending hectic dinner-dances, she loved taking

me out on her motorbike, perhaps to prove her indubitable proficiency in an area previously presumed to be a male prerogative. I had never manipulated any mechanical means of transport. It therefore intrigued me to watch Sylvia straddle the large bike, stand astride to kickstart, settle down and pin the petrol tank between her leather-clad legs, rev the engine and confidently move off with a whoop of joy. The freedom the motorbike offered as it cruised along southern England's undulating country lanes in exceptionally warm April weather proved a new and pleasurable experience. I felt happy and not a little proud to let her lead and liberate us from war's reality.

It also had an erotic dimension. Sylvia soon admitted that the throbbing engine had a stimulating effect on her body, which my male presence behind her converted to exultation. Pillions were not as comfortable as they are today, nor the dress as elaborate. The tight seating arrangements made for intimate bodily contact. With my arms folded around her, my hands often fondled her breasts. She delighted in my response, and sometimes she stopped in some field to enable us to relieve the tensions thus aroused.

For a couple of months we experienced sheer forgetful bliss.

Sylvia was killed on duty, by a bomb in an air raid. I then joined the army just in time for the Normandy invasion and continental Europe's liberation from Hitler's oppression.

Chapter Nineteen

ALEXANDER SLAYS
THE PHANTOM

Alexander was left lying badly wounded in a ditch in Germany. His nazi escort on the train failed to find him. Somehow he got out of the ditch and managed to reach a town and a hospital, where he was kept for several months. He saved himself from detection by pretending to be a Dutch labourer and a victim of the then almost daily bomb attacks on Germany. This explained his lack of personal papers and provided him with a new identity. The ruse succeeded.

Eventually he returned to Holland, determined to solve the mystery that had obsessed him for the last year: who had caused Laura's death? Was there indeed a traitor, as Lady van Alblas had hinted at their last meeting? After some complicated manoeuvres he contrived to meet her in the same wood where they had met last. It was a happy reunion, for Lady van Alblas had given him up for lost. He heard that his brother Peter had been sending witty postcards from Switzerland, but also that Wiardi Beckman had been moved to an unknown destination in Germany, or, as she put it, into the fog of some camp, an unwittingly apt description for the *Nacht und Nebel* (night and fog) camp he had indeed been dumped in, Natzweiler. It did not, however, produce any more than an indication for the cause of Laura's death. But it did suggest an idea which he decided to follow up.

Alexander re-established contact with the OD-chief and found his erstwhile collaborator with whom he had shared death sentence, prison and train jump. To them he mentioned his predicament about Laura's death. It was early 1945, heating in the freezing temperature was non-existent, food almost impossible to get – even tulip bulbs were at a premium – the railways were on strike, bicycles therefore also at a premium. For the resistance these deprivations were compensated for by the availability of the many technical tools so desperately wanted before. These included easy access to personal papers in great variety, an entirely separate – therefore secret – nation-wide telephone system, a shortwave radio network for internal communication, and also – more doubtful – revolvers. They had been used too, for eliminating a few notorious V-men and several other traitors, as well as in self defence. Alexander was pressed to carry one.

One day he boldly bicycled the twelve miles to Luke's parents' house, ostensibly to offer condolences, in reality to see what light they could shed on the tragedy. The visit was full of danger. He had to use his own identity, a serious risk for one of the most hunted men in Holland. He had known Luke only slightly, his parents not at all. Although he assumed the father to be as principled as the son, this was by no means a foregone conclusion. Families were split, as Matthew's was. Even so, word might get round that he was operative again, something the Gestapo did not yet know. He carried the revolver in the inside pocket of his coat, planned various escape routes and timed his unannounced arrival for just after dark at 5 pm, even though the father might not yet have returned from work. It would allow plenty of scope for escape.

He need not have worried: the father was at home and recognized him instantly from Luke's description and his height. That quick identification made him uncomfortable. The father also turned out to be a staunch anti-nazi and mad at the culprits responsible for his son's death. He kept a stiff upper lip throughout their hour-long talk and expressed his gratitude for Alexander's visit in such dangerous circumstances. Near the end he apologized for not offering a meal, not because of the food scarcity but because he wanted to keep his wife out of it. Her involvement would not only increase the chances of Alexander's presence becoming more widely known, but also confuse the issue with emotional scenes. At this he himself nearly broke down. Yes, he had a definite opinion about what had happened but felt it inappropriate to tell Alexander the details. He advised him instead to go to the best source of all: Matthew's father.

At this Alexander stiffened. Matthew had been on his mind, but he had discarded the idea because he trusted Laura's opinion of him as a wet rather than a traitor. Moreover, a traitor would go to the Gestapo, not involve army officers. He did not relish visiting Matthew's father, for although reputedly a patriot he remained a father. He tried to draw out his host. In vain, though Luke's father, sensing the train of Alexander's thoughts, vouched for the reliability of Matthew's father, a great friend of his who as a notary could be trusted to maintain absolute confidentiality. It might be tricky but not an awful dilemma, for both fathers had discussed the events and both were as resolved to establish the truth as Alexander seemed to be. He refused to say more. Perhaps, Alexander thought, it was not Matthew after all. It had seemed unlikely anyhow.

Alexander returned to Amsterdam in two minds. Having given away his identity once, would he get away with it a second time? On the other hand, he had been given a lead and desperately wanted a solution. He owed it to Laura as much as to himself and the families involved. He consulted his comrades. One of them had dug up some information, though not much. It confirmed that Matthew's father was incontestably anti-nazi and reliable. It also established that Matthew had visited his parents again recently. All rather as expected, though not throwing any more light on the riddle. If Luke's father had not been so sure, Alexander would have preferred not to pursue this avenue further but to start again from scratch. His friends counselled caution, leaving the decision to him. Finally, he felt that on balance a visit could be risked. At the very least it might eliminate Matthew altogether, at the most provide a clue to an alternative explanation. He would use the same tactics with more preparation. While familiar with the surroundings, closer inspection of the house and escape routes seemed essential.

Which is why Alexander came to knock on my parents' door. They lived near enough for the house to be used for reconnaissance and as a quick safe-house, yet far enough to avoid immediate suspicion. The unexpected had also proved a good ruse. My parents were delighted to accommodate him, though food was scarce. Alexander could contribute more than his share and supplied them with extra ration cards as well, both of which the resistance could lay hands on for its members. He learned that Amanda and I had reached Portugal and presumably therefore England. He was even tempted to use my cello and with the enthusiastic support of my father tried some of my music, not very successfully. My father took over on his own with great gusto: Beethoven, Chopin and Liszt on the grand piano and to the delight of everyone. For a few hours they forgot the war. He did not volunteer the reasons for his sudden appearance and my parents were too sensible to ask.

Twice on successive afternoons at dusk he went to Matthew's house. It was mid February 1945, the exceptionally cold winter had unexpectedly and blissfully made way for equally exceptional mild weather. It helped the population, starved of fuel for heating, and also allowed Alexander greater mobility. He noticed that the house had a large front garden, that it stood next to a house on the corner of another road which bent sharply and itself spawned crossroads, several of which could be taken to reach my home. That would facilitate escape. He noticed too that the father was at home in the afternoon.

The third day he hid his bicycle just round the corner and knocked on the door at 4.30 pm, as the light was fading. It opened almost immediately. Matthew's father also recognized Alexander instantly, just as Luke's father had done, not unexpectedly for the Paul family were well-known. But it gave him an uncanny feeling. He should not really show himself any more in these familiar parts of his hometown.

To the surprised middle-aged man who hesitated to let him in, he simply said, 'Luke's father told me to talk to you.'

Still hesitant, he let Alexander step into the hall – no further – closed the door, then went to phone Luke's father. After returning he apologized. 'You're like a ghost. Thought you were dead. Well done. Come in.' Alexander was taken upstairs to his study. 'How did you survive?'

'Luck and the holy ghost.' Alexander took a chance on the

assumption that as Luke's family were strict Calvinists, Matthew's could not be far behind.

'A lot of that is needed to save my son.'

It had worked. The subject was now out in the open. Alexander further assumed that Matthew's father would know of his own family's religious inspiration and felt that continuing in this vein might ease the tension. He said: 'A lot will be given to those who want to receive it.'

Matthew's father smiled: 'Young man, there's no need to lecture me on religion. Were you referring to my son?'

'Not really. I was trying to answer your question without going into details.'

'Fair enough. No need to burden me with more secrets. Here's another question: does my son lack the holy ghost?'

'I don't know him well enough. And I didn't come to judge him, simply to find out what caused Laura van Alblas' death. Luke's father seemed to know, but he preferred you to tell me.'

'Why d'you want to know?'

'She was my cousin, in the resistance and at one stage my helper. Like me she detested the nazis as the incarnation of the devil.'

'As I do. Why did Christians perceive the evil so much quicker?'

That was a loaded question. Alexander responded: 'Some did, some didn't. Some Jews did, some didn't. Perhaps more Christians did, but they had political antennae as well.'

'You're evading the question.'

'I'm trying to answer it less simplistically and, I hope, more fairly.'

'What you mean is: my son isn't lost entirely?'

'No one ever is,' said Alexander and he went on to engage Matthew's father in an hour-long religious debate. As a result he made a hit. It took a lot less time to hear the older man's opinion on the cause of Laura's death.

'My son's a good boy basically, honest, with a good brain, but weak, easily swayed by pleasures. He should've listened to us when he met Stephanie.'

Alexander was getting restless. 'Tell me what happened,

please. Perhaps it helps that I don't believe he killed Laura and Luke or had them killed.'

'Of course he didn't. But he was a fool when he married that unbalanced girl. She may not be evil but she certainly lends evil a hand. All the looks and none of the brains of her parents. Add to that a burning desire to dominate and you have someone really dangerous. Why? Because there's no intellect to balance, to restrain. Nor a religious dogma to act as a brake. That makes for ruthlessness. Hitler is like that. So is Stephanie. She likes pomp and prowess, equates one with the other. My son is quite a handsome boy. Isn't that why your cousin fell for him?'

She had not. But Alexander did not want to divert the old man's attention nor destroy his obvious love for his son. So he remained silent.

'He should have married Laura, not Stephanie.' Alexander let that pass too. 'Anyway, Stephanie couldn't stop flirting with the nazis she'd come to know and admire. She went beyond flirting, however, and beyond propriety. Also beyond loyalty to Matthew. It made Matthew very unhappy. That's why he succumbed to Laura's pressure. Though only once he assures me.'

In normal circumstances Alexander would have interrupted and gently tried to point out the error in this judgement. This time he did not.

'When the rows became more frequent and vicious he blamed Stephanie for destroying their marriage by her flagrant extra-marital affairs. I don't know her reply but it hurt him deeply and tempted him into an error. He admitted his infidelity with Laura. She had no right to complain and apparently did not react immediately. But she warned one of her German army lovers and told him to do something about the van Alblases. According to my son he's a young colonel, a fanatical nazi. The colonel passed the message to his general. The general had always wanted a prestigious house in the area like his superiors. So along they went to requisition it, with guns drawn because Stephanie had warned him there might be trouble. Laura mistook them for the Gestapo and started shooting, thereby dragging Luke into the unnecessary fight.'

Alexander had grown tense. The facts sounded true enough,

but the explanation obviously biased. Matthew's version had subtly put part of the blame on Laura. If only he could tell the gullible father that his son had been the rejected suitor, one of the reasons being his failure as a lover, presumably also a cause of his wife's infidelities. No doubt Stephanie had thrown this in his face, no doubt Matthew had then flaunted his escapade with Laura in hers. But Alexander controlled his anger and kept silent.

The father went on to say that Matthew had not seen his parents for three years, not because they refused to meet him but because Matthew respected their anti-nazism and did not want endless verbal fights, as his father put it. He claimed that Stephanie's father was a decent man, who honourably served the Dutch nazi leader in a purely professional capacity. He continued the defence of his son by adding that remorse and reason had brought Matthew back into the family fold. Which is how he came to know what happened. Matthew was due that evening and he hoped it would initiate a permanent stay, away from his wife. The marital conflict could be solved after the war. He even begged Alexander to stay long enough for a talk with Matthew as well.

To Alexander such naivety, such a gloss put by so rational a man on the abject behaviour of his son was the final straw. The father clearly saw it as the return of the prodigal son, whereas Matthew was probably returning in an attempt to avoid postwar retribution and save his skin. However, Alexander now had the answer to his question and did not want to risk any more, certainly not exposure of his whereabouts to so dubious a past rival. He therefore contained his anger, pleaded business elsewhere, thanked his host for his honesty and hospitality, pledged him to secrecy, and left.

Outside it was dark. Alexander walked the twenty-five yards to the gate in deep thought. He felt pity overcome his loathing for what proved to be the weak character Laura had so aptly depicted. The gate opened as he reached for it and he came face to face with the subject of his thoughts.

Although they had barely known each other at Leyden University, recognition was instant. They had a brief chat. Matthew at once apologized for his role in Laura's death, which he assumed his father had explained. He added sympathy for her loss. It sounded sincere enough. He had now finally and irrevocably broken with Stephanie as well as with the false gods of nazism, he said.

Matthew reckoned without his wife's vindictiveness. At that moment footsteps were heard approaching to their left: two people. They peered into the dark. Matthew hissed: 'Stephanie!' She was accompanied by a uniformed nazi.

'He's armed!' Matthew whispered hoarsely. 'Give me your gun, quick,' and his hands were already all over Alexander's coat.

Alexander's own safety demanded immediate flight. He let Matthew take his British revolver, ran to the right, round the corner, jumped on his bike and raced away. Behind him he heard shots. He swept round another corner, took another road and another one and arrived near our home out of breath. Before entering he waited, as much to catch his breath as to make sure no one saw him entering our drive.

Alexander stayed inside our home all of the next day before cycling to Amsterdam under cover of darkness.

Through the resistance grapevine he later learned that both Stephanie and Matthew had been killed. The father had been taken in for questioning but released after a few days. He also learned that Matthew's father somehow blamed him for his son's death. The British weapon found on the scene could only have been his. The father was besotted with his son and could not face up to the truth: that Matthew had himself become the victim of his own weakness. Instead the father put the blame on others: on Stephanie for deserting the matrimonial bed, on Laura for not marrying Matthew and for causing Luke's death, now on Alexander for killing him. These views he spread to outsiders, when soon afterwards the war was over.

By then Alexander was working in Geneva. The news of the rumours came in a letter from Lady van Alblas, who asked whether she should do anything about such silly notions. Alexander would not have left his gun and run away defenceless. Alexander replied that it might be better to let the accusation die a natural death. Laura's death was, after all, sorted out. Shortly after, Matthew's father died of a stroke.

*   *   *

In New York Alexander forgot about the war, until the letter in *The New York Times* thirty-five years later. Even then he could only guess at the connection between the old lady and the events surrounding Matthew's death. He asked his wife to make enquiries in New York with the help of a lawyer friend and arranged for her to follow him to London, where he and I had another day or so on our own. Where in all this lay the act that was 'less than honourable'? Neither of us could explain it. It was then that Alexander recounted briefly what had happened to him after the war. The denouement was yet to come.

Like so many, Alexander was disappointed about postwar developments in Holland. The fighting had stopped, but the future looked bleak, more like clearing up the rubble after a storm to go back to business as usual than a vigorous effort to turn a new leaf. Everyone seemed tired, their earlier ideals like popped balloons.

Some time after the war's end Alexander went to London, to report and be debriefed, and there met again with Adrian Pelt, the press officer of the exiled Dutch government. Pelt had been given the task of setting up a European office for the newly founded United Nations Organization in Geneva, where he had worked before the war for its precursor, the League of Nations. Pelt asked Alexander to join him. After some hesitation he accepted. Although he had been awarded the MWO – the Military Order of William, equivalent of Britain's VC – there seemed little to tie him to his native country: Laura had gone, as had Wiardi Beckman and so many others. His talents could more profitably be employed on an international platform.

In Switzerland a surprise lay in store for him. On his arrival at the hotel in Geneva he found a short note from Irena inviting him to Lausanne. While in London he had been told by Count Vanden Heuvel – MI6 head of station in Bern – that Irena was alive and well and taking courses in Russian and Arabic at the university, in addition to the four languages in which she was already fluent – German, Polish, French and English. It would make her a formidable linguist on top of being a doctor of history. Alexander had done no more than scribble a brief note for Vanden Heuvel to take to her. It had gone unanswered until this invitation. There was no hint of pressure in the note, no reference to the events of four years earlier, simply that uncle, aunt and niece would be pleased to see him. Alexander appreciated the delicacy of this approach, for he was sure Irena had taken a lot of trouble to find him.

All three welcomed him at the front door when he arrived in a newly acquired car that Saturday afternoon. Uncle and aunt seemed little changed, although the uncle must have been nearing ninety and the aunt not far behind. Irena looked different though, somehow more mature, less eager, more self-assured. But it was the mysterious smile that made the real difference. It enhanced her beauty and at once strongly affected Alexander. Remembrance of past pleasures floated through his mind, but he did not show it and his demeanour remained politely non-committal throughout the afternoon and the dinner that followed.

In the familiar surroundings, first in the drawing room, next in the dining room, the talk was all of past experiences and old friends. All those he had known in the German resistance were dead, as were all her colleagues and bosses, her brother too and many of her friends. These sadly included both Rudolph and Emily Smend. Emily had succumbed to injuries during an air raid, Rudolph had been shot by the Russians – by mistake, they said. Irena's fiancé was killed in action on the Russian front.

As Alexander reported on Laura's death nearly two years before, he began to realize that he was falling in love again, deeply so. But still nothing was said to break the unspoken understanding that prevented more personal feelings from spoiling the atmosphere of reminiscence and sadness.

After dinner the mood changed. They had moved to the library, the same place where four years before Alexander had reviewed the German resistance with Irena and Emily. The uncle asked why Alexander had preferred to work at the United Nations – as useless an institution as the League of Nations he felt – instead of helping rebuild his own country. Alexander replied that the structure of the new organization promised it more influence than its precursor. Holland could do without him and he wanted to do everything to prevent another war.

At that moment Irena threw him a glance that conveyed more than mere assent. She interrupted to say that she too wanted to join an international organization as soon as she got her degrees later that year. Alexander returned the glance.

When uncle and aunt repaired to bed, Alexander and Irena remained seated, sipping at their brandies. He had earlier noticed Emily's huge turquoise ring on Irena's right hand fourth finger, but had not remarked upon it. He now did. Irena took it off, turned it round and put it on again. She smiled her mysterious smile. It had been given to her as a present, she said, when she left Berlin for the final journey to Switzerland, her own escape.

'Emily had a premonition of her death,' Irena explained. 'And as I liked it Emily felt I could better preserve it than she herself in the ruins of the Reich. She added that I deserved some lasting memory of my work for the resistance. But there is more,' Irena said, and then fell silent. Her mysterious smile now became positively mischievous.

'Emily hoped the ring would bring luck as well. And it has.'

'What luck?'

'Emily prayed that you too would survive,' she said, slipping the ring off. 'She knew you liked it as well. She hoped you would bring me the happiness I wanted ever since we first met at her home. The ring would be a symbol less overt than a decoration but perhaps more poignant.' She gave it to Alexander, who, taking his cue, ceremoniously slipped it back on her finger.

'Have you also arranged the wedding?' he asked, with a smile.

She burst out in laughter. 'Yes, but not the date.'

When he jokingly continued: 'I can't wait,' Irena pulled him out of his chair. 'You don't have to, stupid,' she said and led him upstairs.

The wedding took place on 31 March 1946. Ten days later the uncle died in his sleep, as if he had been waiting for this happy ending. Indeed it was as if he had planned it. The house and a sizeable fortune were left to Irena and Alexander jointly. The will had originally made Irena sole beneficiary, but when

Vanden Heuvel reported Alexander alive and gave Irena his note, the uncle had at once made a second will.

Irena arrived on the last day of our fortnight's session, unexpectedly, on the afternoon flight in from New York instead of the morning one planned for the next day. She surprised us at dinner in Brown's Hotel, familiar to us from wartime days as the seat of the Dutch prime minister in exile, and Alexander's regular pied-à-terre when in London. He sat with his back to the restaurant's entrance which I faced. I could therefore watch her make her entry: an absorbingly beautiful lady. Although she must have been in her sixties, I could see her as Alexander had described her only a few days ago in her twenties. She caught my eye and put a finger bearing a huge ring to her lips before stealthily approaching our table. Then she quickly put her hands over Alexander's eyes, like newly marrieds. Which is what they still were. She looked radiant and refreshed from the shower that had wiped away her flight fatigue. We had not yet started the meal and she joined us.

'Wonderful timing, darling,' Alexander said. 'I've just finished our life's story with the tale of Emily's ring.'

Irena duly took the uncommon war decoration off for me to admire. Another big ring adorned her left hand.

I had a question. Irena had purposely postponed making any move to approach Alexander for seven months. How could she have waited all those years and then borne waiting another few months instead of jumping at her prey?

The mysterious smile gave way to a chuckle. 'I'm a woman, not a man. You pounce, we stalk.'

'You must have been confident of ultimate success,' I suggested.

'At times yes, at others I wavered, sometimes despaired. Mostly it was just a dream. Doesn't everyone have them, secretly? When life became more complicated and tense I simply clung to the dream. In my dream Alexander represented continuity in the maelstrom of events. It worked wonders while it lasted as a dream. When Fanny Vanden Heuvel delivered Alexander's enigmatic note I woke up and realized the dream might become reality. Then I panicked. Wouldn't

267

you if heaven turned up in hell? With success in sight I was afraid undue pressure might spoil it. So I waited. Also I needed to find out whether I wanted the dream to come true. Perhaps Alexander in the flesh would not match the Alexander of the dream. The strain was alleviated by frequent reports from Fanny about Alexander's movements. He appeared to have no attachments, so my confidence increased. I was about to approach him when Fanny told me of his imminent arrival in Geneva.'

And still together, clearly still happy too.

'Is that surprising? Same interests, similar work, same resistance background, same dreams about a better world. And . . . Alexander's a handsome man, after all.'

'And Irena a very beautiful woman,' I added accurately and gallantly.

Alexander had been listening to our exchanges in silence. 'I can't deny it. She's kept me on my toes. There's no need for a stand-in.'

Irena laughed gaily, putting her left hand on Alexander's. Of course, she also knew the story of Laura and me. With his free hand Alexander touched the huge pearl ring. She took that one off too and showed it to me. 'It's our second decoration, awarded by ourselves, three years ago. To commemorate Hans von Dohnanyi's arrest, my flight to freedom, and our thirty-fifth wedding anniversary.'

With mock ceremonial Alexander put it back on her finger. 'And also to celebrate twenty-five years of the European Community. It has lasted and fulfilled its intended task as peacekeeper. D'you remember what *Het Parool* wrote way back in December 1942?'

Alexander was very serious now and I realized he was on to a peroration. Although he looked at me, the words were no doubt also intended for Irena, to show her that we had not frittered away the days. He wanted to summarize and encapsulate our philosophy as derived from our wartime ideals. Occasionally he smiled at Irena and she smiled in return, encouragingly, to stress her approval of his views. Until near the end.

'I came across that leader article recently. It was signed as usual by Pieter 't Hoen. It couldn't have been Frans Goedhart, nor Stuuf Wiardi Beckman, for both were in prison. But the author doesn't really matter for he voiced the opinion of us all.'

'How did you get hold of it?' I asked.

'I was researching for a lecture, found an old file and there it was: 2,000 words on postwar developments. Stressing the need for a European directorate that would guarantee the German people a place in the European community and thereby divert its creative energy away from military dominance.'

'Uncle Stuuf was already arguing for that in mid-1941,' I interrupted.

Alexander nodded. 'He was, of course, a true pupil of Huizinga, and heeded Huizinga's strictures on hyper-nationalism.'

We were on familiar ground now. Alexander went on. 'Well, that was the first cuckoo. And there were more. Hans von Dohnanyi, Dietrich Bonhoeffer and their intimate and anti-nazi friends had similar ideas, and they surfaced also among resisters in other nazi-occupied countries, like Robert Schuman, born in Luxemburg, minister in France. And this led to the only major breakthrough in international relations this century: the European entity. Step by step, of course, but irreversibly to the European Community. The idea itself was not new, its advocacy in the underground press in the middle of the war under nazi occupation was. The resistance pointed the way, prepared the people for what would otherwise have remained a loftly intellectual exercise, like so many ready for the dustheap. For, whatever the outside influences, it was the willingness of the people of the six original member states – two defeated enemies and four victorious nations – to join together and relinquish part of their sovereignty for a closer co-operation that would prevent future wars. Their elected representatives would have lost office if they had pursued the idea without their consent. And the electors agreed because the resistance spirit provided them with the stimulus. The British never understood that. When they joined it was for so-called practical reasons. But one day they and the other new members will also appreciate that ultimately life can't do without a motivating spirit. Practicalities on their own lead to self-indulgence, re-create hyper-nationalism and lead to war. We were moved to prevent another killer war by co-operation, and our generation actually concocted the machinery. It is the duty of the new generation to adapt that machinery to the new circumstances and thus preserve that warless world. Without such motivated co-operation nuclear weapons wouldn't have deterred.'

Alexander paused, took a sip of wine, looked at his audience of two, then smiled. 'When I had expounded this view at this meeting in New York, someone shouted "bullshit". I asked him to explain his explosive disagreement. He pointed to Marshall aid, the Russian menace and the atom bomb. I then begged him to reflect that none of these created the European Community, nor would any one of these on its own have succeeded in establishing a fairly stable peace. They all contributed, of course. But without the budding European co-operation the Americans wouldn t have been so generous, the Russians might have been tempted to extend their grip one way or another, and the bomb's exclusivity wouldn't have been kept.'

Irena, who must have hard all this before, had become rather restless. 'Well, darling,' she said, changing the subject and glancing at me, 'did you two succeed?'

'Marvellously!' replied Alexander, taking his cue. 'The entire panorama of our wartime traumas surveyed and put into perspective. No more hang-ups.'

'I'm sure you had a lovely time,' she said, laughing. 'It's all right. You deserve it. But that's not what I meant, my love. What about that horrible woman and her vicious attack?'

Alexander: 'Oh, I see. Yes, in a way. We pinpointed the incident she referred to. But we're at a loss why she should have called it "less than honourable". And we still don't understand her connection with it. Did you find out about her?'

'I did. But I'm not much the wiser either. She was born in Holland and came to America in the twenties to marry a lawyer. He died a few years ago after a career as one of the most outspoken members of the Supreme Court. She's no different: opinionated, even bigoted.'

Alexander: 'OK, OK. D'you know her maiden name?'

Irena did and mentioned Matthew's surname. Alexander rushed out of the restaurant, went up to his room and phoned his lawyer friend in New York. He came back after only a few minutes and reported that his hunch had proved to be correct. The lady of the letter turned out to be the sister of Matthew's father. In his only communication with his sister after the war he had vented his warped view of Matthew's death. He had then died before time and talk could alter it. The lady should, of course, have approached Alexander many years earlier. But it is typical of some opinionated people that they avoid testing strongly held views for fear of discovering the flaw. And typical too that the bravado that forms part of their character is rarely expressed honestly and openly but feeds on secretiveness and gossip. Not unlike the myths that have grown up about the resistance by opinionated self-styled experts. Which is why this book came to be written and why it took the form of a dual memoir: to show the many faces of Resistance.

Epilogue

FROM RESISTANCE TO RENAISSANCE

with some statistics

This is a memoir, not a formal history. Yet memoirs and formal history have more in common than is always recognized. Both deal with the past. Historian and memoralist have each developed a view after careful research, and arranged the facts to support that view. The historian selects a subject to which he feels an affinity, but the memorialist is himself the subject, with a closer affinity as a result. While bound to induce greater bias, this should be balanced by greater understanding of the events. Such understanding constitutes the contribution of memoirs to the study of history.

Professional historians are, of course, also susceptible to bias, as one of them – Professor Edward Ingram – has pointed out. 'Evidence of the past is not found in documents, only in what historians decide documents mean.' Still, the credibility of both historian and memorialist depends ultimately on the scrupulousness with which they treat the evidence. Such evidence as exists I have treated with respect. Some historical evidence has been mixed with the adventure story, for our exploits took place within a political context and cannot be separated from it, nor be properly understood without it. But much had to be left out. This Epilogue seeks to make up for such a lacuna with evidence from statistics. In this way I hope to have contributed to an understanding of Resistance which non-participants might find more difficult.

Our story could not have been told without the benefit of

272

hindsight, derived in part from recent publications. Thus such controversial issues as the England Spiel and the influence on posterity of some of our thoughts could not have been properly dealt with much earlier. Our adventures considered in isolation were of little importance anyway, our contribution to 'history' negligible. This is not false modesty, for we felt proud to have participated, and still do. However, it is precisely because of their modesty that the adventures described acquire their importance. Resistance involved ordinary people and affected the great mass of the population. An accumulation of little actions by a lot of people ultimately and profoundly transformed some deeply rooted attitudes.

An assessment of Resistance must take this into consideration. Sadly, several recent publications fail to do so and show a bias that distorts historical reality. As generations born after the war lack the understanding of the participant, such distortions can become alarming. New generations would find it impossible to appreciate the effect of the pressures inherent in living under a nazi dictatorship. All the instruments of the state had failed to stem its tide, the collective nation found itself powerless to protect itself from previously unknown demands and persecutions, at least initially. And who am I, as an individual, to do better? It took time to adjust when the familiar rules of behaviour were suspended, time to discover ways to survive – mentally as well as physically – and to oppose nazi pressures, actively or passively.

A few examples of bogus opinions should suffice.

A professor of modern history at Oxford claimed recently that all resistance was run or dominated by communists. This is complete nonsense, certainly as far as Holland is concerned. Nor does it apply to Germany, Luxemburg, Belgium, France, Denmark or Norway.

Contemporary German historians are at loggerheads about the apportioning of blame for the nazi era to various sections of the German population. But few take any account of their own Resistance, drawn from many sections. As will be seen this was quite substantial.

A well-known British commentator asserts that had the bombplot succeeded on 20 July 1944, a military dictatorship would have followed. His 'evidence' is riddled with factual errors. Unfortunately his conclusion also resurrects the myth of military dominance that could endanger relations with a reborn Germany.

An entry in a reputable Dutch encyclopedia gives a figure of 25,000 resisters and concludes that resistance was negligible. A recent editorial in a leading Dutch weekly compounds this error by stating that 'staunch resistance is a myth'. Both miss the point, both opinions are mistaken as will be seen below.

The respected chronicler of Holland's wartime, Professor de Jong, in a recent interview with a British daily newspaper, recalls that Queen Wilhelmina used to refer to her country as a 'nation of heroes'. 'That, in my opinion, was complete nonsense.' De Jong ignores the fact that such phrases formed part of wartime broadcasts which he himself helped prepare in London and that these royal broadcasts succeeded in their aim of stimulating national resistance. It seems surprising for a historian to confuse propaganda with historical evidence.

These and other bogus opinions tend to focus on one aspect and ignore all other evidence. It is true that one apple from one tree was enough to poison the cosy relationship in the Garden of Eden. But that does not allow contemporary commentators to condemn any tree for a few rotten apples. Scrupulous research should include the study of all apples as well as the tree, its roots, the soil and the weather, before pronouncing a verdict one way or another. Ironically, that is precisely what de Jong has done in an exemplary way for Holland in the 26 volumes of his magnum opus: *The Netherlands in the Second World War*.

My contention is fairly simple: resistance was much more widespread than is generally supposed, had a greater impact than is realized, but contributed little to the military outcome. However, it did have a profound influence on the psyche of the people, and this contributed beneficially to the postwar constellation. There were brave men and cowards, but the majority were neither. Yet many from that majority came to resist because nazism forced them to resist.

One should, of course, distinguish between the fairly small number of active resisters and the large number of passive ones, as will be seen below. There is nothing unusual in that. Often 22 players on the soccer pitch attract 22,000 spectators on the stands without whose financial and other support they would not survive. However, it is the attitude of the majority which contributed to the virtual demise of hyper-nationalism and neutrality as well as to the complete demise of nazism as a form or philosophy of government.

Statistics are, of course, only tools and should be handled with care. The proverbial hammer of bias can so easily hit the thumb of error instead of the nail of truth. It may be relevant to quote Huizinga one last time. 'There is a deep-lying habit common to the whole of modern mankind, the glorification of size and quantity. Ever since the human mind began to lose hold of the old Aristotelian system of measuring the world by quality the opposite tendency set in of over-estimating the importance of quantity.' (*The Fortnightly Review*, April 1940)

World War II Dead

Some sources put the figure as high as 50 million. I prefer the more conservative 40 million. This includes Japan from December 1941 on, but excludes China and Japan pre-1941 as the Sino-Japanese war preceded the world conflagration and in a sense remained a separate local one. The number is still four times as high as in World War I. Even taking into account the increase in population between the two wars, it emphasizes that the technical means for killing were vastly improved.

More interesting is who suffered what. In World War II nearly half (18.2 million) were civilian casualties and of those one third were Jews. There are great differences between nations.

In Britain 0.8% of the total population were killed, in Holland 2.3%. Split into military and civilian casualties the figures are more revealing; military in Britain 326,000, in Holland only 12,000; civilian in Britain 62,000 (air raids), in Holland 198,000 (of whom 104,000 were Jews). The USA lost only soldiers, 250,000 or 0.2%. Russia lost a total of 20 million or 10.5% (13 million soldiers, 7 million civilians). Poland tops the percentage list: 14% (320,000 soldiers, 4.2 million civilians). Germany lost 8.5% (3.5 million soldiers, 2.2 million civilians), Austria 5% (230,000 soldiers, 104,000 civilians), France 2% (340,000 soldiers, 470,000 civilians), Belgium 1% (12,000) soldiers, 76,000 civilians), Norway 0.3% (6,000 soldiers, 3,500 civilians), Italy a surprisingly low 1% (330,000 soldiers, 80,000 civilians), Japan 3% (1.7 million soldiers, 360,000 civilians).

German Resistance
In 1954 German government figures put the number of Germans convicted by courts of resistance activities and subsequently executed at 33,000. Of these 13,000 were civilians, but many of those classified as military were civilians working for defence establishments, among them Hans von Dohnanyi and Dietrich Bonhoeffer. In addition many people were executed without trial, like the family mentioned on page 155, four out of five of whom were shot dead. Others were thrown into concentration camps without trial and did not survive. Professor Peter Hoffmann in his authoritative *History of the German Resistance* produced many more figures. 'Official data show that between 1933 and 1945 about three million Germans were held at some stage in a concentration camp or prison for political reasons, some only for a few weeks, some for the whole twelve years! He points out that many people were killed 'while attempting to escape', others 'starved or beaten to death in camps', or 'executed under camp justice'. These figures do not even attempt to explain why nazism happened, nor why it could last for twelve years. They do, however, confirm that there was widespread resistance to the nazi regime.

Dutch Resistance
The figure of 25,000 mentioned in the encyclopedia comes from one of the 26 volumes of Professor de Jong. It applies to the most active resisters up to September 1944 and is no more than a – carefully considered – guess. Within the same limited, stringent criteria de Jong adds another 15,000 for the nine succeeding months, as well as 5,000 'who committed individual acts of sabotage and spying rather than in groups' and 3,500 'who by escaping abroad took great personal risk'. That already nearly doubles the figure misquoted in the encyclopedia.

Moreoever, when de Jong was asked in 1982 to advise a Committee set up to award Resistance Crosses to the then still surviving active resisters, he suggested a maximum of 10,000. By the end of 1983 the Committee had handed out £5,000 awards, nearly forty years after the war. Whether this will move de Jong to increase his guesstimate to, say, 75,000 will have to await his final volume which is intended to answer all questions raised in previous volumes. And, after all, an underground government (the College of Confidants) came into being which co-ordinated active resistance, was stimulated and sanctioned by the exiled cabinet and they paved the way for a smooth postwar transition.

However, the exact number is not material to my argument, as will have become clear. I refer to civilian resistance. And, after the same scrupulous research, de Jong elsewhere mentions that during the last year of the occupation '350,000 people are known to have been in hiding'. Most of them – including 35,000 Jews – had not taken an active part (as narrowly defined) in the resistance, but by evading nazi instructions risked unknown penalties including their lives. They were sheltered by an estimated 200,000 families who thereby accepted similar risks. Some of these families also sheltered Allied military personnel such as pilots and remnants of the airborne troops at Arnhem, among them a wounded Brigadier John Hackett. The families were in turn supplied with life-saving gadgets like ration cards and money by countless others. Sadly, one of those tireless organizers of this huge evasion operation – known as Tante (Aunt) Riek – could not figure in my narrative as neither Alexander nor I came across her. If we estimate a family conservatively at two persons, the number involved in what I define as civilian resistance rises considerably. A family, of course, usually consists of more than two persons.

And this still does not include those doctors, artists, police and workers, who refused to comply with nazi instructions in minor and more stealthy ways. Nor my mother. Her imprisonment was, of course, not a result of her activity but of mine. However, her subsequent adoption of a Jewish baby falls within my definition of civilian resistance. The total number can thus safely be put at one million or 12½% of the total population, probably over 20% of adults.

The picture is not all pure white. 25,000 Dutchmen put on nazi uniform. Many of them fought on the Russian front, some even against the Allies – including me – on the western front in 1945. There were also 50,000 members of the Dutch nazi party. In addition numerous people collaborated with the nazi regime in one way or another, some out of conviction, some because they felt Germany would win, others to preserve their lifestyle. No reliable figures exist for this group or will ever be known. Some even collaborated while engaged in active resistance. Undeniably they represented a large enough section of the population to have created controversies that persist to this day. However, my concern is with balance, as mentioned in my Preface and Prologue. Collaborators no more represent a nation than criminals do, nor do bad policemen make the police bad. For people in exposed positions, opposition and active resistance was more complex than for the many of us without such constraint. And, after all, we do not measure men by their failures but by their achievements.

The figures show no more than what my narrative seeks to show, that Resistance to nazism in its varied forms – active as well as passive, early as well as late – gradually encompassed a major part of the Dutch population. Resistance can, of course, be depicted as an essentially negative response to circumstances, as the word implies. And so it was, in a sense. But it had a positive effect. That should be borne in mind by postwar generations, including academics.

People had come to reflect on human principles that previously were taken for granted, steadily and profoundly. They had the time, of course, as well as the provocation of an amazing antagonist. Thus tolerance came to be re-appraised and an ancient truth re-discovered, that more unites men than divides them. Differences in temperament and in religious, social or political beliefs were found to be less divisive than supposed. One could actually agree on a whole range of practical issues and still retain one's own ethos, whether as an individual or as a group. This had enabled Wiardi Beckman to build a political bridge after reducing a multiple of fiercely held

credos to what Queen Wilhelmina called 'just five commandments', supported by rigid Calvinists, wily Catholics, fuzzy
liberals and dogmatic socialists alike.

The process of reflection also resulted in an awareness that
some of the roots of the nazi evil lay in our own society, our
own fallibility. Consequently, much of the bigotry inherent in
confrontation went out of the window. And one came to look
out of the window beyond nazism's defeat. What started as a
ploy to parry the opprobrious oppressor evolved into an urge to
improve postwar society.

While writing these flamboyant sentences in the quiet of my
study I can hear the howls of laughter and derision outside:
idle idealism. It had happened before, in 1918, when the world
would be made safe for democracy, and the result was the
Treaty of Versailles, the subsequent economic calamity and
hyper-nationalism, all of them incitement to nazism. Did not
many people happily go along with the nazis or hide their
heads in the sand? The euphoria that follows victory and relief
from tyranny would not last long. It never had. Nor did the
euphoria last long this time. Yet the laughter is hollow, and the
derision misplaced cynicism. Cynics may have their use for
pointing out weaknesses, but they rarely contribute to positive
steps forward. It was, after all, the cynicism of the silent
majority that allowed nazism to establish itself.

The underlying feelings did not disappear with the euphoria.
The credibility gap between lofty ethics and daily chores had
narrowed immutably. Sadly the renewal of the national
democratic machinery in Holland – though not in France – fell
by the wayside where its creators – among them Uncle Stuuf –
had been interred. Their postwar successors were less bold: safe
administrators rather than visionary leaders. But those reflective
years had produced another common goal in addition to the
defeat of nazism: international integration. No doubt inspired
by Huizinga, hyper-nationalism like individual selfishness had
come to be perceived as another evil. The common European
heritage had again been recognized. Therefore the nation-
states of Europe should co-operate in some effective, practical
way, 'not to form coalitions between states but union among
people'. And they did.

The Benelux led the way: conceived in 1944 it was sanctioned in 1947. There followed the European Coal and Steel Community (ECSC), conceived in 1950, operative in 1952, and the European Economic Community (EEC), conceived in 1955, operative in 1957. For the masses this common international goal may have been amorphous, but none of these institutions could have been set up without their support and ultimate consent through the ballot box. Qualified majorities in the various parliaments were required too, for some national sovereignty was to be transferred to international bodies. And such majorities were achieved.

To return to the statistics: the figures for the resistance do not, of course, add up to a 'nation of heroes'. The concept of heroism is ambiguous and has an emotional content that ill fits my pretention to scrupulously assess events that happened half a century ago. It reflects neither my intention nor the considered opinion of Queen Wilhelmina, however lavish her praise for resisters and Resistance. The concept is wrong. Saints are recognized in heaven, sinners in hell, whereas we on earth have to make do with more mundane conceptions. Or, to put it differently, heroes like sinners are in the eyes of the beholder, never in their own.

Some 400,000 British died during World War II and very nearly the entire population supported the war effort, which cannot be said for the Dutch. Both British and Dutch may well have had no option but to act as they did. There is, though, one difference: continental Europeans faced nazis and nazism day in day out for all those years. That did not make them any better but it did influence their attitude, permanently. Perhaps that is one reason for Britain's lacklustre response to postwar European integration, replete with pragmatism but lacking in emotional conviction.

This may have been inevitable – though not for want of trying by a few visionary British politicians – but it is not irreversible. The EEC appears to have lapsed into a debilitating debating society where tribal (farmers, road-hauliers, etc.) and national (currency, defence, etc.) considerations too often prevail over international requirements: the close integration that the founders envisaged. Present national policy makers might usefully remember those early sentiments: the urge to root out hyper-nationalism as one of the causes of nazism and its accomplices. And remember too that not all its creators lived under nazi occupation. None of the three men who prepared the Treaty of Rome did. The Frenchman Jean Monnet – the Father of Europe – was in Washington; the Belgian foreign minister Paul-Henri Spaak – Mr Europe – was in London, as was his Dutch colleague Jan Willem Beyen, who had there helped evolve the pragmatic functional approach to European integration that was at the core of the Treaty of Rome.

However that may be, Holland certainly abandoned its prewar neutrality, both as a state and in the minds of its citizens. And Germany certainly pursued exemplary democratic procedures within its reduced boundaries and adopted a flexible cooperative attitude internationally, as Hans von Dohnanyi and other members of the German Resistance had suggested. Neither happened only as a result of power politics. Presumably that is the reason why General Sir John Hackett, after reading an earlier version of this book, encapsulated what happened to the Dutch nation as 'the sleeping beauty woke up'.

A NOTE ON THE AUTHOR

Having escaped to England in 1943 to avoid execution following his involvement
in the Dutch Resistance, Herman Friedhoff worked at the Dutch Foreign Office
before joining the Dutch Army in time to participate in the Allied invasion of
Europe.

The deep-seated concern with international relations fostered in him by the
Resistance movement led him to join the Royal Netherlands Institute for
International Affairs, where he worked until 1947 when he embarked on a
career in publishing.

After travelling widely and working for a wide range of publishers, in the late
Sixties Herman became Managing Director of the company Elsevier
International Projects Ltd, a post he held until 1981. Since that time he has
acted as a consultant publisher and is still involved in marrying video discs and
encyclopaedias internationally.

Herman Friedhoff lives in Oxford with his wife Polly and two of his six sons.
Requiem for the Resistance is his first book.